ISBN 978-1-330-58231-2
PIBN 10023743

OUTLINES

OF

CONSTITUTIONAL LAW

WITH NOTES ON LEGAL HISTORY.

BY

DALZELL CHALMERS, B.A.
(Law Tripos, Cambridge) Barrister-at-Law,
Author of "The Students' Guide to Roman Law,"

AND

CYRIL ASQUITH,
Barrister-at-Law,
and late Fellow of Magdalen College, Oxford,

LONDON:
SWEET & MAXWELL, LIMITED,
3 CHANCERY LANE, W.C. 2.

—

1922.

PRINTED AT READING, ENGLAND
BY
THE EASTERN PRESS, LIMITED.

PREFACE.

We have been asked to prepare for press a second edition of this work, and had we not been requested to make it a cheap work we should have doubled the length of it.

We hope that the Student will not treat this unpretentious volume as a *vade mecum*, but merely use it to condense knowledge previously obtained from the standard works.

Anyone desirous of obtaining a creditable knowledge of constitutional law and our ancient institutions should read the works of Maitland, Professor Dicey, Dr. Carter, Dr. Holdsworth, and Lord Courtenay, and also extracts from the commentaries on the common law by Dr. Blake Odgers and Mr. Odgers, whose lucid style will commend itself to beginners and will impart in a pleasant manner much information as to Constitutional Law and Legal History.

D. C.
C. A.

I have written a few chapters of this work, and given what assistance I could in regard to the remainder to my learned collaborator. Any merit which the book may be found to possess is to be ascribed to him.

C. ASQUITH.

December, 1921.

TABLE OF CONTENTS.

Part I.—INTRODUCTORY.

Part II.—THE SUBJECT.

Part III.—THE CROWN.

Part IV.—JUDICATURE.

Part V.—PARLIAMENT.

TABLE OF CASES.

ADDENDUM.

Under the Parliament Act, 1911, the Maximum duration of Parliaments is reduced from seven to five years. It is also provided that measures extending the duration of Parliaments are excluded from the operation of the Parliament Act.

Outlines

OF

CONSTITUTIONAL LAW.

PART I.

Introductory.

CHAPTER I.

INTRODUCTORY DEFINITIONS.

The State.—A State is an independent political society, occupying a defined territory (*a*), and the members of which are united together for mutual protection and assistance. Its function is to repel aggression from without, and to maintain law and order within its own dominions.

Government defined.—The Sovereign, according to Austin, is the person or persons having supreme authority in an independent political society, and in every State there must be a sovereign power which exercises and controls the functions of government, and conducts and regulates the intercourse with other political societies. "The aggregate of powers," says Sir William Markby, "which is possessed by the rulers of a political society is called sovereignty. A single ruler, where there is one,

(*a*) The territory of a State includes its territorial waters. As to the British doctrine of territorial waters and the marine league limit, see the Territorial Waters Jurisdiction Act, 1878 (41 & 42 Vict. c 73), passed in consequence of the conflicting opinions in the *Franconia Case* (1876) 2 Ex. D , p 62 (a case of manslaughter on a foreign ship by a foreigner) It has recently been decided that an island which comes into existence within the marine league limit belongs to the British Crown. (*Secretary of State for* India v *Sri Raja Rao* [1916] 85 L J. P. C 222)

is called the Sovereign; the body of rulers, where there are several, is called the Sovereign Body, or the Government, or the Supreme Government. The rest of the members of a political society, in contradistinction to the rulers, are called the subjects." (Elements of Law.)

The internal functions of government are commonly divided into three categories, namely—(1) legislative, (2) judicial, and (3) executive. The legislature makes, alters and repeals the laws. The judicature, or judicial bench, interprets and applies those laws; the executive carries those laws into effect. The sovereign power of a State may be vested in a single individual, as in an autocratic State, or in a smaller or larger body of citizens, as in the case of an oligarchy or of a democracy. The allocation of sovereign powers may vary indefinitely, but whatever the form of government may be, its functions must, in a modern State, be delegated to a large number of persons. Sir William Anson divides those persons into the following classes, namely, legislators, maintainers of order, and protectors of State independence in dealings with other societies.

Constitution defined.—The particular form of government adopted by a particular State is called its Constitution. By the Constitution of a country, says Paley, is meant so much of its laws as relates to the designation and form of its legislature, the rights and functions of the several parts of the legislative body, and the structure, office, and the jurisdiction of the courts of justice (Moral Philosophy, Book VI. Chapter VII.). A more adequate definition is suggested incidentally by Chancellor Kent in his commentary on American laws. The power of making laws, he says, is the supreme power in the State, and the department in which it resides will have such a preponderance in the political system that the law of separation between that and other branches of the Government ought to be marked with the most careful precision. The Constitution of the United States has effected this purpose with great felicity of execution. It has not only made a general delegation of the legislative power to one branch of the Government, of the executive to another, and of the judicial to a third, but it has specially defined the general powers and duties of each of these departments.

Professor Ahrens defines the Constitution of a country as "that *tout ensemble* (entirety) of fundamental institutions and laws by which the action of government (administration) and all the citizens are regulated" (cited Holland on Jurisprudence, p. 306).

Constitutions, rigid or flexible.—Constitutions may be classified in various ways, such as federal or non-federal, autocratic or democratic. But from the legal point of view the division into rigid and flexible is the most important (cf. Bryce's Studies in History and Jurisprudence, Chap. III.). A rigid Constitution is one which is founded on fundamental written laws, whilst in a flexible Constitution all laws can be altered by the same machinery. By a fundamental law is meant a law dealing with the framework of the Constitution, which can only be altered by a special machinery provided by the Constitution for that purpose. The United States furnishes a typical example of a rigid Constitution. Its Constitution, as framed in 1787, can only be altered on the proposition of two-thirds of each House of Congress, and the proposed alteration must be ratified by the legislatures of three-fourths of the States composing the Union. In England, on the other hand, an alteration in the Constitution, such as an amendment in the rules relating to the succession to the Crown, can be effected by exactly the same machinery as an alteration in any ordinary law. But whenever a Constitution is reduced into a written law, it must contain a certain element of rigidity even though it can be altered by the ordinary law-making procedure. It can only be altered consciously and intentionally, whereas in so far as a Constitution depends on custom or conventiou, it may be altered gradually and imperceptibly by the adoption of new precedents, or by old precedents becoming obsolete. The main characteristic of a Constitution founded on fundamental laws is this : the laws passed by the legislature may conflict with the fundamental law, and in that case it becomes the function of the courts of justice to declare their invalidity. If a law passed by a State in America contravenes any provision of the Federal Constitution, the Supreme Court of the United States condemns it as *ultra vires*, just as the English Judicial Committee of the Privy Council declares invalid any colonial law which conflicts with the provisions of an imperial statute. In the allocation of sovereign powers under a rigid Constitution, the judicial bench, for certain purposes, is put in a position of superiority over the legislative department of government. (Cf. Lecky's Democracy and Liberty, Chap. I. p. 64.)

The earliest important instance of a written Constitution, so far as modern times are concerned, is that of the United States. It was a written Constitution, and necessarily rigid. One great feature of the American Constitution, following the doctrine of Montesquieu, was the "séparation des pouvoirs," *i.e.*, the laying down of a strict line of demarcation between legislature, judicature, and executive.

Though these functions are separate, overlapping occurs occasionally, *e.g.*, the President cannot declare war or make peace without the consent of two-thirds of the Senate, and the Senate also must be consulted as to high patronage.

A written Constitution drawn on the lines of separation of powers places the head of the Executive in a difficult position. The American President goes down to Congress at its opening, and states the requirements of the Government, but his speech bears no resemblance whatever to the *oratio principis in senatu habita*, or even to the Speech from the Throne in the English Parliament. The President is not a member of the legislature, nor can he procure the passing of any law unless he can obtain the help of influential coadjutors in Congress.

Again, in rigid Constitutions the judges can disregard any statute not in accordance with the written Constitution. There is, accordingly, a danger of their causing mischief by overzeal for its observance, or, on the other hand, though it may seldom happen, by their misinterpreting the law owing to party bias or influence.

Flexible Constitutions are characterised by (1) adaptability to changed conditions, the legislature being able to destroy the whole fabric of the Constitution by a single enactment. (2) The relationship between rulers and ruled, and the fundamental rights of citizens, are scantily defined, much being left to conventional rules of positive morality. (3) They are relics of antiquity.

Federal States.—All States are either unitary or federal. In a unitary State, though it may contain partially self-governing entities, there is one supreme Government.

Federal States, again, consist of confederated States, and States strictly federal. Confederated States possess a supreme Government, with only sufficient power to secure " union as opposed to unity " (cf. Dicey), each State composing the union desiring, and to a large extent possessing, independence with protection, whereas in States strictly federal even the subjects of local sovereigns feel the hand or, more than that, the pressure of the supreme Federal Government.

There are probably also States which are neither federal nor confederate, which are marching by gradual steps from " union to unity " (cf. Dicey).

(In Germany, there was first a military union for protective purposes, " the Bund "; later, for governmental purposes, a formal Constitution, headed by an Emperor; and then came a criminal code, followed after some years by a civil code of ordinary law binding on all Germans. All German soldiers, whatever their State, owed allegiance to the Kaiser.)

A federal State is an amalgamation of two or more States which unite for the purpose mainly of protecting themselves against other political societies, and which desire, according to Mr. Dicey, " union as opposed to unity," and which, though they desire union as opposed to unity, wish to preserve wholly or partially the political independence of each State forming the union. The Constitution, moreover, must be written, and therefore the judges can pronounce invalid any given law which is at variance therewith.

The self-governing dominions of the Crown are now departing from the old colonial status and are approaching the status of federated States.

Requisites of a successful Federation.—The following are the requisites of a successful federation :—

1. A group of States banded together by a common nationality, physical contiguity, or long historical association.
2. A federal *esprit de corps*.

3. Such judicious distribution of sovereign powers between the Federal Government on the one hand and the States forming the union on the other as to obviate friction.

4. A carefully selected bench of judges, who should be well paid and be permanent officials not changing with the Government.

5. It being difficult to provide for every possible contingency in framing a Constitution, there should be a clear understanding as to legislation on topics not specifically allocated either to the supreme Government or the individual States.

Federalism, according to Professor Dicey, has the following characteristics :—

(A) The Constitution is supreme.

(B) The powers of government are split up amongst bodies with limited and co-ordinate authority.

(C) The duty of interpreting the Constitution falls upon the judicial bench.

These characteristics necessitate a written Constitution dividing the ordinary powers between the Federal Government and the State legislatures. Again, federal Constitutions must be rigid in the sense that special machinery must be employed to change fundamental or, rather, constitutional laws. Finally, each State must be a subordinate law-making body (Dicey, Part I. Chap. 3).

In the federal State, as compared with the State which is unitary, there is weak government, a tendency to conservatism and a predominance of the judicial bench (Dicey, Part I., Chap. 3).

Constitutional law.—Constitutional law, according to Austin, consists in the rules of positive morality, or the compound of positive morality and positive law, which fixes the constitution or structure of a given supreme government (Jurisprudence, Lecture VI.). Professor Dicey substantially adopts this definition, substituting the happy phrase " the conventions of the Constitution " for the Austinian " positive morality." He concisely defines constitutional law as that body of rules which relates to the exercise and distribution of sovereign power in a State.

Professor Holland approaches the question from a somewhat different standpoint. He divides the realm of law into public and private, and attributes this classification to the Romans, who define public law as follows: *Ad statum Rei Romanæ spectat, in sacris, in sacerdotibus, et magistratibus consistit.* Public law, according to that learned writer, that is to say, "the law between the State and the subject," may be divided into six heads, viz.:—1. Constitutional law; 2. Administrative law; 3. Criminal law; 4. Criminal procedure; 5. The law of the State in its quasi-private personality; 6. The procedure relating to the State, so considered. It is obvious that the line of demarcation between these different heads must be drawn more or less arbitrarily, according to the opinion and convenience of the writer who is dealing with them. We may take as an example offences against the State as such, *e.g.*, treason and sedition. They are a part of criminal law, but the punishments awarded for them are among the sanctions of constitutional law.

Administrative law.—Again, the line between constitutional law and administrative law is a hazy one. By administrative law is meant the body of rules which govern the exercise of executive functions by the officers to whom they are entrusted by the Constitution. But it is usually confined to the action of individual departments of the executive, including those local bodies to whom certain public functions are delegated. It does not extend to action on behalf of the sovereign body as a whole. For instance, treaties according to English law are made by the executive, but the rules regulating the treaty-making power belong to constitutional rather than to administrative law. On the other hand, the relations between the Local Government Board and local administrative bodies, such as county councils or boards of guardians, were a branch of administrative law. Administrative law is, in effect, a subordinate branch of constitutional law, and any line of demarcation must be more or less arbitrary.

Field of constitutional law.—It follows from what has been already stated that constitutional law, in relation to the State, deals with the distribution and exercise of the functions of government, while in relation to the subject, it is concerned with him in his civic capacity, that is to say, in his capacity as a citizen. Constitutional law comprises that part of a country's laws which relates to the following topics, amongst others :— The mode of electing the chief magistrate of the State, whether he be emperor, king, or president : his powers and prerogatives; the constitution of the legislative body : its powers and the privileges of its members; if there be two chambers, governs their relations *inter se*; the status of ministers and the position of the civil service which acts under them; the armed forces of the State and the liability of the citizens to be called on to serve in the army or navy; the relations of Church and State, if these be formally recognised; the relations between the central government and local bodies to whom subordinate functions of government are delegated; the relations between the mother country and its colonies or dependencies; the treaty-making powers, and the rules which regulate intercourse with other States; the persons who are to constitute its citizens, and the terms on which foreigners may be admitted to its territories and the privileges which they are permitted to enjoy; the mode in which taxation may be raised and the revenues of the State may be expended; the constitution of the courts of justice and the tenure and immunities of the judges; the right to demand a jury where trial by jury exists; the limits of personal liberty, free speech, and the right of public meeting or association; the rights of the citizen to vote for elective bodies, central or local, and his liability to perform civic duties, such as serving on juries or aiding in maintaining order. (Cf. Dicey, Const. Law, ed. 1, p. 24 : Holland's Jurisprudence.)

Conventions of the Constitution.—As it has already been stated, constitutional law consists partly of positive laws, cognizable and enforceable by courts of justice, and partly of customs and traditions, which Austin calls rules of positive morality and Professor Dicey calls conventions. So far as it consists of positive laws, it is to be found in Acts of Parliament and decisions of the law courts. The Acts of Union with Scotland and Ireland, and the Act which vacates a seat in the

Commons when a member accepts an office of profit under the Crown, are instances of constitutional statutes. The decision in *Somerset's Case*, where it was held that slavery cannot exist in England, and that a slave became a freeman as soon as he touched the English shore, established an important constitutional doctrine.

But the greater part of English constitutional law consists of conventions founded on custom, tradition, and precedent. The Ministry must resign if the Prime Minister (an officer unknown to the law) cannot command a majority in the House of Commons: but no court could enforce their resignation or restrain them from continuing to act. The conduct of a Ministry which refused to resign would be a breach of constitutional law, but it would more properly be described as unconstitutional than as illegal. So far as the conventions are protected by sanctions, the sanctions consist in a sense of honour, respect for tradition, and the fear of popular resentment. Like all customary rules, the conventions of the Constitution vary in vitality. Some are of increasing vigour, some are obsolete, and some are obsolescent. No court would recognise as an Act a Bill which had not received the Royal Assent, but it is difficult now to imagine circumstances under which the King would veto a Bill which had passed both Houses. It is a constitutional rule that a peer shall not interfere in the election of a member of the House of Commons, but this is a rule which is now observed better in the letter than in the spirit. Mr. Dicey in an illuminating chapter, which should be read and re-read by every student, discusses the conventions of the Constitution, and formulates the more important of them. Among others, he refers to the rule of collective responsibility among the members of the Cabinet (a rule by no means always adhered to in the present day); the rule that a treaty should not be concluded or a war entered upon against the wishes of the legislature; the right of ministers to a statutory indemnity when, in a public emergency and for the public safety, they have acted outside the bounds of law. It may be noted that some of the conventions of the Constitution are framed like written laws; for example, the Standing Orders of the two Houses of Parliament. But their conventional character is shown by the fact that either

House can at will suspend its Standing Orders. After the dynamite outrages the Explosives Act was passed through both Houses in a single day.

Characteristics of the English Constitution classified.—The characteristics of the English Constitution are as follows :—
1. Parliament is absolutely sovereign (Dicey); 2. The Constitution is the outgrowth of the law of the land, and not its source, as is the case where the Constitution is written; 3. The conventions of the Constitution depend on the law of the land (Dicey); 4. The English Constitution is convenient rather than symmetrical (Anson); 5. The theory and practice of the Constitution are divergent (Anson); 6. Legislature and executive are joined by a connecting chain (the Cabinet).

CHAPTER II.

PARLIAMENTARY SOVEREIGNTY.

Parliamentary sovereignty.—The expression "parliamentary sovereignty" means that the King, the House of Lords, and the House of Commons can make new laws and repeal and alter old laws, speaking in a legal sense, at will, and there are no fundamental laws which Parliament cannot interfere with. The enacting formula of an Act of Parliament clearly shows the corporate character of the three branches of the Legislature and their interdependence. It runs as follows :—" Be it enacted by the King's most excellent Majesty, by and with the advice and consent of the Lords spiritual and temporal, and Commons, in this present Parliament assembled and by the authority of the same, as follows." Since the Parliament Act, 1911, however, the enacting words of a Money Bill are somewhat different.

Parliamentary sovereignty has a positive as well as a negative aspect. In its positive aspect it means that the King, the Lords, and the Commons acting together can make, alter or repeal any law; in its negative aspect it means that there is no legislative authority which can compete with Parliament (Dicey).

Though by the Parliament Act, 1911, the veto of the Lords over Money Bills has been abolished, and as to other Bills they have only a suspensive veto, it is probably still true to say that King, Lords and Commons are still the legal sovereigns, since there is no extraneous legislative authority which can compete with them, but this is a point on which many political authorities differ and it is somewhat hazardous to form an opinion.

In England the nominal sovereignty is in the King, the legal sovereignty is in Parliament, and the political sovereignty is in the Electorate.

" When the ' referendum ' comes there will be an end to the sovereignty of Parliament " (Pollard, Evolution of Parliament, p. 1).

Mr. Dicey abundantly illustrates the fact of parliamentary supremacy, and the student who desires to thrash out the subject is referred to the chapter on "The Sovereignty of Parliament" contained in his most able work. He gives as illustrations the disestablishment of the Irish Church (a direct contravention of the Act of Union); the Septennial Act, whereby Parliament extended its life from three to seven years; and he also tells us that the Scotch Act of Union has been tampered with. As there are no fundamental laws, there is no judicial or other authority which can declare any given Act of Parliament invalid.

It has been suggested by certain writers that there are legal limits to parliamentary sovereignty.

(1) It is said that Parliament cannot legislate against the laws of morality. But clearly that is not so. Many people hold that the Divorce Laws contravene both the Divine and the moral law, but the courts must enforce and give effect to those laws, just as they give effect to any other law.

(2) It is said that Parliament cannot legislate against international law. But this is not so. There is a strong presumption that Parliament does not intend to infringe the rules of international law, and the courts sometimes put a forced construction on a statute in order to give effect to this presumption. If an Act of Parliament contravenes any principle of international law, the only remedy is by diplomatic action on the part of any State which may be injuriously affected.

(3) It is said that a statute cannot interfere with or derogate from the Royal Prerogative. The Act of Settlement is an answer to this contention. The alleged limitation is little more than a rule of construction. Parliament presumably legislates for the subject and not for the Sovereign, and the Crown can only be bound by express words or necessary implication. The usual formula for so doing runs: "The provisions of this Act shall bind the Crown." (Cf. Craies' Statute Law, Chap. VII.)

In addition to the foregoing alleged limitations to parliamentary sovereignty, certain ancient limitations deserve notice. Among these were: (1) The King; (2) The judges; (3) Resolutions of either House of Parliament (*b*).

(*b*) The word "Parliament" in old days meant a "parley," or "talk," and the expression was first applied by monastic Statutes of the thirteenth century to the post-prandial discourses of monks, when they met in the refectory, which discourses, according to the Statutes, were unedifying After this

(1) *The King.*—Till there was a Parliament the King was absolute, and Parliament, as we understand it, did not, according to the prevailing opinion, exist till 1295. Before 1295, it may be contended that Parliament was not a representative body. There was a great Council of Tenants *in capite*, but whether tenure *in capite* up to the reign of Edward I. was, or was not, a *sine quâ non* is open to considerable doubt. (See Ilbert on Parliament, p. 11.) According, however, to the Magna Charta of 1215, the King's Council was at that time an assembly of tenants *in capite*. (Cf. Pollard, Evolution of Parliament.)

The Model Parliament of 1295 was, if we except the so-called Parliament of Simon de Montfort, probably the first really representative assembly. It included, besides the Earls and Barons, the Archbishops and Bishops, who were summoned by the King's writ, and each prelate, whether bishop or archbishop, was enjoined to bring with him the deans and archdeacons, one proctor for the clergy of every cathedral, and two proctors for each episcopal diocese to represent the inferior clergy. The sheriff was, moreover, to summon two knights for each shire, two citizens for each cathedral city, and two burgesses for each borough. (Ilbert on Parliament, p. 13.)

This was a Parliament of the estates of the realm, viz. : the Clergy, the Baronage (including other Lords) and the Commons. Edward I. was tired of barons, of whom his father as well as himself had had such unpleasant experiences. He wanted, as Professor Maitland says, clergy who prayed, barons who fought, and commoners who worked.

It is noteworthy that there were only forty-one barons at the Model Parliament, and Professor Pollard thinks that " the receipt of a writ at that time depended on the caprice or discretion of the Crown (*c*).

the word was used in connection with conferences between sovereigns After a further interval the word, in England, was applied to meetings of great men to discuss grievances either with or without the King, *e g* , Simon de Montfort's Parliament, Henry III 's Parliament Lastly, Parliament denoted the body of persons assembled to confer (See Ilbert on Parliament, p 1)

(*c*) Ninety nine barons were summoned to the Parliament of 1300 To the Parliament of 1321 Edward II summoned fifty two barons (Pollard on Evolution of Parliament, p 99) Probably Edward I summoned only those barons to whom he was partial

Parliament, when summoned, soon asserted its power in various ways, *e.g.*, the establishment of impeachment in the reign of Edward III.; and in the reign of Henry IV., during the golden age of the later Plantagenets and Lancastrians, the Lords and Commons framed the Statutes, from which circumstance flowed rules of debate and procedure generally, and the King assented to Statutes in much the same fashion as at the present day.

But the King continued to legislate by ordinance. He was supposed thus to legislate on matters of trifling moment: matters of importance required, or were supposed to require, a Statute. What was trifling, however, and what was important occasioned many a serious conflict, as will hereafter appear (cf. Maitland, Const. Hist., p. 18). A Statute was recorded on the Statute Roll, and could be revoked only by an Act of Parliament, whereas an ordinance could be revoked by the King in Council at any time. (*Id.*)

The King had two modes of legislating. When he wished the law to be promulgated to the public he made use of a proclamation, and in other cases he made use of an ordinance.

On the accession of Henry VII. there were supposed to be the following restrictions on the royal power:

No tax could be levied or law passed without consent of Parliament ·

No man could be imprisoned without a legal warrant specifying his offence:

Ministers infringing the rights of the public could be sued, and could not plead, by way of defence, the royal authority:

Ministers could be impeached for high misdemeanours:

Civil and criminal cases were triable before a jury of twelve men as regards facts. (Hallam's Const. Hist., Vol. 1.)

Henry VIII. obtained from Parliament the right to legislate by proclamation, and the famous Statute of Proclamations was enacted which gave to such instruments the force of law. Though this Act was repealed in the first year of Edward VI., Edward VI.'s regents, Mary and Elizabeth, enforced proclamations, notwithstanding that it was agreed by the judges in the reign of Mary that no proclamation could make a new law

(Thomas's Const. Cases, p. 15), but only confirm and ratify an ancient one (*d*).

In the reign of James I. the Commons complained of the abuse of proclamations (Langmead, p. 402), and Coke's (*e*) opinion and those of four of his colleagues were asked for, and were to the following effect :

(A.) No new offence could be created by proclamation.

(B.) The only prerogative possessed by the Crown is such as is conferred by the law of the land :

(C.) To prevent offences the King can by proclamation warn his subjects against breaches of the existing law.

This decision was disliked by James I., who wanted to prohibit by proclamation the building of new houses in London (to check the overgrowth of the capital), and the manufacture of

(d) The proclamations of Mary and Elizabeth were respecting imports and also religious matters.

(*e*) Sir Edward Coke (1552—1631) was the most hard-working of English jurists, his contributions to the legal literature of the period being colossal. He was educated at Norwich Grammar School and Trinity College, Cambridge, and was called to the Bar at Lincoln's Inn in 1578 His skilful handling of the cases of Cromwell and Shelley brought him into prominence, and in 1586 he became Recorder of London. In 1592 he was appointed Solicitor-General, in 1594 Attorney-General, in 1606 Lord Chief Justice of the Common Pleas, and in 1613 Lord Chief Justice of the King's Bench. He is chiefly celebrated for obstinacy, pride, and for literary ability, but, to do him justice, he had principles, and acted on them His celebrated dispute with Lord Ellesmere, when the latter attempted to restrain a man from enforcing a King's Bench judgment obtained by fraud, brought him into disfavour with James I. The King also sided against Coke in his dispute with Bancroft, the Primate, relative to prohibitions directed against the Courts Christian The *Case of Commendams* lost Coke his position. He refused to allow Bishop Neale to hold livings in conjunction with his See, and this James I. considered to be an attack on his prerogative. The other Judges agreed with Coke, but, when summoned before James and the Council, relented Coke remained obdurate, and was dismissed a few weeks afterwards (Langmead, p 414) Maitland says that four " P's " ruined Coke, namely, pride, prohibitions, praemunire, and prerogative Coke was the author of the celebrated Institutes bearing his name, in which were incorporated Littleton's celebrated Treatise on Tenure He was also the author of eleven volumes of reports and the reputed author of two more such volumes. These reports disclose a remarkable knowledge of the Year Books, which were reports of legal cases containing arguments of counsel and judgments in almost unbroken succession from the reign of Edward I to that of Henry VIII Littleton was a judge in Edward IV's reign, and the chief cause of his name being handed down to posterity was the treatise above mentioned

starch from wheat (so as to preserve wheat for human consumption) (Langmead, p. 404).

The decision of Coke had little effect, and time-serving judges continued to uphold proclamations, disobedience to which in the reign of Charles I. was punished in the Star Chamber.

The last instance occurred during Chatham's Ministry, when, owing to bad harvests, exportation of wheat was prohibited; but on this occasion the Ministers of the Crown were covered by an Act of Indemnity. George V., during the recent war, obtained a limited statutory power to legislate by proclamation, *e.g.*, the Trading with the Enemy Act.

The Suspending and Dispensing Powers.—These were great impediments to parliamentary sovereignty. By virtue of the suspending power the King was able indefinitely to nullify the operation of any given Statute; by virtue of the dispensing power he could do away with statutory penalties in favour of any particular individual or individuals.

The later power, if not the former, was derived from the Papal practice of issuing bulls *non obstante statuto*, "any law to the contrary notwithstanding."

Henry III. first made use of the *non obstante* clause, and, in fact, exercised both powers.

The Commons in the reign of Richard II. accorded to that King the like privilege as to the Statute of Provisors, a Statute restricting the Papal power of nominating foreign clerics to English livings and dignities, but stipulated that it should not become a precedent. Henry IV. had similar indulgences from Parliament. In the reign of Henry V. the Commons prayed for a statute to expel aliens from the country, and the King granted their petition on condition that he might dispense with the statute at his discretion.

In the reign of Henry VII. it was decided that the King could at common law dispense with *mala prohibita* but not *mala in se* (Langmead, p. 253), and, subject to this restriction, both the suspending and dispensing powers were treated as parts of the prerogative during the sixteenth and seventeenth centuries. The Stuarts used these so-called prérogatives to subvert fundamental laws, and the unscrupulous use of the suspending power cost

James II. his throne. The circumstances of the case were as follows : James II. issued a proclamation that a Declaration of Indulgence in matters of religion should be read in the churches and that the bishops should distribute copies of the declaration in their dioceses. The Primate and six bishops signed a petition that his Majesty should not insist on the declaration being read, on the ground of its being illegal and against their consciences.

This petition was printed and circulated by sympathisers, and their conduct resulted in a criminal information for libel against the bishops. They were summoned before the King and his Council and, on admitting their signatures, were committed to the Tower for seditious libel. At the trial they were acquitted by the jury, the right of the subject to petition the King, which was afterwards contained in the Bill of Rights, being admitted.

Charles II. made use of the suspending power on two occasions : (1) When he successfully suspended the operation of the Navigation Act. (2) When he unsuccessfully issued a declaration similar to that of his successor, on which occasion he prudently gave way to Parliament.

The first important case on the dispensing power occurred in the reign of Henry VII., when it was held by the judges that although a Statute forbade any man to hold the office of sheriff for over a year and expressly barred the operation of a *non obstante* clause, nevertheless the grant of a shrievalty for life if it contained such a clause would be valid. This case was approved by FitzHerbert, a judge who flourished in the reign of Henry VIII., the author of a celebrated treatise known as "De Naturâ Brevium," and the reputed editor of Bracton's Note-book, containing numerous reports of decisions in the reign of Henry III.

In the case of *Thomas* v. *Sorrell* (1674) (Thomas's Constitutional Cases, p. 16), the plaintiff claimed a large amount for selling wine without a licence contrary to a Statute of 12 Charles II. The jury returned a special verdict that they had found a patent of 9 James I. incorporating the Vintners Company and granting them permission to sell wine without a licence, *non obstante* an Act of 7 Edward VI. forbidding the same.

The judges decided to the following effect. That the King might dispense with an individual breach of a penal statute by which no man was injured, or with the continuous breach of a penal statute enacted for the King's benefit (cf. Anson, Vol. 1., p. 314).

In *Godden* v. *Hales* (1686, 11 St. Tr. 1165) a collusive action was brought to test the King's dispensing power. Sir Edward Hales, the defendant, was sued for that he, after being appointed colonel of a Foot Regiment, had neglected to take the oaths of supremacy and allegiance and to receive the Sacrament according to the Test Act of 25 Charles II. The defendant had been convicted under the above Act at Rochester Assizes, and the plaintiff sued him for a penalty recoverable thereunder.

The defendant pleaded a dispensation of James II. discharging him from taking the oaths and also the Sacrament. The Court held, by twelve judges, that the dispensation barred the right of action.

This decision nearly coincides with the view of Coke (see Co. Litt. 120 A and 3 Inst. 154 and 186).

Blackstone says that the doctrine of *non obstante*, which sets the prerogative above the law, was effectually demolished by the Bill of Rights, and " abdicated Westminster Hall when James II. abdicated the Kingdom " (Bl. Coms. I. 342).

This is true as to the suspending power, but there may be still perhaps left to the King not only the power to pardon but also a limited amount of dispensing power. (Halsbury says there is none.)

The clauses as to the dispensing power in the Bill of Rights are as follows : (a) That the pretended power of dispensing with laws or the execution of laws by regal authority, *as it hath been assumed of late*, is illegal; (b) that no dispensation by *non obstante* be allowed, but that the same shall be held void except a dispensation be allowed of in such statute.

The words " *as it hath been assumed and exercised of late* " deserve attention, as thereby the King's prerogative right to pardon was retained (Thomas, p. 25). These words were also utilised to procure a dispensation in the *Eton College Case*, where, owing to their insertion, a fellow of Eton College was allowed to hold a living in conjunction with his fellowship (Broom's Const. Law, p. 503).

There is a distinct contrast between pardon and dispensation, the former condoning past offences only, whilst the latter condones future ones as well. (Cf. Maitland, Const. Hist., p. 303.)

2. *The Judges.*—The judges of the seventeenth century, at all events, held that the Common Law was of superior efficacy to an Act of Parliament, and even Blackstone in the eighteenth century does not treat a Statute with the respect it deserves. He says, *e.g.*, that Statutes contrary to Divine law should be disregarded. Coke certainly, and according to the soundest view consistently and persistently, stated that "when an Act of Parliament is against common right and reason, or repugnant or impossible, the Common Law will control it." Elsewhere Coke says of the power and jurisdiction of Parliament for the making of laws in proceeding by bill, "it is so transcendent and absolute as it cannot be confined either for causes or persons within any bounds of this "*Court*," of which it is truly said, *si antiquitatem spectes est vetustissima*, si dignitatem est honoratissima, si *jurisdictionem* est capacissima."

The chapter in which these words occur is headed "High Court of Parliament," and this perhaps shows, in conjunction with the words "*Court*" and "*jurisdictionem*," that Coke was not considering the word "Parliament" from a legislative standpoint. The first reference comes from Dr. *Bonham's Case.*

Sir Thomas Smith, one of Elizabeth's Secretaries of State, judging from his "Commonwealth of England," emphatically endorses the view that Parliament is legally sovereign (Ilbert on Parliament, p. 26). Hobart, J., in the case of *Day* v. *Savage* (1615, Hobart's Reps.), takes Coke's view, as also does Bacon. Hobart said, "Even an Act of Parliament made against natural equity as to make a man a judge in his own cause is void, for *jura naturalia sunt immutabilia*, and they are *leges legum*." Blackstone and his editor, Stephen, agree that Statutes are to be construed not according to the mere letter but the intent and object with which they were made. "It occasionally happens that the Judges who expound them are obliged in favor of the intention to depart in some measure from the words" (Stephen's Coms. (3rd ed.), p. 72). The proper rule is strictly to follow the Statute, and only to give weight to the intent with which it was passed when its language is ambiguous. In *Lee* v. *Bude &c. Mg. Co.* ((1871), L. R. 6 C. P., at p. 576) Willes, J., a very high authority indeed, said, " Acts of Parliament are laws of the land and we do not sit as a Court of Appeal from Parliament."

Equity judges have at times shown a tendency to disregard a Statute; in fact, they look at a Statute from the standpoint of the evil it seeks to remedy, *e.g.*, the Statute of Frauds to prevent fraud prescribes (see section 4) writing as to contracts relating to sales of land and hereditaments. To prevent fraud Equity judges have held that such a contract may be enforced even though not in writing where there has been part performance (see Strahan and Kenrick on Equity, Art. 99). In *Caton* v. *Caton* (1866), 1 Ch. 137, Cranworth, L.C., said : " When one of two contracting parties has been induced or allowed by the other to alter his position on the faith of the contract, as, for instance, by taking possession of land or expending money in building or other like acts, it would be a fraud on the other party to set up the legal invalidity of the contract on the faith of which he induced or allowed the person contracting with him to act or expend money." Again, where, according to the Wills Act, a person would naturally be presumed to hold a legacy for his own benefit, yet he may be declared by a Court of Equity to be a mere trustee for a person not named in the will where the legatee was previously informed of the particular trust intended.

3. *Resolutions of either House.*—The two great cases as to the legal effect of a resolution of either House are *Stockdale* v. *Hansard* and *Bowles* v. *The Attorney-General.* In *Bowles* v. *The Attorney-General* Mr. Justice Parker held to the effect that a resolution of either House in the absence of statutory authority to that effect does not legalise the collection of a tax, or, in other words, the decision in *Stockdale* v. *Hansard* that a resolution of either House cannot alter the law of the land was upheld.

By the Provisional Collection of Taxes Act, 1913 (3 Geo. V. c. 3), temporary legal validity, to wit, four months, was given to the Budget Resolutions so as to allow time for the Finance Act for the year, which is retrospective, to come into force.

Actual limitations to parliamentary sovereignty.—Mr. Dicey intimates that when he says Parliament is legally sovereign he is speaking in a legal sense only. He affirms that there are actual limitations to parliamentary sovereignty. He says that there is "an external limit which consists of fear of insurrection," and also an internal limit, which consists in the fact that the dispositions of Sovereigns are moulded by the times and circumstances under which they live.

But there are further actual limitations to parliamentary sovereignty :—

(A.) *The growth of the power of the Crown.*—The power of the King has, conventionally speaking, decreased, but the power of the Executive (*i.e.*, the Cabinet) has increased. The Cabinet now practically monopolises legislation, and a member of the House of Commons is at present little more than a pawn for the purpose of recording a vote for his party. The receipt of a salary of £400 a year renders many persons undesirous of a change of Ministry.

(B.) *The Electorate.*—The electorate are the political sovereigns of the country, and in the end can enforce their will.

(C.) *Leagues for political purposes.*—This concerns the right of association, for political purposes or otherwise. No free State will deny to its subjects the right of the citizens to associate in a non-political sense, *e.g.*, to form a railway company, and, to a modified extent, to associate for political objects; *e.g.*, an association like the Primrose League.

The British Government has been very favourable to combinations of workmen and to combinations of employers, and even international combinations of workmen have been tolerated to such an extent as to tie the hands of the Government and Parliament.

(D.) *The League of Nations.*—Professor Vinogradoff has stated in a lecture delivered at Oxford that the League of Nations is a super-Parliament, and though such a League does not affect the legal sovereignty of Parliament, it must be admitted that some of its provisions must sway the minds of members of either House and might impede their free judgment. Having regard, however, to the immense importance of the objects which the League of Nations is intended to serve, its maintenance is well worth the sacrifice of national pride, and even independence, involved. But there can be no doubt that where a league can interfere in the internal management of the affairs of a State it must prove deleterious to parliamentary sovereignty. Article 8 of the Covenant provides that maintenance of peace requires the reduction of national armaments to the lowest point consistent with national safety, and it also suggests the checking of private manufacture of munitions. Again, our Dominions can, at the sittings of the Assembly appointed by the League, if they choose to do so, oppose our interests.

(E.) *A free* Press, *which can ventilate its opinion fearlessly.*—The Press was not always free. Ever since the invention of printing in the reign of Edward IV. it was considered a monopoly out of which the Crown could make a profit, and it was also dreaded as forming a possible instrument of heterodoxy. It was from the date of its birth subjected to censorship, and such censorship was continued throughout the Tudor period.

During the reign of Mary the mere possession of heretical or treasonable books was punishable under martial law. During the reign of Elizabeth no man could print either a book or paper without the licence of a bishop or the Council, and the ordinance further provided that the possession of Catholic writings involving controversy was to be punishable.

Printing was checked by the Star Chamber during the reigns of Elizabeth, James I. and Charles I. (Fielden, Const. Hist., p. 244).

On May 23rd, 1623, the *Weekly News*, the first of English newspapers, appeared. The Long Parliament, though it abolished the Star Chamber (*f*), placed restrictions on printing.

(*f*) This Court derived its name from the fact that the King's Council sat in a room known as the "Camera Stellata," or Star Chamber. Henry VII. created a Court inaccurately, perhaps, called the Star Chamber, but though its members were on rare occasions not members of the Council, still, in the main, they were so. The tribunal could inflict any punishment, death excepted. Defendants were examined on oath, and also had to answer interrogatories, *i e*, questions in writing to be answered on oath. On its civil side the Court took cognisance of disputes between alien merchants, and between alien merchants and Englishmen; questions of prize; unlawful detention of vessels; maritime questions not within the purview of the Admiral; suits between corporations; and appeals from the plantations, as the colonies were then called. On its criminal side, jurisdiction was exercised in cases of

In 1662 the first Press Licensing Act was passed and, although it remained in force only three years, was periodically renewed until 1679, when it was suspended for a time.

In 1680, in *Carr's Case*, Scroggs, C.J., said : " If you write on the subject of the Government, whether in terms of praise or censure it is not material, for no man has a right to say anything of the Government " (Langmead, p. 609). In 1685 the Press Licensing Acts were renewed for seven years, and again once more in 1692 for one year, and till the end of the following session of Parliament (*ibid.*, p. 609).

After this the Press was supposed to be free, but it was fettered by the imposition of stamp duties and a straining of the law of libel (*ibid.*, p. 610). Nevertheless, newspapers multiplied. The first Stamp Act was passed in Anne's reign, and in George III.'s reign stamp duty was extended to other printed matter.

In 1763, owing to the attacks on the Government made by Wilkes in the *North Briton*, proceedings were taken against that paper. By straining the law, a general warrant (*g*) was brought into play, *i.e.*, a warrant issued by a Secretary of State for the arrest of the unnamed authors of No. 45 of the *North Briton*. Under this warrant Wilkes and others were arrested.

The Court held that a general warrant to search for and seize the papers of the unnamed author, printer or publisher of a seditious libel was illegal (*Wilkes* v. *Wood* (1763), Thomas, p. 76).

In *Leach* v. *Money* ((1765), 19 St. Tr., p. 1001), a general warrant to search for and seize the unnamed author of a seditious libel was declared illegal by Mansfield, C.J.,

In *Entick* v. *Carrington* ((1765), 19 St. Tr., p. 1036; Broom's Const. Law, p. 555), it was held that a warrant to search for and seize the papers of the named author of a seditious libel was illegal.

As to straining the law of libel, it was held in *Almon's Case*—
(1) That the publisher of a libel was criminally responsible for

forgery, perjury, riot, maintenance, fraud, libel, conspiracy and all misdemeanours (Langmead (7th ed), p 149)

(*g*) General warrants were warrants issued by a Secretary of State to seize a person or his papers and were probably initiated by the Star Chamber They were made use of until the above cases were decided

his servant's acts unless proved to be not privy thereto, and that exculpatory evidence not being admissible, publication by the servant was evidence of the master's guilt. (2) That it was for the judge to determine the criminality of a libel, and for the jury to determine the fact of publication and whether the libel meant what it was alleged in the indictment to mean (Langmead, p. 612).

These trials encountered severe public criticism, and in the end Fox's Libel Act, 1792, enabled the jury to return a general verdict of guilty or not guilty in a libel case.

The French Revolution brought about a temporary reaction, but after 1832 the Press was practically free. The publicity of all proceedings, including parliamentary debates, influences Parliament and perhaps somewhat fetters its action, and although Parliament can avoid this type of control by holding its debates in secret, yet secrecy is so repugnant to English ideas that secret debates (which have been held once or twice during the recent war) are a luxury which a modern Parliament cannot frequently afford.

Subordinate law-making bodies.—Legislative powers may be delegated as well as any other sovereign powers. *Prima facie,* the Crown legislates for colonies, but very wide legislative powers have been delegated in many instances to British colonies. The powers of the Australian and Canadian Legislatures are almost as wide as those of the Imperial Parliament; but what an Act of Parliament bestows it can in theory take away; and all British courts would be bound by an Imperial Act abrogating the powers of those Legislatures. Again, partly to save parliamentary time, and partly to provide for greater flexibility, a statute often delegates to a department of government or to a local authority a power of making rules or by-laws to carry out the provisions of the Act. So, too, the power of making rules of practice and procedure is usually bestowed on courts of justice. All statutory rules and orders of general application are collected and published annually by the Stationery Office.

PART II.

The Subject.

CHAPTER III.

LEGAL STATUS OF THE SUBJECT.

General equality of all persons.—The subjects of the Crown cannot be punished or deprived of their possessions except by due course of law, and all subjects, whether they be officials or non-officials, are, as a rule, liable to trial in the ordinary courts by the ordinary magistrates and in the ordinary manner.

All men (the King excepted) are, in the main, equal in the eye of the law, and this means that if they break the law they are liable to punishment in the ordinary courts of justice. The maxim of the law is that the King can do no wrong, but the reason is that he acts through ministers, who are personally responsible for their advice and acts. But in all well-regulated States it is impossible to place all the citizens on an absolute equality in respect of all their actions—*e.g.*, A., in discharge of a public duty, may do a particular act with impunity which B. cannot do when acting in a private capacity. To begin with, there must be certain classes privileged as to official acts; and, again, there must be classes whose privileges are less extensive than those of the ordinary subject. Officials must differ from ordinary citizens to a limited extent, and in England they are, in a very limited sense, deemed a privileged class, but they do not possess anything like the same immunities as they do in France.

In that country, according to Mr. Dicey, a system known as "Droit administratif" prevails, and official courts have been established where officials are tried before an official bench for acts done in an official capacity. As it is well known that there is a fellow-feeling amongst officials, this system tends at times to gross miscarriage of justice, so much so that the ordinary individual frequently endeavours to get his cause heard before the ordinary courts, and the "Tribunal des Conflits," which decides whether or not a particular case is to go to an official court or the ordinary court, has considerable work to do.

In the days of the Stuarts we had something like "Droit administratif," for in cases where the rights of the subject clashed with the royal prerogative the writ "de non procedendo rege inconsulto" was often utilised to the subject's prejudice. (Dicey, Law of Constitution, Chap. XII.) (*h*).

Public Authorities Protection Act.—By the Public Authorities Protection Act (56 & 57 Vict. c. 61) no person can sue another in respect of any official act, or in respect of any neglect or default, whilst in the execution of any statutory duty, or of any public duty, except within six months after such act, neglect, or default, or in case of a continuance of injury or damage within six months after the ceasing thereof. Furthermore, opportunity

(*h*) It is worthy of remark that Professor Dicey, in the latest edition of his work, has modified to some extent his earlier criticisms of the French system of "Droit administratif." Doubtless he has been led to do so on account of what he calls the "judicialising" process to which this system has been subjected. In other words, it has lost its elasticity in a way analogous to that of our own system of equity, and consequently is not now characterised by that appearance of arbitrariness that seemed so much to favour the State at the expense of the individual. But even now it is undoubtedly true that at bottom the "Droit administratif" rests upon principles radically antithetical to those of our own *corpus juris*, which is permeated by the "Rule of Law" and Ministerial Responsibility.

It is hardly necessary to point out that the term "Droit administratif" finds no equivalent in English law, far less does it signify "administrative law" as described in a previous chapter of this book.

In a manner of speaking, we have faint adumbrations of such a notion even in our own system; for example, the subject cannot take legal proceedings against the Crown according to the ordinary forms of action, but must proceed by way of Petition of Right, and then only after obtaining the leave of the Attorney-General. Still, even here, there is lacking the primary characteristic of the French "Droit administratif," which, even if its principles have hardened into the technical certainty of a code, is the co-existence of State or official courts side by side with the ordinary courts.

must be given of tendering amends by the official, and when an action is commenced after tender of amends, or proceeded with after a payment into court, if the plaintiff does not recover more than the sum tendered or paid into court, he shall not recover costs incurred after such tender or payment into court. Where an action against an official is unsuccessful he can recover against the plaintiff costs on a higher scale than the ordinary individual can under similar circumstances.

Immunities of high officials.—There are other classes occupying important positions who must, for obvious reasons, have special privileges. A Viceroy, it seems, can commit certain wrongs on an individual with impunity, for which even ordinary officials could be penalised. (*Luby* v. *Ld. Wodehouse*, cited and commented on in *Musgrave* v. *Pulido* (1879), 5 App. Cas. 111.)

Acts of State.—The expression "act of State" is used in various senses. It is used to denote important State documents or important executive acts. But in law it has a special meaning. It denotes an act of State policy done under the authority of the Crown which would otherwise constitute a wrong, but which, being an act of State, is not cognizable by any municipal court. (Cf. *Musgrave* v. *Pulido* (1879), 5 App. Cas. 111.) Sir FitzJames Stephen defines an act of State as "an act injurious to the person or to the property of some person, who is not at the time of that act a subject of Her Majesty; which act is done by a representative of Her Majesty's authority, civil or military, and is either sanctioned or subsequently ratified by Her Majesty." (Stephen's Hist. of Crim. Law, vol. 2, p. 61.)

In *Buron* v. *Denman* (1859) 2 Ex. Rep. 167, the defendant, a naval captain, made a treaty with the chief of an uncivilized country for the abolition of the slave trade without the authority of the Crown, and then, in pursuance of the treaty, committed acts of aggression on the plaintiff's property. The court held that the subsequent ratification by the Crown of an unauthorized treaty made what would otherwise have been illegal an act of State, and that consequently no right of action lay.

See, further, *Salaman* v. *Secretary of State for India*, (1906) 1 K. B. 613, C. A.; and Fraser on Torts, pp. 13—17.

Judicial immunities.—Where a judge acts either without jurisdiction or in excess of jurisdiction, a civil action lies at the suit of the person injured (*Houlden* v. *Smith* (1850), 14 Q. B. 850). But if the judge had no means of knowing that he lacked jurisdiction, *aliter* (*Calder* v. *Halkett*, 3 Moo. P. C. 28); and where, whilst acting within his jurisdiction, he makes a mistake, he is not civilly responsible (*Kemp* v. *Neville* (1861), 16 C. B. N. S. 523); and it has even been held that where a judge acts maliciously whilst within his jurisdiction, he is not civilly responsible (*Anderson* v. *Gorrie*, [1895] 1 Q. B. 670, C. A.).

The reason for this immunity, as Lord Esher points out, is that otherwise judges would lose their independence, and that the absolute freedom and independence of the judges is essential to the due administration of justice. (*Anderson* v. *Gorrie*) (*i*).

The rule in England is that judges hold office during good behaviour and are not dependent on the will of the Executive. If a judge of the Supreme Court is guilty of gross misconduct he may be removed by the Crown on an address moved by both Houses of Parliament. Judges of inferior courts are, as a rule, removable by the Lord Chancellor for inability or misconduct. See, *e.g.*, County Courts Act, 1888, s. 15; Coroners Act, 1887, s. 8. In the case of other judges, as, for instance, recorders, the power of removal is somewhat obscure, but probably can be exercised by the Crown. Magistrates are removed by the Lord Chancellor by striking their names out of the commission of the peace.

Inferior courts are also controlled and kept within the bounds of their jurisdiction, even where no appeal lies, by the writs of mandamus, procedendo, certiorari, and prohibition, issued by the High Court as the successor of the old Court of King's Bench.

Official immunities.—Certain high officials are not civilly liable for the acts of their subordinates as ordinary persons would be: thus, in the case of *Lane* v. *Cotton* (1700), Salkeld, p. 17, the Postmaster-General was not deemed, as an ordinary employer of labour would have been, legally responsible for the acts of

(*i*) The late Mr. Justice FitzJames Stephen, in his Digest on Criminal Law, mentions a crime called "oppression," for which a punishment is prescribed against judges who act oppressively; but this offence is now, perhaps, obsolete.

employés who had, under circumstances of carelessness, lost some valuable exchequer bills. Where, however, a public official is personally guilty of breach of a legal duty, he incurs civil liability in the event of an action, as a rule (*Henley* v. *Mayor of Lyme* (1828), 5 Bingham, 17).

In general, an agent who exceeds his authority is personally liable, but when the agent happens to be a colonial governor the rule is different. Thus, in an old case where the Governor of Quebec contracted with a tradesman in his capacity of governor for the purchase of certain commodities, and the Treasury, deeming his conduct imprudent, disallowed a considerable portion of the price, he (the governor) was not held civilly responsible for the excess (*McBeath* v. *Haldimand* (1786), 1 T. R. 172; see also *Dunn* v. *Macdonald*, [1897] 1 Q. B. 555).

A public official is not responsible where he enforces in a regular and reasonable manner any sentence or legal process, provided that he acts under an order or warrant purporting to be regular on the face of it, and that it is his duty to obey such order or warrant (*Lord Mayor of London* v. *Cox* (1867), 2 House of Lords, p. 269) (*k*).

Members of both Houses of Parliament possess certain immunities (see *post*), and so do clergymen.

Officials "inter se."—Where government officials deal with subordinates a considerable amount of latitude is allowed in certain cases, and they can go scot free from liability in respect of actions which would subject others to severe legal penalties. In the case of *Sutton* v. *Johnstone* ((1787), Bro. P. C. 76) the plaintiff was arrested at the instance of the defendant and detained in custody for a considerable time, and though he was ultimately acquitted by a court-martial, which exonerated him from all blame, it was held that no action lay against the defendant. Again, in the case of *Dawkins* v. *Lord Paulet* ((1869), L. R. 5 Q. B. 94), it was held that no action lay in

(*k*) A public officer who acts under a warrant issued by a magistrate is exempted from civil liability by 24 Geo II c 44, s 6, on production of a copy of his warrant six days after demand being made for same See Fraser on Torts, p 18

respect of what would otherwise have been libellous statements contained in a report made by a superior officer against his subordinate. See also *Dawkins* v. *Lord Rokeby* (1875), L. R. 7 H. L. p. 744; also cases collected in Fraser on Torts, p. 112.

In the case, however, of *Warden* v. *Bailey* ((1811), 4 Taunt. p. 67), it was held that an action for damages lay where a man was imprisoned because he disobeyed an order made by a military superior, which that military superior had no jurisdiction to make (*l*).

Immunities of Trade Unions.—Two Acts have been passed exempting trade unions from criminal and civil liability to which ordinary persons are subject. As to criminal liability, " an agreement or combination by two or more persons to do or procure to be done any act in furtherance of a trade dispute shall not be indictable as a conspiracy if such act when committed by one person would not be criminally punishable " (Conspiracy and Protection of Property Act, 1875, s. 3).

By the Trades Disputes Act, 1906 (6 Edw. VII. c. 47), any act done in pursuance of an agreement or combination by two or more shall, if done in contemplation of a trade dispute, not be actionable in a civil court unless the act complained of, if done without such agreement or combination, would be civilly actionable. Nothing in the Conspiracy and Protection of Property Act is to affect the common law as to riot, unlawful assembly, breach of the peace, or sedition, or any offence against the King or the State (section 3). The word " crime " for the purposes of the Act is to include summary offences.

By section 3 of the Trades Disputes Act, 1906, any act done in contemplation or furtherance of a trade dispute is not to be actionable by reason only that it induces any person to break a contract of employment or interferes with any person's liberty to dispose of his labour or capital as he wills, and by section 4 actions of tort against trade unions, whether of workmen or masters are prohibited.

(*l*) Magistrates and others who act without jurisdiction, or in excess of jurisdiction, are liable to actions for damages. Accordingly, members of a court martial who pass a sentence they have no power to pass are all civilly liable (Manual of Military Law, Chap. VIII.)

Persons who labour under legal disadvantages.—We will now turn to those classes whose position in the social community brings them under special laws, or exposes them to certain disadvantages. Examples of these are :—

(A.) Those belonging to certain callings, *e.g.*, the Army, the Navy, the Church. Soldiers and sailors are subject to military law, and clergymen are subject to the discipline of the ecclesiastical courts, and also to restrictions in trading.

(B.) Those who, owing to previous convictions, must of necessity be placed under certain restrictions.

(C.) Paupers, who are subject to certain electoral and other disabilities.

(D.) Aliens. (An alien is any person who is not a British subject.)

(E.) Bankrupts, who are ineligible for certain public offices and franchise.

(F.) Outlaws.

The legal disadvantages of persons exercising particular callings need no comment here; but where persons have been previously convicted, they may be rendered liable to imprisonment in respect of conduct which would be readily explainable in the case of the ordinary citizen; *e.g.*, being found on someone else's premises without being able to give a satisfactory account of themselves. (Prevention of Crimes Act, 1871, s. 7.)

For the protection of society it is often necessary to punish conduct which is merely suspicious. By 5 Geo. IV. c. 83, s. 4, every person wandering abroad, and lodging in any barn or outhouse, or in any deserted or unoccupied building, or in the open air, &c., not having any visible means of subsistence, and not giving a good account of himself, may be punished as a rogue and a vagabond.

The section further provides that every suspected person or reputed thief frequenting any river, &c., or any place of public resort, &c., or any street or highway, &c., with intent to commit a felony, may be punished as a rogue and a vagabond. In proving the intent to commit a felony, it is not necessary to prove any act tending to show the purpose, but the prisoner may be convicted if, from the circumstances of the case and his known character, it appear that he contemplated a felony. There must be evidence that the prisoner was there more than once (*R.* v. *Clarke*, Metropolitan Police Guide).

Aliens.—By the common law aliens could not hold land or fill public offices or possess civic rights (Langmead, p. 533, 7th ed.). Magna Charta (Art. 41) provided that all merchants should have liberty to enter, dwell, and travel in and to depart from England for purposes of commerce without being subject to any evil tolls but only to the ancient and allowed customs, except in time of war. On the breaking out of war merchants of the hostile States shall be attached, if in England, without damage to body or goods until it be known how our merchants are treated in such hostile State, and if ours be safe, the others shall be safe also. In the first re-issue of Henry III.'s charter the words " nisi publice antea prohibiti fuerint " were added after the opening words " Omnes Mercatores " (Langmead, p. 108, 7th ed.) (*m*).

By 32 Henry VIII. c. 16, aliens could neither rent a shop nor a residence, but the statute was silent as to pre-existing restrictions. Higher taxation was imposed on aliens. At common law they could be expelled at the royal pleasure, this prerogative right being last exercised in 1575.

An alien could always be made a denizen by royal prerogative, or a British subject by a private Act. 7 James I. c. 2 provided that no alien should be naturalised until he took the Sacrament according to the rites of the Church of England, and the oaths of supremacy and allegiance in the presence of Parliament. These restrictions were avoided by private Acts. In 1708 an

(*m*) Jews in Norman and Plantagenet times were counted as aliens with the exception that their position was not so secure

The Norman Kings utilised the Jews to feed upon the people so that the King in his turn might feed upon them, which he did by tallages. In the reign of Henry II the Jews must have been profitable to the King, for we hear of the " Scaccarium Judaismi," supervised at first by Jewish but afterwards by Christian judges. Magna Charta (article 10) provided that debts due to Jews were to bear no interest during the minority of the heir. In 1290 Edward I. banished the Jews, but Cromwell allowed them to visit England, and they were allowed to settle in England in the reign of Charles II. (Langmead)

Act, 7 Anne c. 5, which only lasted three years, was passed which provided that all foreign Protestants could be naturalised (*n*).

During the wars with France in the eighteenth and nineteenth centuries aliens were placed for a time under severe restrictions, but these gradually disappeared after Waterloo.

In 1844 aliens obtained certain advantages under Hutts' Act, which enabled them (*inter alia*) to be naturalised under a certificate of the Home Secretary on taking the oath of allegiance, but they could not become members of Parliament or of the Privy Council, neither could they enjoy rights excepted by the certificate. (As to subsequent Acts affecting naturalisation, see *post*.)

In *Speyer*'s *Case* (*R.* v. *Speyer*, [1916] 2 K. B. (C. A.) 858) it was held that a naturalised alien could be a member of the Privy Council.

In *R.* v. *Arnand* ((1846), 19 Q. B., p. 806) it was held that a company which had been registered in this country could own a British ship although all its members were aliens. Putting aside the case of war and the status of alien enemies, an alien in England enjoys full civil, as opposed to civic, rights. He owes temporary allegiance, and as he is subject to our laws, he enjoys their protection, *e.g.*, he can bring and defend actions and institute prosecutions. He can acquire land, has full personal liberty, and can generally do as he pleases; but though he must pay taxes when domiciled in England, he cannot exercise either the parliamentary or municipal franchise; neither can he own a British ship or any share therein.

Undesirable aliens.—For many years this country has been infested with criminal aliens and aliens who come over here without any visible means of support, and common sense has therefore dictated summary methods of dealing with these people. The Aliens Act of 1905 provides that an alien who is classed under the Act as " undesirable " may, under certain conditions, be prevented from landing, and the following are denominated undesirable aliens :—

(*n*) In 1753 an Act was passed permitting the naturalisation of Jews without taking the Sacrament.

1. Those who (not being political or religious refugees) cannot show that they have in their possession, or that they are in a position to obtain, the means of supporting themselves and their dependants.
2. Lunatic or idiot aliens, or those suffering from any disease or infirmity by which they may become detrimental to the public.
3. Those who have been sentenced for an extraditable offence in a foreign country.
4. Those against whom an expulsion order has been made.

Under the regulations of the Secretary of State, the Act at present is only directed against the importation in bulk of undesirable aliens. Ships which bring more than twenty alien steerage passengers can only land them at certain named ports. Before landing the immigrants are inspected by the immigration officer, who rejects those who appear to be undesirables, subject to appeal to an Immigration Board appointed by the Home Secretary.

The Act further provides for the expulsion of aliens who abuse our hospitality, and the following are liable to expulsion :—

(A.) Aliens who have been convicted of felony, misdemeanour, or any other offence punishable with imprisonment without the option of fine, and disorderly prostitutes, provided that the convicting court recommends them for expulsion, and that the Home Secretary confirms the recommendation.

(B.) Where it has been certified to a Secretary of State by a magistrate after proceedings taken for the purpose within twelve months after the alien has last entered the United Kingdom that such alien has—

α. Been in receipt of such parochial relief as would, if he were a natural-born subject, disqualify him for the parliamentary franchise.

β. That he has been living under insanitary conditions, or wandering without visible means of support.

γ. That an alien has entered the United Kingdom after the passing of the Act, having been sentenced in a foreign country in respect of an offence for which he could be extradited.

Provision is made by the Act for the detention in custody of undesirable aliens till the Secretary of State has made an order concerning them, and afterwards till their embarkation.

During the late war the following restrictions were imposed on aliens generally. By the Aliens Restriction Act, 1914, his Majesty was empowered in case of war or any national emergency to make orders—(a) prohibiting or restricting the landing of aliens in the United Kingdom, (b) for the departure of aliens from the United Kingdom, (c) for deportation of aliens, (d) to prescribe for aliens' residence within certain areas, (e) for registration of aliens, (f) for appointment of officials to supervise movements of aliens, (g) for imposition of penalties for non-compliance with orders, (h) for the arrest, detention, and searching of premises of aliens. Provision is also made for the summary punishment of persons offending against the Act. By the Aliens Restriction Continuance Act, 1919 (9 & 10 Geo. V. c. 92), certain emergency powers were to be exercisable as to aliens, and by section 3 of the Act any alien who either attempts to do or does any act calculated or likely to cause sedition or disaffection amongst any of his Majesty's Forces or the forces of his Allies or amongst the civilian population shall be liable to penal servitude up to ten years, or to imprisonment on summary conviction up to three months.

A penalty of up to three months' imprisonment is imposed where an alien promotes or attempts to promote industrial unrest in any industry in which he has not been *bona fide* engaged within two years prior to the summary proceedings being instituted against him.

The Act also prohibits an alien, subject to certain exceptions, from holding a pilotage certificate, or acting as master or chief officer of a merchant ship, or as skipper or second hand of a fishing boat.

Restrictions are also placed on aliens changing their names. Where, again, an alien sits on a jury, as he is liable to be called upon to do after ten years' residence in this country, any party to the proceedings may challenge him and so get him removed from the panel.

The Crown has, by its prerogative, right to detain an alien enemy during time of war.

Alien enemies.—An alien enemy is a person who voluntarily resides or carries on business in enemy territory. Local and not natural allegiance furnishes the test. But during the recent war an extended meaning was given to the term; at any rate, for trading purposes. Under the Trading with the Enemy Act, 1915 (5 & 6 Geo. V. c. 98), enemy nationals and other persons having hostile associations may be treated as enemies though not residing in hostile territory.

As a general rule, except under licence from the Crown, an alien enemy cannot sue or initiate any proceeding in a British court. He may be sued, and therefore may appeal. If a cause of action has accrued to him before war, it is only suspended till peace comes, but no right of action can accrue to him during war.

When war is declared by this country the declaration operates as if it were an Act of Parliament prohibiting all intercourse with the enemy except under licence from the Crown. In the case of contracts made with an enemy before war, the contract is dissolved if the fulfilment of its conditions would involve any intercourse or dealings with the enemy during war.

For leading cases, see *Driefontein Consolidated Mines* v. *Janson* [1902] A. C. 384 (enemy status); *Porter* v. *Freudenberg* [1915] 1 K. B. 857 (legal proceedings); *Ertel Bieber & Co.* v. *Rio Tinto Co.* [1908] A. C. 260 (trading with enemy).

Under the Aliens Act of 1919 before mentioned ex-enemy aliens are to be deported unless the Secretary of State, on the recommendation of a proper advisory committee, permits them to remain.

Until after the expiration of three years from the passing of the aforesaid Act ex-enemy aliens are prohibited from acquiring land in the United Kingdom, having any interest in a key industry, or a share in a British ship.

Lastly, the Act repealed the Aliens Act, 1905, from such dates as might be specified by Order in Council, and such order was allowed to repeal any of its provisions on different dates, and, on the other hand, could incorporate any of the provisions of the repealed Act.

Women.—Women in England before the Sex Disqualification

Removal Act, 1919 (9 & 10 Geo. V. c. 71), had full civil rights, though their civic rights were somewhat restricted. A woman may be a peeress in her own right, but, though it may have been occasionally allowed in old times, cannot now sit in the Lords; formerly she could not be elected for the House of Commons or vote at a parliamentary election. Women have for some time been able to hold certain local offices, and under recent legislation they can vote at almost all local elections and hold nearly every local office. Where a woman was elected as mayor of a borough, she could not formerly, but can now, act as a magistrate. Married women possess certain advantages when judgments have been signed against them, and it is only when they engage in trade that they can be made bankrupts (Bankruptcy Act, 1914).

By the Act of 1919 women, whether married or single, are no longer disqualified from exercising any public function or from being appointed to any civil or judicial office, or for admission to any incorporated society (*e.g.*, Inns of Court), or from serving as jurors. Rules under the Act are to be made as to the admission of women to the civil service. Women can be admitted solicitors upon three years' service under articles, provided that they have taken the qualifying university degree required of a man, or have qualified for that degree at any university not admitting women to degrees. Power is given to universities by the Act to admit women to membership or to any degree. Women are by the Act liable to service on a jury in certain instances.

CHAPTER IV.

THE LIBERTY OF THE SUBJECT.

Personal freedom of subject.—Mr. Dicey commences his able discussion on personal liberty by impressing upon us a very valuable fact. What he says amounts to this. After telling us that the Belgian Constitution has a special clause (or clauses) whereby personal liberty is guaranteed to the subject by the written Constitution, he goes on to show that if the reader were to expunge the clause or clauses, the liberty of the subject would be a thing of the past, but that in England the unwritten law is so full of subject-matter dealing with liberty that it would be very difficult to get rid of it. Mr. Dicey further tells us that in France there is a special provision in the written Constitution for proclaiming a state of siege, and that when a state of siege has been proclaimed the military tribunals can try civilians by martial law. This, in fact, is martial law in the strict sense, and some authorities are of opinion that no such thing exists in England, and that it has not existed since the Petition of Right. Recently, however—during the South African War—Mr. Marais, a civilian, who had been placed under military arrest, appealed against such arrest to the Privy Council, with the result that the course pursued was deemed justifiable on the ground that war was raging in the colony. *Inter arma silent leges.* (*Marais* v. *General Officer Commanding*, [1902] A. C. 109, 115.) The Privy Council there say : " No doubt has ever existed that where war actually prevails the ordinary courts have no jurisdiction over the action of the military authorities. Doubtless cases of difficulty arise when the fact of a state of rebellion or insurrection is not clearly established."

Redress of subject when deprived of liberty.—On wrongful deprivation of liberty, the following remedies are open to the citizen or the alien, viz. :—

1. The taking of civil proceedings for damages either in respect of malicious prosecution or false imprisonment or assault;

2. A criminal prosecution for assault, battery, or even in respect of false imprisonment itself (*o*).

3. In certain cases a summons can be taken out before a magistrate, under the Summary Jurisdiction Act, to recover costs incidental to defending irregular and unjustifiable proceedings.

4. Obtaining one's release by suing out a writ of habeas corpus.

5. In certain exceptional instances a writ of certiorari or prohibition can be sued out (*p*).

6. Appealing from the verdict of a jury to the Court of Criminal Appeal under the new Criminal Appeal Act, or from magistrates to quarter sessions.

Redress for false imprisonment and malicious prosecution.— As to redress for false imprisonment and malicious prosecution, the damages which are awarded may be vindictive, *i.e.*, the jury are permitted to mark their disapprobation of defendant's conduct by awarding damages which will punish and not merely compensate. No damages, however, can be recovered unless it can be shown that the defendant has acted maliciously, and without reasonable and probable cause.

It is a generally accepted opinion that where a man puts in motion the criminal law against another man the accused must be acquitted before he can sue for damages; it may be noted that where a statute provides a particular method of arrest, and an irregular arrest has been made in violation of the statute, the accused can recover damages. (*Justice* v. *Gosling* (1852), 12 C. B. 39.)

(*o*) See Archbold's Criminal Pleadings, p 89

(*p*) Statutory provision has also been made for obtaining one's liberty when sentenced to imprisonment by a magistrate for a summary offence, whereby release is obtained pending appeal, if one tenders recognizances or proper bail.

Power has also been given for the Metropolitan Police to discharge from custody on bail or on recognizances persons arrested for trifling misdemeanours when twenty-four hours must elapse before such persons can be brought before a magistrate. (10 Geo. IV. c 44)

Arrest.—The general rule is that no man can be arrested or imprisoned except under due process of law. Where a person is suspected of serious crime, the usual course is to apply to a magistrate for a warrant for his arrest. That warrant can only be granted on a sworn information. In minor cases a summons is usually applied for, and if the person summoned does not appear a warrant can then be issued. But there are many cases where a person can be arrested without warrant, especially by a peace officer.

A constable may arrest where he has reasonable suspicion that his prisoner has committed felony, but a private person cannot do so unless he can show by way of defence that a felony has been in point of fact committed, or unless he does the act when called upon to assist the constable, or perhaps a justice of the peace; or there has been a hue and cry (a general chase of a suspected person) (*q*).

The writ of habeas corpus and kindred writs at common law.—Prior to the Habeas Corpus Act there were various old writs designed to secure personal liberty to the subject under certain circumstances.

1. The writ of mainprize, whereby the sheriff was directed to take sureties for the appearance of a prisoner on a given occasion, and subject to such sureties (mainpernors) being forth-

(*q*) Where an affray or breach of the peace accompanied by violence has been committed, any person present may interfere to part the combatants, and onlookers may hold a combatant till the temper of that combatant cools down, and they may also detain the combatants and afterwards hand them over to a constable at the first convenient opportunity. A mere threat to fight will not justify interference, for till it actually begins no arrest can take place, either by a constable or anyone else.

A person attempting to commit a felony may be arrested by a private person present at the time, and a policeman may arrest to prevent a breach of the peace, and on all occasions where a breach of the peace has been committed before him.

Where an indictable offence has been committed between 9 p m. and 6 a.m., it appears that any person can arrest. (14 & 15 Vict. c. 19, s. 11) Again, where an offence is committed directly against a person, a power to arrest is in many cases given to that person, and also to his servants. A magistrate may either arrest or order the arrest of a person committing a breach of the peace in his presence. (Metropolitan Police Guide, 4th ed., p. 397.)

There are also many statutes giving a power of arrest for particular offences either to constables or the public generally, or to specified persons.

coming to set him temporarily at liberty (Blackstone, 21st ed., Vol. 3, p. 121).

2. The writ *de odio et atiâ*, bidding the sheriff to hold an inquiry whether a prisoner accused of murder was committed on reasonable grounds for suspecting guilt or *propter odium et atiam*, and, if the sheriff found that prisoner was committed *propter odium et atiam*, to admit him to bail. (Blackstone, 21st ed., Vol. 3, p. 128.)

3. The writ *de homine replegiando*, directing the sheriff to replevy a person just as goods were and are repleviable in the action of replevin; sureties bound themselves before the sheriff that prisoner should appear and answer the charge against him.

4. The following habeas corpus writs were designed to secure temporary liberty, and for other purposes.

(A) *Habeas corpus ad respondendum*, to bring up a prisoner in the custody of an inferior court to charge him with a fresh action in the superior court.

(B) *Habeas corpus ad satisfaciendum*, to bring up a prisoner against whom an adverse judgment had been obtained in an inferior court. (Blackstone, 21st ed., Vol. 3, p. 129.)

(C) *Habeas corpus ad recipiendum*, alias *habeas corpus cum causâ*, to bring up a defendant already in custody in an inferior court to do and receive what the King's Court shall deliver in that behalf. (*Ibid.*)

(D) *Habeas corpus ad subjiciendum*, directed to the person who had the prisoner in custody, commanding such person to produce the prisoner in court with the day and cause of detention, *ad faciendum subjiciendum et recipiendum*, whatever the court should ordain in that behalf. This was the writ which was improved upon by the Habeas Corpus Acts.

At common law there was a writ of *habeas corpus cum causâ*.

Where a prisoner was brought into his presence the judge, on release being demanded, had to satisfy himself that the captive was detained on some ground which would hold water in a court of law. The writ, however, was not particularly efficacious, as the gaoler to whom it was addressed could evade liability by proving change of prison as an excuse for non-production of the accused.

The ways in which the right to a release could be evaded caused a great commotion in the reign of Charles I., when Sir Thomas Darnell demanded his freedom on the ground of illegal detention. In this case venal judges held that the fact of Sir Thomas being detained by the royal command was quite sufficient, irrespective of any question of legality. Later on the Petition of Right settled once for all the question that the orders of the Sovereign were not in future to be sufficient grounds for incarcerating his subjects. In the reign of Charles II. (1676 A.D.), a man named Jenks was arrested, and afterwards, on a writ of *habeas corpus* being applied for, the court held that change of prison quarters amply exempted the governor of the prison from liability for not delivering up the prisoner. The proceeding excited sympathy, as the prisoner had been confined during the Long Vacation. This circumstance brought about the passing of the Habeas Corpus Act, 1679, which applies to criminal cases only.

Habeas Corpus Act, 1679.—This statute provides :—

1. That on complaint in writing by or on behalf of any person charged with any crime (unless committed for treason or felony plainly expressed in the warrant, or as accessory, or on suspicion of being accessory, before the fact to any petit treason or felony, &c., or unless he is convicted or charged in execution by legal process), the Lord Chancellor, or any of the judges in vacation, upon viewing a copy of the warrant, or upon affidavit that a copy is denied, shall (unless the party has neglected for the two whole terms after his imprisonment to apply to any court for his enlargement), award a writ of habeas corpus for such prisoner, returnable immediately before himself or any other of the judges, and upon service thereof the officer in whose custody the prisoner is shall bring him before the said Lord Chancellor, or other judge, with the return of such writ, and the true cause of the commitment, and thereupon, within two days after the party shall be brought before them, the said Lord Chancellor, or other judge, shall discharge the prisoner if bailable, or on giving security, to be fixed according to their discretion, to appear and answer to the accusation.

2. That such writs shall be endorsed as granted in pursuance of the Act and signed by the person awarding the same.

3. That the writ shall be returned and the prisoner brought up within a limited time, according to the distance, not exceeding in any case twenty days after service of writ.

4. That officers and keepers neglecting to make due returns or not delivering to the prisoner or his agent within six hours after demand a true copy of the warrant of commitment, or shifting the custody of the prisoner from one prison to another without sufficient reason or authority (see section 8), shall for the first offence forfeit £100 and for the second offence £200 to the party aggrieved, and be disabled to hold his office.

5. That no person once delivered by habeas corpus shall be re-committed for the same offence on penalty to the party aggrieved of £500.

6. That every person committed for treason or felony shall, if he requires it, the first week of the next term, or the first day of the next session of oyer and terminer, be indicted in that term or session, or else admitted to bail, unless it appear on oath made that the King's witnesses cannot be produced at that time; and if acquitted or not indicted or tried in the second term or session, he shall be discharged from his imprisonment for such imputed offenee; but that no person after the assizes shall be open for the county in which he is detained shall be removed from the common gaol by habeas corpus till after the assizes are ended, but shall be left to the justice of the judges of assize.

7. That any such prisoner may move for and obtain his *habeas corpus* as well out of the Chancery or Exchequer as out of the King's Bench or Common Pleas, and the Lord Chancellor or judge denying the same on view of the copy of the warrant or oath that such copy is refused shall forfeit severally to the party grieved £500.

8. That this writ of habeas corpus shall run in the counties palatine, the cinque ports and other privileged places, and the islands of Guernsey and Jersey.

9. That no inhabitant of England (except as in this section excepted) shall be sent prisoner to Scotland, Ireland, Jersey, Guernsey, Tangier, or other place beyond seas within or without the King's dominions, on pain that the party committing, his

advisers, aiders and assistants shall forfeit to the party grieved a sum not less than £500, to be recovered with treble costs, shall be disabled to have any office of trust or profit, and shall incur the penalties of a praemunire, and shall be incapable of receiving the King's pardon for any of the said forfeitures, losses and disabilities (*r*).

The defects of the above Act were as follows :—

1. There was no protection where the bail was fixed too high.
2. The return to the writ might not be truthful.
3. Illegal civil detention was ignored.

The Bill of Rights provides that bail be not excessive, and the Bail Act, 1898, gives power to magistrates to admit persons to bail, with or without sureties, when such magistrates have power to grant bail under section 23 of the Indictable Offences Act, 1848; and by the Criminal Justice Administration Act, 1914, a magistrate who issues a warrant is empowered to state in writing on the back of such warrant the amount of bail he is prepared to accept, which bail may be taken before the superintendent of police.

By 56 Geo. III. c. 100, the Habeas Corpus Act has been extended so as to embrace cases of civil detention. By this Act judges are required, upon complaint made to them, to issue in vacation writs of habeas corpus returnable immediately, in cases other than for criminal matter, or for debt, or on civil process. Any person disobeying a writ sued out under the above Act is to be deemed guilty of a contempt of court, and becomes liable to be sent to prison for such contempt. Provision is further made that where on the face of it the return to the writ, which is addressed to the person detaining, shows a valid ground for the course pursued, the judge may yet go into the merits of the case.

Habeas corpus to places abroad.—The writ runs to the Channel Islands and Isle of Man (31 Car. II. c. 10, s. 10; 56 Geo. III. c. 100, s. 5), but it cannot issue into a British colony or foreign dominion of the Crown where a court of competent jurisdiction has been established. (See 25 & 26 Vict. c. 20.)

(*r*) This summary of the Habeas Corpus Act has been, by permission of the proprietors of the copyright, taken from Taswell-Langmead's Constitutional History, pp. 520, 521, ed. V.

Uses to which the writ of habeas corpus has been put.—The writ of habeas corpus has been used to set free slaves during the period when slavery was lawful in England (*s*).

The provisions of the second Habeas Corpus Act have been made use of to restrain the rights of a parent over a child and a guardian over his ward. Where a father, as is almost universally the case, is the guardian of his child, he can generally enforce his rights to the custody of such child, though by comparatively recent legislation the rights of the mother are recognized also. Again, the mother of a bastard child can claim the custody of such child as against the reputed father by suing out a writ of habeas corpus. Where a father is unfit to have the custody of a child, the court will deprive him of such custody.

Modern practice as to writs of habeas corpus.—Where a writ has been sued out, the modern practice is either to instruct counsel to move the Divisional Court of the King's Bench Division or to apply by summons to a King's Bench Division judge sitting in chambers; but where the case is one of extradition, a motion must, except in vacation, be made by counsel to the Divisional Court (Crown Office Rules, 1906, r. 219). At the hearing the court may make either an order

(*s*) Slavery was a legal institution in our country till the days of James I. In this reign one Caley claimed the horse of one Pigg, whom the defendant (Caley) alleged was his *villain regardant*. Pigg brought an action, and the court held in doubtful cases that slavery was obsolete, and that law was "in favorem libertatis" In or about 1772 A D. one *Somerset*, the slave of an English colonist, came to England with his master. As the master put him under arrest a writ of habeas corpus was applied for, and the court held that any slave who set foot in England became ipso *facto* free (Broom, Constitutional Law, p 59) In the case of *The Girl Grace*, a female slave accompanied her mistress to England, and then returned with her to the colony where she had been a slave Here the court held that the fact of such voluntary return caused her to relapse into the *status* of a slave ((1827), 2 Hogg, Adm p 94) Slavery in English colonies has now been abolished, and Englishmen are forbidden, under pain of severe criminal punishment, to traffic in slaves, fit out ships to be used in the slave trade, or do various other things connected therewith. (See Stephen's Digest of Criminal Law, pp 82—86)

In the case of *Forbes* v. *Cochrane* (1824), 2 B & C. 448, the liberty of a slave who escaped to a British ship was expressly recognized

absolute for the issuing of the writ "*ex parte*," or may make an *order nisi*, thus giving an opportunity for the person detaining the prisoner to oppose. Where time is not of grave importance, a *rule nisi* is made, and the applicant then issues a summons, which is served on the respondent, at the hearing of which the judge determines whether or no he will accede to the application. The person to whom the writ is addressed, *i.e.*, the person detaining the prisoner in civil or criminal custody, is obliged to state in his return to the writ all causes for detention, if more than one, and it is not necessary to endorse these causes on the writ, as they may be set out in a schedule which must be annexed to the writ (Crown Office Rules, 1906, r. 222).

A prisoner or anyone suing out process on his behalf may impeach the return to the writ by affidavit. (*The Canadian Prisoners' case* (1839), 3 St. Trials, N. S. 963.)

When the person detained is produced in court or chambers the judge may either—

1. Make no order at all.
2. Discharge the person detained.
3. Award bail.

In the case of *R.* v. *Richards* (1844), 5 Q. B. p. 926, it was held that where a commitment order is disputed for a reason which is purely technical, a properly drawn up warrant or order may be substituted for the original one. In the above case the return stated that the prisoner was committed to gaol for three months by the order of a magistrate. The warrant of commitment recited a conviction which was bad on its face. The return further stated that a week after the committal, whilst the prisoner was still in custody, the same magistrate delivered to the gaoler a fresh warrant of committal relating to the same offence, in which the matter was put right. The court held that the prisoner was not entitled to be discharged from custody, as the return disclosed a good warrant for his detention. (See *R.* v. *Allen* (1860), 30 L. J. Q. B. 38, as to warrant irregularly signed.)

Appeal to the Court of Criminal Appeal.—The new Criminal Appeal Act (7 Ed. VII. c. 23) does not interfere with the right of the Crown to pardon or commute criminal sentences. It provides, *inter alia*, that a person convicted on indictment may appeal to the Court of Criminal Appeal against his conviction on any ground of appeal involving a question of law; and where the leave of the Criminal Appeal Court has been obtained, or the judge who tries the case awards to the prisoner a certificate authorizing appeal, such prisoner may appeal on any question of law and fact, or fact alone, provided the court is satisfied that the ground of appeal is a sufficient one. A convicted man may also by leave appeal against his sentence, unless such sentence is one fixed by law; but where a sentence is appealed against, a more severe one may be passed by the Appeal Court.

Persons found by the magistrates at petty sessions to be incorrigible rogues, after being sentenced at quarter sessions can appeal to the Court of Criminal Appeal (see Criminal Appeal Act, 1907), and by the Criminal Justice Administration Act, 1914, persons sentenced to Borstal treatment have the like privilege.

The court has power, whenever a conviction is appealed against, to dismiss the appeal, notwithstanding the fact that they are of opinion that the point raised in the appeal might be successful, where they also think that no substantial miscarriage of justice has occurred (section 4, sub-section 3).

Notice of appeal must be given within ten days after conviction, and no sentence either to death or corporal punishment can be executed till the time for giving notice of appeal has expired, or, where notice of appeal has been given, until the appeal has been heard. The court may examine witnesses if they think fit, and may admit the prisoner to bail pending appeal. An appeal lies from the Criminal Appeal Court to the House of Lords in certain cases.

Where the Home Secretary has received a petition for pardon on behalf of a convicted prisoner, he may submit the case, or any point arising thereon, for the opinion of the Court of Appeal. (Section 19.)

Appeals from sentences to imprisonment passed by magistrates.—By the Summary Jurisdiction Act, 1879, s. 19, an appeal lies to the Court of Quarter Sessions on the merits where a person has been sentenced to imprisonment without the option of a fine by magistrates.

There are also, in certain cases, remedies against erroneous convictions by writs of certiorari, and magistrates may furthermore be required to state a case on a point of law for the opinion of the High Court.

The right to trial by jury.—By the Summary Jurisdiction Act, 1879, s. 17, a person charged with an offence in respect of which he is liable to be imprisoned for a term exceeding *three months* (cases of assault excepted) can demand to be tried before a jury, and magistrates have to inform prisoners of their rights in this respect, and where the accused is a child of tender years his parent or guardian may exercise this option of trial by jury on his behalf. For the history of criminal and civil juries, see Appendix C.

Powers of detention in non-criminal cases.—Children, lunatics and persons incapable of taking care of themselves—as, for instance, a man suffering from delirium—can, of course, be restrained for their own protection. So, too, persons suffering from dangerous infectious illness may, under recent legislation, be compulsorily isolated, and habitual drunkards may, under certain conditions, be committed to a reformatory or, with their own consent, be detained for a specified period in a retreat.

Use of force.—The Criminal Code Bill Commissioners, in their report dated 1878, state as follows :—" We take one great principle of the common law to be that though it sanctions the defence of a man's liberty and property against illegal violence, and permits use of force to prevent crimes, to preserve the public peace, and bring offenders to justice, yet all this is subject to the restriction that the force used is necessary ; that the mischief sought to be prevented could not be prevented by less violent means, and that the mischief done be only what might be reasonably anticipated from the force used, and not be disproportionate to the mischief which it is intended to prevent."

Mr. Serjeant Stephen, in his Commentaries, states as follows : —" In the case of justifiable self-defence the injured party may repel force by force in defence of his person, habitation, or property against anyone who manifestly intends, or endeavours with violence or surprise, to commit a felony upon either. In these cases he is not obliged to retreat, but may pursue his adversary till he find himself out of danger, and if in a conflict between them he happens to kill, such killing is justifiable."

Stephen, J., says :—" The intentional infliction of force is not a crime when it is inflicted by any person to arrest a traitor, felon, or pirate who has escaped, or is about to escape, from such custody, although such traitor, felon, or pirate offers no violence to any person " (Stephen's Digest of Criminal Law, p. 158).

Force, again, may be used by a father to protect a son; by a husband to protect a wife; by a son to protect a father; and generally the strong may come to the assistance of the weak without breaking the law.

Reasonable assault and battery may be committed with impunity when one is acting (1) in defence of person or property; (2) when one occupies a peculiar relationship to the person assaulted or beaten, *e.g.*, a father may moderately chastise his child; (3) in the preservation of the public peace (Fraser on Torts).

CHAPTER V.

LIBERTY OF DISCUSSION.

British subjects in the United Kingdom may speak and publish what they choose provided that the law is not infringed.

The law of liberty of discussion is chiefly concerned with defamation, sedition, blasphemy, and obscenity. Defamation consists of libels and slanders and denotes publishing, orally or in writing, defamatory matter concerning a person, such defamatory matter being calculated to prejudice him in his calling or trade or to hold him up to ridicule, hatred or contempt.

Where the defamatory matter is either written, printed, or consists of a picture, effigy, or assumes some other permanent form, it is libel, but where it is oral, it is slander.

Defamatory libel calculated to bring about a breach of the peace is a criminal as well as a civil offence, but slander, except in rare instances, is only a civil wrong.

(For the distinctions between libel and slander and other useful information, see Odgers's Common Law, Chap. X.)

Truth, again, is a defence to a civil action for libel, and also to one for slander, but it is no defence to a criminal libel unless defendant can prove truth and that publication was for the public good.

Publication is the communication of defamatory matter to a person other than the one defamed, and affects the author, the printer, the publisher, the communicator, and even the careless seller of a libel, and also the originator and the repeater of a slander. No publication to a third person is necessary to obtain a conviction for criminal libel.

Privileged communications.—Certain communications are absolutely privileged, *i.e.*, they are under no circumstances punishable civilly or criminally, whilst other statements are only privileged if they are not malicious in fact.

The following are absolutely privileged :

(1) Judicial proceedings, and these include documents necessary to the case of a litigant, and also all proceedings in a court, freedom of speech being accorded to judges, counsel, and other advocates, litigants conducting their cases in person, and witnesses (cf. *Royal Aquarium Co.* v. *Parkinson*, [1892] 1 Q. B. p. 451). But a witness is not protected as to statements made before he is sworn or after leaving the box (*Trotman* v. *Dunn* (1815), 4 Camp. p. 211). As to privileges of judges, see p. 28.

(2) Words uttered in either House of Parliament by members (see p. 243, *post*).

(3) State communications, which include, possibly, statements made by all persons in government employ as to State business.

(4) Proceedings at a court-martial or a military enquiry (*Dawkins* v. *Rokeby* (1875), 7 H. L. p. 544).

(5) Reports made in pursuance of military duty (*id.*).

(6) Fair and accurate reports in newspapers of proceedings publicly heard before a court exercising judicial authority if published contemporaneously and neither blasphemous nor indecent.

(7) Reports and other documents published by order of either House of Parliament (see p. 252).

The following communications are privileged in a qualified sense :—

(A.) Communications made in pursuance of a legal, social, or moral duty (cf. *Stuart* v. *Bell*, [1891] 1 Q. B. p. 530). This may possibly include communications by a government official to his superior.

(B.) Statements in his own defence by a man who has been attacked (cf. *Koenig* v. *Ritchie* (1862), 3 F. & F. 413).

(C.) Communications between persons possessing a common interest (*Hunt* v. *G. N. Railway*, [1891] 2 Q. B. p. 191).

(D.) Reports of judicial proceedings not covered by section 3 of the Law of Libel Amendment Act, 1888. These are not privileged if inaccurate, biased or not published *bona fide*, or when blasphemous or indecent. This privilege is not confined to newspapers, and includes reports of *ex parte* proceedings.

No protection exists when the publication of proceedings is prohibited by order of court.

(E.) Faithful and correct reports of parliamentary debates, and also fair and reasonable comments by public writers on matters of public interest (see *Wason* v. *Walter* (1868), L. R. 4 Q. B. p. 73) (*t*).

(F.) Fair and accurate reports in any newspaper of the proceedings of a public meeting or (except where neither the public nor newspaper reporters are admitted) of a meeting of any vestry, town council or other public body mentioned in section 4 of the Law of Libel Amendment Act, 1888, or of documents published at the request of any government department or any official specified in the Act. A public meeting, for the purposes of the Act, is any meeting *bona fide* and lawfully held for a lawful purpose, whether admission thereto be general or restricted.

Press privilege.—The statutory defence of apology is an important concession to the Press and persons interested in periodical publications. Defendant may prove by way of defence absence of malice and gross negligence, and also that a full apology has been inserted at the earliest opportunity or, where the above course is impossible, the making of a full apology has been offered.

Payment of money into Court by way of amends must also be made. (For further particulars, see Order XXII., R. S. C., rule 1.)

When journalists are charged with criminal libel they may be dealt with summarily where the libel is trivial, and fined up to £50 (Newspaper Libel, &c., Act, 1881 (44 & 45 Vict.), ss. 4 and 5).

In newspaper actions defendant may prove in mitigation of

(t) It is perhaps doubtful whether the defence of fair comment comes under the heading of qualified privilege, but it is one of those topics which concern the constitutionalist and yet cannot be dealt with conveniently in outline The reader is therefore referred to Odgers on Common Law, Vol. 2, pp. 527 to 530, 2nd ed.).

damages that plaintiff has received, or has agreed to receive, compensation from other sources (Law of Libel Amendment Act, 1888, s. 6).

Censorship of stage plays.—From the time of Henry VIII. downwards, the drama has been controlled by the Executive. Under the Theatres Act, 1843, the Lord Chamberlain has a jurisdiction—(1) to forbid the performance of unlicensed stage plays anywhere; (2) to license theatres in certain places. He has an arbitrary right under the Theatres Act, 1843, to prohibit any stage play whenever he thinks its public performance would militate against good manners, decorum and the preservation of the public peace; and in order that he may exercise complete supervision, all new plays and all old plays which have been altered must be submitted to him, and fees for perusal paid. He has local jurisdiction to license all theatres in the cities of London and Westminster, in Finsbury, Marylebone, the Tower Hamlets, and also in Windsor and other places where the King possesses a royal residence.

The county councils license places to be used in their counties, and at Oxford and Cambridge the university authorities possess a veto as to the performance of plays within their respective jurisdiction. (Report of the Joint Committee of the Lords and Commons, 8th November, 1909.)

Blasphemy.—The late Mr. Justice Stephen says:—"Every publication is said to be blasphemous which contains matter relating to God, Jesus Christ, the Bible, or the Book of Common Prayer, intended to wound the feelings of mankind, or to excite contempt and hatred against the Church, or to promote immorality.

"Publications intended in good faith to propagate opinions on religious subjects, which the person publishing them regards as true, are not blasphemous within the meaning of the definition merely because their publication is calculated to wound the feelings of Christian people, or because their general adoption might tend by lawful means to alterations in the constitution of the Church as by law established." "Blasphemous writings," the learned judge continues, "are libels, and also misdemeanours" (Stephen's Digest of Criminal Law, p. 125).

Denial of Christian truths.—The learned judge also mentions another offence dealt with by 9 Will. III. c. 32, whereby persons educated in or professing the Christian doctrines incur various disabilities and punishments when they, by writing, printing, teaching, or ill-advised speaking, deny the truth of the Christian religion or the Holy Scriptures or their Divine authority. He also mentions the misdemeanours of depraving the Lord's Supper (see Digest of Criminal Law, p. 128; see also 1 Ed. VI. c. 1, s. 1) and defaming the Book of Common Prayer (see Digest of Criminal Law, p. 128).

Blackstone mentions the offence of apostacy or denial of the Christian truths, and also heresy or denial of some essential doctrine of Christianity; but all these offences are now practically obsolete, blasphemy excepted (*u*).

The offence of profane and common swearing is quoted by Blackstone, and also Stephen, as an offence against religion, and they tell us that it is a misdemeanour punishable by a small fine or a short alternative period of imprisonment. This offence is obsolete, save in so far as it may come within the range of certain bye-laws.

Obscenity.—It is a misdemeanour to write, make and publish obscene and criminal books, pictures, &c., when the writing, picture, effigy, &c., has a tendency to deprave and corrupt those whose minds are open to immoral influence (*R.* v. *Hickling* (1868), 11 Cox, p. 26). Purity of motive is no excuse for the publication of indecent matter (*ibid.*).

Uttering obscene words before a large number of persons may also constitute a misdemeanour (Odgers on Libel, 5th ed., pp. 505 *et seq.*).

Exhibiting publicly for sale or otherwise indecent writings, &c., is criminal, but not mere possession of same (*ibid.*).

(*u*) Persons are still, in theory, liable to censure and punishment at the instance of an ecclesiastical court for fornication, adultery, and other deadly sins, and also for heresy, according to Prof. Maitland; but these proceedings are also obsolete. (See Stephen's Digest of Criminal Law.)

In *R.* v. *Bradlaugh and Besant* ((1878) 3 Q. B. D., p. 569) an indictment for obscene libel was quashed because the indecent matter constituting the libel was not set out at full length, but by the Law of Libel Amendment Act, 1888, it appears to be no longer necessary to do this.

By the Post Office Act, 1870 (33 & 34 Vict. c. 79), the Postmaster-General, with the consent of the Treasury, may make regulations for stopping in the post the transmission of indecent matter.

It is also a misdemeanour to send by post indecent writings, prints, cards, &c. (Post Office Protection Act, 1884 (47 & 48 Vict. c. 76)).

By the Indecent Advertisements Act, 1889 (51 & 52 Vict. c. 18), it is a summary offence to place an indecent advertisement or to write indecent words or otherwise publish indecent matter on any building, wall, gate, public urinal, &c.

By 20 & 21 Vict. c. 83, s. 1, any court of petty sessions on complaint on oath being made that any obscene documents are in any house or other place for sale or other purpose of gain may issue a search warrant to have such articles searched for, seized and brought into court. A summons can then be issued against the occupier of the place in question to show cause why such articles should not be destroyed, and they may be destroyed after the time for appeal has expired unless cause be shown to the contrary.

There are certain formalities to be complied with as to the drawing up of the order, and the court must be satisfied that the works, &c. are obscene before granting the search warrant, and there must be some evidence of sale or exhibition for purposes of gain.

CHAPTER VI.

THE RIGHT OF PUBLIC MEETING.

Liberty of association.—The general rule of English law allows complete liberty of association for any lawful object—*e.g.*, people may combine to form a club or society or a partnership without any permit from the Government and without fulfilling any legal formality. But various statutes have restricted this common law freedom—*e.g.*, a club which supplies intoxicating liquors must be registered and comply with certain formalities; a trading company must not consist of more than twenty members, or a banking company of more than ten, unless it registers under the Companies Acts.

General right of public meeting.—It is a rule of English law that any given person can meet another given person or an indefinite number of persons at any appointed place so long as the law is not thereby broken. As a rule, people may assemble in any numbers in a *private* place for a lawful object, provided they do not become a nuisance to others or break the law. To understand the legality of any given public meeting it will be necessary to enquire into the law as to unlawful assemblies, routs and riots. (Cf. *R.* v. *Vincent*, 9 C. & P. at p. 109.)

Unlawful assemblies.—Mr. Serjeant Stephen defines an unlawful assembly as "a meeting of great numbers of people with such circumstances of terror as cannot but endanger the peace, and raise fears and jealousies amongst the subjects of the realm."

It has been decided that where persons assemble to witness a prize fight the assembly is an unlawful one (*R.* v. *Billingham* (1825), 2 Carrington & Payne, p. 234).

Where, however, people assemble for a lawful object without intending to commit a breach of the peace, though they have reason to believe that there will be such a breach in consequence of their meeting being opposed, such persons do not, according to the decision in *Beattie* v. *Gillbanks*, constitute an unlawful assembly (*Beattie* v. *Gillbanks* (1882), 9 Q. B. D. 308).

In this case a certain section of the Salvation Army marched about the streets of Weston-super-Mare singing hymns and disturbing the tranquillity of owners and occupiers of property in that town. An opposition army, called the Skeleton Army, was accordingly raised to oppose them. Fearing a disturbance, the local magistrates caused a notice to be served on the Salvationists not to assemble. In spite of this notice the assembly was persisted in. The two armies met, and a breach of the peace occurred. One Beattie, the commanding officer of the Salvationists, was convicted of being a member of an unlawful assembly by the bench, but the conviction was upset on appeal by the Divisional Court for the reason above stated.

The case of *Wise* v. *Dunning* presents the law in a different aspect, however. Here the plaintiff was a conscientious but violent denouncer of "the scarlet woman and her creed." Got up in a peculiar costume, he gave religious addresses in places of public resort in Liverpool.

Certain Roman Catholics taking umbrage at these meetings and street rows resulting, the magistrate bound Wise over to keep the peace and be of good behaviour. Proceedings were taken, on the hearing of which Darling, J., gave a very lucid judgment to the following effect :—"To begin with, we have the appellant's own description of himself. He calls himself a crusader who is going to preach a Protestant crusade. In order to do this he supplied himself with a crucifix, which he waved about. . . . Got up in this way he admittedly made use of expressions most insulting to the faith of the Roman Catholic population. . . . There had been disturbances and riots caused by this conduct . . . and the magistrate has bound him over to be of good behaviour, as he considered that the conduct was likely to occur again. Large crowds assembled in the streets, and a riot was only prevented by the police. The kind of person which the evidence here shows the appellant to be I can best describe in the language of Butler. He is one of—

'That stubborn crew
Of errant saints whom all men grant
To be the true church militant;
A sect whose chief devotion lies
In odd perverse antipathies.'"

Finally the learned judge upheld the opinion of the magistrate. This case (*Wise* v. *Dunning*, [1902] 1 K. B. 167) probably overrules the earlier decision in *Beattie* v. *Gillbanks*.

Forbidden acts in places of public resort.—A crowd of persons cannot block up public thoroughfares or interfere with the general comfort of other persons lawfully using such place; neither can a man cause a crowd to assemble to the annoyance of owners and occupiers of adjacent land or houses.

By the Parks and Gardens Act (35 & 36 Vict. c. 15) provision is made for, *inter alia*, securing the enjoyment of the ordinary frequenters by giving power to make bye-laws; and as to several of these parks penalties are imposed under bye-laws for the delivery of any public address.

By the Municipal Corporations Act, 1882, borough councils can make bye-laws for the general good government of the borough.

The same sweeping power has been conferred on county councils by the Local Government Act, 1888.

By the Local Government Act, 1894, certain powers of making bye-laws respecting recreation grounds have been accorded to parish councils.

Meetings in London.—Some persons are under the impression that meetings may be held in Trafalgar Square to discuss grievances, but a reference to the case of *R.* v. *Graham and another* will convince them that they are wrong (16 Cox (1888), p. 420) (*x*).

(*x*) The case of *R.* v. *Graham and another* (16 Cox, p. 420) is most important on account of the dicta of Mr. Justice Charles. One of the principles the learned judge laid down was to the following effect: "The law recognizes no right of public meeting in a public thoroughfare—a public thoroughfare

By 57 Geo. III. c. 19, the convention, or giving notice for the convention, of any meeting consisting of more than fifty persons, or for more than fifty persons to assemble in any street, square, or open space in the city or liberties of Westminster or county of Middlesex, within the distance of *one mile* from the gate of Westminster Hall, except such parts of the parish of St. Paul's, Covent Garden, as are within the said distance, to consider or prepare any petition or address to the King or either House of Parliament for the alteration of matters in Church or State, on any day on which the two Houses shall sit or be adjourned to sit, or on any day on which His Majesty's Court of Chancery, King's Bench, Common Pleas and Exchequer, or any of them, shall sit in Westminster Hall, is to be deemed unlawful, and the meetings, if held, are unlawful assemblies.

It is doubtful whether a meeting can be held within a mile, as the crow flies, of the Law Courts, as the Judicature Act, 1873, says that expressions in former Acts of Parliament referring to the old courts are to refer to the new High Court of Justice.

Tumultuous petitioning.—By 13 Car. II. stat. 1, c. 5, no person shall solicit the signatures of upwards of twenty persons to any petition to the King or either House for alteration of Church or State matters without previously obtaining the consent of one or other of the authorities mentioned in the Act. Furthermore, no persons above the number of ten shall repair to His Majesty or both Houses or either House of Parliament

being dedicated to the public for no other purpose than that of providing a means for the public passing and repassing along it. A place of public resort is analogous to a public thoroughfare; and although the public may often have held meetings in places of public resort without interruption by those having control of such places, yet the public have no right to hold meetings there for the purpose of discussing any question whatever, social, political, or religious" (see headnote from which this extract is taken, *R.* v. *Cuningham Graham and another*, 16 Cox, p 420).

In the same case the same judge defined a riot as "a disturbance of the peace by three persons at least, who act on intent to help one another against any persons who oppose them in the execution of some enterprise (lawful or unlawful), and actually execute that enterprise in a violent and turbulent manner, to the alarm of the people" (*R.* v. *Graham and another*, 16 Cox, p. 420).

upon the pretence of delivering any petition or complaint, &c. The penalty for this offence is a fine up to £100 or three months' imprisonment, and the offender is to be tried within six months after committal of offence. Three witnesses are necessary to secure a conviction.

Revolutionary and dangerous meetings.—In order to put a stop to meetings of a mischievous character at which oaths are administered to members of a particular society, the following statute was passed. 37 Geo. III. c. 123, provides that "Every person who shall in any manner or form administer, cause to be administered, or aid or assist or consent to the administering of any oath or engagement, or shall take any oath or engagement to embark in any seditious or mutinous purpose, or to break the peace, or belong to any society formed for such purpose, or to obey any leader or body of men not having by law authority for that purpose, or not to reveal any unlawful federation or combination, or any unlawful act done or to be done, shall be guilty of felony." The punishment prescribed is penal servitude not exceeding seven years. (See further Russell on Crimes).

Unlawful drilling.—By 60 Geo. III. & 1 Geo. IV., c. 1, s. 1, persons attending illegal meetings for drilling or training in the use of arms, or practising military evolutions without authority from the King, or the lords lieutenants, or two justices for the county, riding, or borough, are liable to fine and imprisonment not exceeding two years.

A prosecution must take place within six months, or not at all.

Public Meeting Act.—By the Public Meeting Act, 1908 (8 Edw. VII. c. 6), disorderly conduct at any lawful public meeting is punishable by fine not exceeding £5 or imprisonment not exceeding one month, and in the case of a political meeting between issue of the writ for the return of a Member of Parliament and the return, the offence is an illegal practice within the meaning of the Corrupt Practices Act of 1883.

CHAPTER VII.

ROUTS AND RIOTS AND MARTIAL LAW.

A rout is defined by Mr. Serjeant Stephen in his Commentaries as a disturbance of the peace by persons assembling together with an intention to do a thing which, if it be executed, will make them rioters, and actually making a motion towards the execution thereof (Stephen's Commentaries, 14th edit., vol. 4, p. 174).

There must be three or more persons engaged to constitute a rout. The same learned author defines a " riot " as a tumultuous disturbance of the peace by three persons or more assembling together of their own authority with an intent mutually to assist one another against anyone who shall oppose them in the execution of some enterprise of a private nature, and afterwards actually executing the same in a violent and turbulent manner to the terror of the people, whether the act intended be of itself lawful or unlawful. A rout is a misdemeanour, like an unlawful assembly, and so is a riot in the first instance, though a riot may very easily become a felony, *e.g.*, where rioters burn a house or injure property.

The Riot Act.—Some persons think that before a riot can exist it is necessary to read the Riot Act. This is not so, as the effect of the statute is to constitute the rioters felons if they do not comply with the proclamation. (See 21 Howell's State Trials, 493).

The Act (1 Geo. 1, st. 2, c. 5) is to the following effect : Where twelve or more persons, being unlawfully and riotously assembled together to the disturbance of the public peace, are commanded by a magistrate, county sheriff or under-sheriff, mayor of a borough or a borough justice where such assembly shall be, by proclamation in the form thereinafter set forth to disperse themselves, and such persons shall to the number of twelve or more unlawfully and tumultuously remain together for one hour after the reading of the proclamation, such persons shall be guilty of felony.

The person authorized by the Act to read the proclamation shall go among the rioters, or as near to them as he can safely come, and with a loud voice command silence or cause silence to be commanded during the reading of the proclamation. The form of the proclamation is to be as follows : " Our Sovereign Lord the King chargeth and commandeth all persons being assembled immediately and peaceably to depart to their habitations or lawful business upon the pains contained in the Act, made in the first year of King George, for preventing tumults and riotous assemblies. *God save the King* " (*y*).

Section 3 provides that if the twelve or more persons in question do not disperse within the hour, any justice, constable and such other persons as shall be commanded to be assisting unto such justice may seize and apprehend the rioters, and if any be killed or hurt when resisting apprehension the persons so killing are to be indemnified.

Section 5. Wilful opposition by force of arms to the reading of the proclamation is to be felony.

Section 8. Offences under the Act are to be prosecuted within twelve months.

Persons who happen to be on the spot are not to be treated as felons, unless evidence be forthcoming of some participation in the riot (*R.* v. *Atkinson* (1869), 11 Cox, 330).

Military and other force in riots.—The duty of maintaining order and restraining disorder rests with the local authorities, and not with the central government. Sheriffs, mayors of boroughs, and magistrates, are bound to suppress rioting, and they are also charged with the duty of dispersing unlawful assemblies. When the critical moment for the use of force arrives, force must be used, but not till then.

(*y*) *R* v. *Child*, 4 Carrington & Payne, p. 442. This case is referred to in the last edition of Archbold, and, from the way the editor deals with it, it may be inferred that the omission of the words "God Save the King" might save the prisoner from capital punishment, but would not exonerate him from penal servitude, perhaps for life (see Archbold's Criminal Pleadings, p. 1169).

Military force may be resorted to when a riot is likely to be of a serious kind.

The primary duty of preserving order rests with the civil power. An officer should, where practicable, act under the orders of the magistrate, but when from fear of responsibility he abstains from acting because no magistrate is at hand, he does wrong.

Where officer and magistrate are acting in concert the former must take the latter's orders, and must not either fire without orders or refuse to fire when ordered. Still, circumstances may exist under which an officer may refuse to fire when ordered to do so. (Cf. Manual of Military Law, ed. 1907, p. 219.)

In the case of *R.* v. *Pinney* Littledale, J., made the following remarks : "A person, whether a magistrate or not, who has the duty of suppressing a riot, is placed in a very difficult situation, for if by his acts he causes death he is liable to be indicted for murder, and if he does not act he is liable for an indictment on information for neglect. He is, therefore, bound to hit the precise line of his duty. . . . Whether a man has sought a public situation or not . . . or whether he has been compelled to take the office which he holds, the same rule applies, and if persons were not *compelled* to act according to law there would be an end of society" ((1866), 4 F. & F. 763).

In *Keighly* v. *Bell* ((1832) 5 C. & P. 254), Mr. Justice Willes stated as follows : "I hope I may never have to determine how far the orders of a superior officer justify force. If compelled to determine that question, I should hold probably that those orders were an absolute justification in time of riot, at all events as regards enemies and foreigners, and probably also against natural-born subjects, unless the orders were not legally given. I believe the better opinion is that a soldier acting under the orders of his superior officer is justified unless the orders be *manifestly* illegal."

Soldiers refusing to obey orders of superiors are liable to be tried by court-martial. The whole question of calling in military force is discussed in the report of the Commission on the Featherstone Riots, cited at p. 220 of the Manual of Military Law.

Martial law.—Martial law is a term somewhat loosely employed to denote a number of quite distinct things. Chief among these are :—

(1) The law formerly administered by the Court of the Constable and Marshal.

(2) What is properly termed Military Law—the code governing the soldier, in war and peace, at home and abroad.

(3) The suspension of the ordinary law and the substitution for it of discretionary government by the Executive exercised through the military.

(4) The common law right and duty to maintain public order by the exercise of any necessary degree of force in time of invasion, rebellion, riot or insurrection.

(5) The law administered by a British general in occupied enemy territory in time of war, and

(6) (possibly) The law administered by a British general in an occupied district of ex-enemy territory.

Of (5) and (6) it is unnecessary here to say more than that the law so administered amounts to arbitrary government by the military, tempered by international custom (*e.g.*, The Hague Conventions) and such disciplinary control as the British War Office or home Government think fit to exercise.

(1), (2), (3) and (4) call for further remark.

(1). *The Constable and Marshal.*

Reeves says little is known of this court till the time of Richard II., when, he alleges, it is alluded to as a court which decided cases of contract concerning deeds of arms. He says that in the second year of Richard II. the Commons petitioned that the Constable and Marshal should surcease from holding pleas of treason or felony, which matters should be determined before the King's justices. In consequence of the continued remonstrance of Parliament 8 Richard II. c. 5 was passed, which provided that divers common law pleas should not be brought before the Constable and Marshal, but that the law should stand as it was in the reign of Edward III. The offices of Constable and Marshal were then hereditary and the heirs being infants their duties were discharged by the King. Another Act was passed after the heirs came of age (13 Richard II.) defining the jurisdiction of the court in the following way: "To the Constable belongs cognisance of contracts touching deeds of arms and war out of the realm, and also of things which touch war within the realm which cannot be determined or discussed by the Common Law with other usages to the same matters appertaining which other Constables before that time had duly and reasonably used." Maitland says that from a very early period the offices of Constable and Marshal were hereditary, and that they devolved on Henry IV. on his accession. The Constable and the Marshal were the leaders of the army and, as early as Edward I.'s reign, declined to lead the army to France. Edward IV. by letters patent in 1462 and 1467 conferred on the Court power to try all cases of treason by two commissioners. The tribunal "came to an end" with the accession of the Tudors, but in the reign of Mary there were trials by martial law, and Elizabeth and James I. granted commissions for trial of persons by martial law which were then not resisted (Maitland, Const. Hist., p. 217).

(2). *Military law* is a code embodied in the Army Act, 1881 (*z*), the King's Regulations and Army Orders. It is a code to which soldiers alone are subject, and it constitutes a number of acts "military offences." These are mainly offences against discipline and offences committed by one soldier against another, but include also certain acts which are civil crimes (*a*). In respect of military offences a soldier is subject to the jurisdiction of the courts-martial, and in the case of minor military offences, to the summary jurisdiction of his company commander and commanding officer. It is important to note that the code does not divest the soldier of his rights or relieve him of his duties as an ordinary citizen. It merely imposes on him, in addition to those duties, a number of obligations and burdens peculiar to his class. A civilian striking an officer may expose himself to nothing more than an action for a common assault, but similar action by a soldier may call down upon him, under military law, penalties of extreme severity. A civilian refusing to pay a debt of honour

(*z*) The Army Act is re-enacted yearly by the Army Annual Act

(*a*) There are, however, certain grave crimes in respect of which soldiers can only be tried by the ordinary Courts—*e g*, treason, murder, and rape

incurs only social penalties; an officer guilty of such a refusal may be convicted by court-martial of "conduct unbecoming an officer and a gentleman." Again, many offences can from their nature be committed only by a soldier, *e.g.*, desertion, or being drunk on sentry duty. Courts-martial must proceed in dealing with matters within their cognisance on the same principles of evidence and procedure as civil courts.

Three points should be noted in regard to military law:—(i) that it governs only soldiers (in which term are included Regulars, Territorials when embodied or in training, and Royal Marines when on shore); (ii) that the only acts of soldiers in respect of which they are amenable to military law are those which are constituted military offences by the Army Act; (iii) that military law does not confer on the soldier any privileged position *vis-à-vis* of civilians, or relieve him of any duties to which they are subject. It merely imposes on the soldier burdens from which civilians are exempt. By this means the existence of a standing army is reconciled with the preservation of civil liberty. This, while a blessing to the public, is very embarrassing to the soldier when, as not infrequently happens, his duties as a soldier and as an ordinary citizen come into apparent conflict. As a soldier he must obey all lawful orders: as a civilian he must commit no crime or tort. If, therefore, he is ordered to commit some act which would in normal circumstances amount to a crime or a tort (*e.g.*, to fire on a mob) he must often at a moment's notice decide whether the special circumstances of the case make the order a lawful one—a duty calling for considerable tact, judgment and knowledge of jurisprudence; while, if in the course of this intricate calculation he makes a mistake, he exposes himself either to the risk of being court-martialled for disobeying a lawful order or of being indicted for obeying an unlawful one. In practice *bonâ fide* miscalculations are excused by the tribunal, whether civil or military, and obedience to an order not manifestly unlawful is treated as an answer to proceedings in the civil courts. It is a little difficult to gather from the decisions whether a soldier who has reasonably obeyed an order which was in fact unlawful is relieved of legal liability in respect of such obedience, or is excused by an act of clemency though technically liable. (See *Keighly* v. *Bell* (1832), 5 C. & P., p. 254.)

(3). This is martial law in the strict sense of the term. It is equivalent to what is known in some Continental countries as a "state of siege" or "the suspension of the constitutional guarantees," and amounts in effect to the temporary supersession of ordinary law by unlimited government at the will of the executive. Once it has been validly proclaimed, civilians can be tried by courts-martial, the most extensive interferences with the subject's normal rights of liberty and property can be practised with impunity by the government and its servants, and the victims of such interferences can obtain no redress in the ordinary courts of law, either at the time or later. Martial law in this sense is, in fact, no law at all. High authorities, notably Prof. Dicey, assert that it is unknown to our Constitution. Other eminent lawyers draw a sharp distinction between martial law in time of peace and in time of war, and assert that while the petition of right makes it illegal in the first case, it may still validly be proclaimed in the second.

In Great Britain, at any rate, the Crown cannot proclaim martial law by prerogative in time of peace. Nor has the Crown purported to proclaim it in time of war since the time of Charles I. Outside Great Britain martial law has been proclaimed in a few cases, but in these cases powers have, as a rule, been obtained from Parliament (*e.g.*, in Ireland, 1899, and in Jamaica, 1865).

Some authorities hold, nevertheless, that martial law may validly be called into operation in time of war both in Great Britain and outside it, and that when this has been done, the civil courts have no authority to call in question the actions of the military authorities. They rely on the preambles to certain Irish Acts of Parliament (*e.g.*, 39 Geo. III. c. 11, which refers to "the wise and salutary exercise of his Majesty's undoubted prerogative in executing martial law.") They also pray in aid language used by Lord Halsbury in *Ex parte* D. F. *Marais* ((1902) A. C. 109), "The framers of the Petition of Right well knew what they meant when they made a condition of peace the ground of the illegality of unconstitutional procedure." One answer to this line of reasoning was anticipated by Lord Blackburn when he said, in his charge in *R.* v. *Eyre* ((1868), Finlason 974), "It would be an exceedingly wrong presumption to say that the Petition of Right, in not condemning martial law in time of war, sanctioned it." Another is afforded by the circumstance that when martial law has been proclaimed, the Crown has almost invariably protected its servants after the event by Acts of Indemnity. It is, at least, difficult to see why Acts of Indemnity should be needed if the actions which they retrospectively legalise were by virtue of martial law legal all the time and could not be reviewed or questioned by the civil courts (*b*).

It is sometimes difficult to determine when a state of war exists in a particular district. It was formerly supposed that in answering this question the test to be applied was whether the civil courts were open. It is now, however, established by the decision of the Privy Council in *Elphinstone* v. *Bedreechund* ((1830), 2 St. Tr. N. S. 379) and in *Ex parte* D. *F. Marais* that this test is not conclusive and that the existence of a state of war in a given district is compatible with the continued functioning for some purposes of the civil courts within that district. These judgments should be studied in detail (*c*).

(4). *The common right to maintain public order by the exercise of any degree of necessary force.*

Every citizen both may, and in the last resort must, preserve the king's peace by the exercise of any degree of necessary force in time of riot, insurrection or invasion.

The degree of force thus properly applicable may extend to the destruction of life and property to any extent. Nor must it be supposed that because this duty devolves in practice mostly on the servants of the Crown—magistrates, soldiers and police—it is not binding also on the ordinary citizen. All must, if necessary, co-operate in re-establishing public order. Martial

(*b*) See on this part of the subject *R.* v. *Nelson and Brand* (1867) F. Cockburn's Reports, pp. 59, 79; and Forsyth, "Cases and Opinions on Constitutional Law," pp. 198, 199, 553, 556, 557.

(*c*) The student is recommended also to note carefully the results of certain proceedings, which are *sub judice* as this Book goes to press, regarding the legality of so-called martial law in Ireland.

law in this sense does not need to be proclaimed. The moment public order is disturbed all citizens are entitled to suppress the disturbance (*d*). In doing so they must apply neither more nor less force than a reasonable man would judge necessary to restore peace. If they adopt excessive or cruel measures they will be criminally answerable in the ordinary courts (*Wright* v. *Fitzgerald* (1789), 27 St. Tr., p. 65), and they are bound when the actual conflict is at an end to hand over prisoners to the civil powers (Forsyth: Opinion of Edward James and FitzJames Stephens, p. 554; and *cf. Wolfe Tone's Case* ((1798), 27 St. Tr. pp. 624-5). If the right amount of force is applied, and in the course of its application acts are committed which in normal times would amount to assaults or trespasses, the courts will regard the acts as justified and required by a state of public disorder, and will give no relief to their victims. Not merely so, but they will, as the case of *R.* v. *Pinney* (5 C. & P. 254) shows, punish severely a magistrate who hesitates, in the course of a riot, to commit acts illegal in ordinary circumstances but necessary to the restoration of order. Martial law in this sense differs from martial law in sense (3) in the following important respects:—

(A) The amount of force of which it justifies the exercise is strictly limited to the necessities of the case.

(B) In respect of acts which purport to be justified by virtue of it, an aggrieved party can have recourse to the ordinary courts and will in a proper case obtain redress.

(C) It need not be "proclaimed."

There is a current superstition that such acts may not be done until "the Riot Act has been read." This is not so. It may be, and often is, the duty of a magistrate to order troops to fire on a riotous crowd without previously reading the proclamation set out in the Riot Act. The effect of reading this proclamation is not to legalise an exercise of force which previous to such reading would be illegal, but simply to constitute any twelve rioters who remain assembled one hour after the reading a "felonious assembly."

(*d*) In *R.* v. *Brown* it was held that it was an indictable misdemeanour to refuse to aid a police officer in suppressing a riot (*R.* v. *Brown* (1841) C & Mar, p. 314. See also Archbold (25th ed), p 1169)

On this part of the subject the student is referred to the statements of the Commissioners for enquiring into the disturbances at Featherstone in 1893 (C. 7234).

The Emergency Powers Act, 1920, is dealt with in the Appendix.

CHAPTER VIII.

TREASON AND SEDITION.

Treason (*proditio*) denotes a betraying, treachery or breach of faith against the Sovereign (Stephen's Commentaries, vol. 4, p. 146).

The earliest statute on the subject is 25 Edw. III., st. 5, c. 2, which constitutes the following offences treason :—

1. Compassing or imagining the death of the king, queen, or their eldest son.
2. Violating the king's companion or the king's eldest daughter unmarried or king's eldest son's wife.
3. Levying war against the king in his realm.
4. Adhering to king's enemies in his realm by giving them aid or comfort in realm or elsewhere.
5. Counterfeiting the king's seal or money, or importing false money.
6. Slaying chancellor, treasurer, king's justices of the one bench or the other, justices in eyre (on circuit), justices of assize, and other justices assigned to hear and determine in their places doing their offices.

Compassing death of Sovereign.—The word "compass" imports design which must be manifested by an overt act. The following are overt acts according to Blackstone, viz. : providing weapons, conspiring to imprison king though not intending his death, assembling and consulting to kill king. Idle words are not now treason, though they were formerly deemed so, but they are high misdemeanours.

Treasonable writings constitute treason, even without publication, as Blackstone says that in arbitrary reigns people were punished for unpublished treasonable writings, *e.g.*, Peacham (afterwards pardoned) for an unpublished sermon, and Algernon Sydney for treasonable unpublished papers found in his closet. Blackstone considers both Peacham and Sydney guiltless of treason.

Levying of war.—This includes not only levying of war to dethrone king, but levying war to reform religion, remove councillors, or redress grievances, as private persons cannot forcibly interfere in grave matters. Resistance of the royal forces by defending a castle against them is levying war, and so is an insurrection with an avowed design to pull down all chapels and the like.

During Anne's reign *Damaree* and *Purchas* were convicted of treason for burning meeting-houses, the court being of opinion that the design was a general one against the State, and therefore a levying of war ((1710), 15 St. Tr. 521).

Blackstone says that merely conspiring to levy war is not a treasonable levying of war, but that it constitutes compassing the king's death where it is pointed at the royal person or government.

Adhering to the king's enemies.—Pirates and robbers who invade our coasts are king's enemies, and so also are foreign enemies and our fellow-subjects in rebellion at home. Where, according to Blackstone, a rebel flees the realm, he is not an enemy within 25 Edw. III. (Hawke, P. C., Bk. 1, c. 17, s. 28).

Persons acting under duress as regards life or person cannot be convicted as traitors, provided that they leave the king's enemies at the first opportunity (Stephen's Com., vol. 2, p. 146).

The facts of modern civilisation and the overshadowing power of present-day central governments make it extremely difficult for any individual to hope to approach a project of rebellion, or of " levying war against the king in his realm," with the slightest prospect of even partial success. Furthermore, attacks on the person of the monarch or other royal personages are extremely rare in England, a fact which has often been ascribed to the great freedom of English institutions. Be that as it may, we hear but little of charges of high treason of this nature (or indeed any other), and when *R.* v. *Lynch* came before the Courts, there had not previously been a charge of high treason tried for sixty-two years. That case is important on the construction of that section of the statute of 1351 which deals with adhering "to the king's enemies in his realm by giving them aid or comfort in the realm or elsewhere." At the outset of the trial it was moved to quash the indictment on the ground that each count charged an adhering "without the realm," and therein disclosed no offence under 25 Edw. III., stat. 5, c. 2. The Court, while leaving the accused the right to move in arrest of judgment should he choose to do so, were of the opinion that the words in question were governed by *R.* v. *Vaughan* (13 St. Tr. 525), and that the words "be adhering to the king's enemies in his realm" did not mean that the "accused person *being in the realm* has been adherent to the king's enemies *wherever they were*," to the exclusion of such a case as that before the Court. It is clear that so narrow a construction not only would enable an Englishman to engage with a foreign hostile power against his own country so long as he took care to remain abroad, but also ignores the words "or elsewhere" in the same sentence of the section. The case also decided that section 6 of the Naturalisation Act, 1870 (33 & 34 Vict. c. 14), does not enable a British subject to become naturalised in an enemy State in time of war and, further, that the very act of becoming naturalised under those circumstances constitutes an overt act of treason. (*R.* v. *Lynch*, L. R. (1903), 1 K. B., p. 444.)

In *R.* v. *Casement* ((1916), 2 K. B., p. 858) it was decided that a man may adhere to the king's enemies and be found guilty of treason whether the act complained of was committed within or without the realm. In the case of *R.* v. *Ahlers* (C. C. A. (1915), 1 K. B., p. 616) the facts were as follows. The accused was German Consul at Sunderland and it was therefore part of his ordinary duty to give to compatriots assistance, monetary and otherwise. Ahlers on August 5th, 1914, on the day after the outbreak of war, took steps to assist German subjects of military age to return home to fight in the German army. On the 5th of August an Order in Council was made under the Aliens Restriction Act, 1914, which limited the time of departure for alien enemies to the 11th of August; of this accused knew nothing, but, as he afterwards stated in his evidence, he believed he was acting in accordance with international law. The accused was indicted for treason and convicted of adhering to the King's enemies, but the conviction was quashed by the Court of Criminal Appeal on the ground that proof was wanting that in acting as he did he was not simply carrying out his duties and also that he was aware that he was assisting the King's enemies.

Slaying the chancellor, &c.—As the chancellor and judges represent the King in court, Blackstone considers them entitled to equal protection. Attempted murder of the chancellor and judges in court is, according to Blackstone, not treason, though murdering the lord keeper (in court) was. These technical treasons the criminal code commissioners consider should be turned into murder (*e*).

By 1 Anne, st. 2, c. 21, s. 3, endeavouring to deprive or hinder any person next in succession to the throne under the Act of Settlement from succeeding thereto, and maliciously and directly attempting same by any overt act, is treason (Stephen, vol. 4, p. 143).

By 6 Anne, c. 41, maliciously and directly by writing or print maintaining and affirming that any other person hath any right to the Crown other than in accordance with the Act of Settlement, or that Parliament has not power to make laws to bind the Crown and the descent thereof, is treason (Stephen, vol. 4, p. 149).

The compassing, or imagining or intending, either within the realm or without, of the King's death, destruction, or bodily harm tending to death or destruction; maiming or wounding, imprisonment or restraint of the King's person, his heirs and successors; and uttering or declaring any such treasonable intent by any overt act, is treason (36 Geo. III. c. 7, and 57 Geo. III. c. 6).

The punishment for treason is death by hanging (Felony Act, 1870), but formerly the traitor was hanged, drawn and quartered, after being dragged on a hurdle to the place of execution.

(*e*) For what was treason in medieval times the student is referred to Stephen's Commentaries, vol. 4, p. 143.

Treason cannot be committed against a King *de jure* who is not King also *de facto*.

According to Hale, a king who has abdicated is no longer protected by the law of treason.

Procedure in treason.—By an Act of Edward VI. two witnesses are necessary to a conviction for treason, but where there is more than one overt act the two witnesses may prove one overt act apiece.

The offence must be prosecuted within three years after its commission, save in the case of compassing the King's death (7 & 8 Will. III. c. 3).

Misprision of treason.—Misprision of treason is bare concealment thereof, as where there is an assent the offence is treason.

Treason-felony.—By 11 & 12 Vict. c. 12, if any person shall, within or without the realm, compass, imagine, invent, devise, or intend to depose the Queen, her heirs or successors, from the throne of the United Kingdom, or any of her Majesty's dominions, or to levy war against the Queen, her heirs or successors, within any part of the United Kingdom, in order to compel by force a change of counsels or measures, and in order to put any constraint upon either House of Parliament, or move any foreigner to invade the realm, or other part of her Majesty's dominions, and shall express such compassing, &c., by publishing any print or writing, or any overt act, such person shall be guilty of felony.

The maximum punishment is penal servitude for life, and if a person is indicted for treason-felony, and the offence turns out to be treason, such person may be convicted of treason-felony.

Every person accused of treason is entitled to be defended by counsel, and also to give evidence on his own behalf, just like any other person accused of crime can now do.

By an Act of the year 1870, no forfeiture of property is now entailed by a conviction for treason.

By 7 & 8 Will. III. c. 3, persons accused of treason can challenge thirty-five jurors; and by 7 Anne, c. 21, a panel of

A copy of the indictment must also be furnished ten days before trial.

Inciting the King's soldiers to mutiny.—By 37 Geo. III. c. 70, s. 1, persons maliciously endeavouring to seduce the King's soldiers or sailors from their duty and allegiance, or to commit an act of mutiny or traitorous practice, are to be guilty of felony, and may receive a maximum punishment of penal servitude for life.

Sedition.—Sedition is the attempt to bring into hatred and contempt the person of the reigning monarch, or the government and Constitution of the United Kingdom as by law established, or either House of Parliament, or to incite his Majesty's subjects to attempt the alteration of any matter in Church or State (Criminal Libel Act, 1819, c. 8), or to incite any person to commit any crime in disturbance of the peace, or to raise discontent or disaffection amongst his Majesty's subjects, or to promote feelings of ill-will and hostility between different classes (Strode's Legal Dictionary, sub. tit. "Sedition").

In the case of *R.* v. *Burns and others*, tried at the Central Criminal Court, Mr. Justice Cave stated that "sedition embraces everything, whether by word, deed or writing, which is calculated to disturb the tranquillity of the State, and lead ignorant persons to endeavour to subvert the government and law of the empire" (*R.* v. *Burns* (1886), 16 Cox, 355).

A meeting lawfully convened may become an unlawful meeting if, during its course, seditious words are spoken of such a nature as to produce a breach of the peace, and those who do anything to assist the speaker in producing upon the audience the natural effect of their words, as well as those who spoke the words, are guilty of sedition (*R.* v. *Burns* (1886), 16 Cox, 355).

Criminal slander.—It is a misdemeanour to slander any member of either of the two legislative chambers, when the defamatory words in question are published and would be libellous supposing they were written concerning a private individual touching his calling in life (Odgers, p. 493).

Ribald and insulting verbal abuse of either of the legislative chambers *en bloc* or of Parliament generally, are also criminal misdemeanours.

One may criticise either House, or Parliament generally, and great latitude is permitted; but insulting language calculated to inspire contempt is criminal. The same remarks apply to published verbal abuse of High Court judges (Odgers on Libel, p. 493).

Official secrets.—An old Official Secrets Act has been repealed and is now replaced by the Official Secrets Act, 1911, which provides for the prosecution of persons who for any purpose prejudicial to the State approach a place thereby defined to be a prohibited place, or who make sketches of such prohibited place, or take copies of any prohibited document or who communicate any sketch, documents or information, &c., or who receive such sketch, &c. Such persons are by virtue of the statute guilty of a felony.

Persons again are guilty of a misdemeanour under the Act who carelessly part with any sketch, documents or information, &c., to any unauthorised person, or who retain sketches, plans or documents or information too long after the time has arrived for handing them over. Attempts to commit the above offences are to count as the commission of such offences. Persons are to be guilty of a misdemeanour, again, who either harbour spies or wilfully refuse to give information to a police superintendent respecting spies where they have harboured spies.

A prohibited place includes any arsenal, munition works, camp, fort, workshop or any place where munitions, &c., are made. By the Official Secrets Amendment Act, 1920, the following offences have been made punishable :—

(1) Wearing an unauthorised uniform for the purpose of gaining admission to a prohibited place.

(2) Making false declarations, oral or written, with the same object.

(3) Forging passports, passes or permits.

(4) Pretending to be a government official or in the employ of one.

(5) Communicating with foreign agents, *i.e.*, persons authorised by foreign powers, with a view to doing acts prejudicial to the State.

(6) Interfering with the police or the military with such purpose. The Act empowers the Government to intercept telegrams. Receivers of letters are to be registered and they are required to give information on demand as to their customers, and it appears to be an offence to give receivers of letters false information.

No member of the public is to refuse to give information respecting a suspect spy if asked to do so by certain specified police officials.

CHAPTER IX.

ALLEGIANCE—NATURALISATION—EXTRADITION—FOREIGN JURISDICTION OF CROWN—FUGITIVE OFFENDERS.

What allegiance is.—Allegiance has been defined as the "natural and legal obedience which every subject owes to his Prince" (*Termes de la Ley*) in exchange for the protection extended by the Prince to the subject (Blackstone I., p. 369). In addition, however, to subjects who owe permanent or natural allegiance, there are those who owe local allegiance, namely, aliens resident in the dominions of the Prince so long as they reside there. Allegiance is correlative with treason, in the sense that treason can only be committed against the Sovereign by a person owing allegiance to him, either natural or local. Allegiance is, moreover, due to the *de facto* Sovereign (*Calvin's Case* (1608), St. Tr. 559), even though he be an usurper.

(The case of Calvin was formerly of great constitutional importance. James I. was anxious to emphasise the fact that allegiance was a personal tie binding the subject to the Sovereign, and that English and Scotch subjects should be mutually naturalized. This idea was begotten of the idea of divine right. The Commons opposed James in the matter, and two collusive actions were therefore brought. Land was bought in the name of John Calvin, an infant. Calvin was a *post natus* (*i.e.*, born after the accession of James I. in 1603) and claimed as such *post natus.* In the first action the land was claimed for Calvin as a natural-born subject of the King, and in the second action the title deeds were claimed in Chancery. The defendant claimed that Calvin was an alien. This plea was demurred to, and in the hearing of the demurrer the court held that it was bad. Thus the case terminated in Calvin's favour.)

And when the Crowns of two countries which have formerly been united are severed, allegiance automatically reverts to the place of birth. Thus, when William IV. died, Hanoverians ceased to be British subjects (*Stepney Election Petition*, 17 Q. B. D., p. 54).

British subjects and aliens.—All persons are either :—

(1) British subjects; or

(2) Aliens.

(1) British subjects are either :

(A) Natural born; or

(B) Naturalized; or

(C) Have acquired British nationality owing to a British conquest or cession of territory to Great Britain or, if a woman, by marrying a British subject.

The last clause includes denizens.

(2) Aliens are either :

(A) Friendly aliens; or

(B) Enemy aliens.

Both of these classes, so far and so long as resident in the British dominions, owe local allegiance.

1. *British subjects.*

(A) *Natural born.*—By the British Nationality and Status of Aliens Act, 1914 (4 & 5 Geo. V., c. 19) (which codifies and to some extent modifies the pre-existing law), s. 1, the following persons are deemed to be natural-born British subjects :—

(i.) Any person born within his Majesty's dominions and allegiance.

(ii.) Any person born out of his Majesty's dominions whose father was a British subject at the time of that person's birth, and either was born within his Majesty's allegiance or was a person to whom a certificate of naturalization had been granted (*f*).

(iii.) Any person born on a British ship, whether in foreign territorial waters or not.

But nothing in this section affects the status of any person born before the Act comes into operation. Such persons are subject to

(*f*) Or, by the Act of 1918 (8 & 9 Geo. V. c. 38), had become a British subject by reason of any annexation of territory, or was at the time of that person's birth in the service of the Crown.

the pre-existing law, which is not substantially very different. One difference which may be noted is that before the Act of 1914, not only the children of a male British subject born abroad, but his grandchildren so born were British subjects (see 7 Anne c. 5, 4 Geo. II. c. 2, and 13 Geo. III. c. 21, which Acts perhaps applied only to Protestants).

By the law of nations the children of ambassadors born abroad retain the nationality of their father.

(B) *Naturalized British subjects.*—At common law no alien could by any voluntary act become a British subject, nor could any British subject became an alien (*Nemo potest exuere patriam*) (see *Fitch* v. *Weber*, 6 Hare). Up to 1844 private Acts of Parliament were from time to time passed naturalizing individual aliens. Since that time the joint effect of a number of statutes is to enable any alien complying with certain conditions to apply for, and in suitable cases to obtain, a certificate of naturalization. A person obtaining such a certificate enjoys, so long as it is in force, to all intents and purposes the full political and civil status of a natural-born British subject (4 & 5 Geo. V., c. 17, s. 3 (i)). The application must be made to a Secretary of State, who before granting a certificate must be satisfied (i) that the applicant has resided in his Majesty's dominions or has been in the service of the British Crown for not less than five years; (ii) that he is of good character, and has an adequate knowledge of English; and (iii) that he intends, if his application is granted, to reside in his Majesty's dominions or to enter or continue in the service of the Crown.

The five years' residence in condition (i) must be five years within the last eight years preceding the application. The last year's residence before the application must be in the United Kingdom. The other four may be in the United Kingdom or elsewhere within his Majesty's dominions.

As the law stood before 1914 a British colony could, in certain cases, naturalize an alien so as to make him a British subject within that colony. The Act of 1914 has, in this respect, made an important innovation. Section 8 (i) of the Act provides in effect that the Government of India and of any self-governing dominion may grant certificates in the same way and with the same effect as a Secretary of State, *i.e.*, can confer full imperial naturalization. A similar grant by the Government of any of the other British possessions must be confirmed by the Secretary of State.

No certificate takes effect until the applicant has taken the oath of allegiance (section 2 (4)).

The Secretary of State may at his discretion grant a certificate to any person with respect to whose nationality as a British subject doubt exists.

An alien applying for a certificate may ask that any infant child of his may be included in the certificate, and if the request is granted such child is naturalized as from the same date as the parent, subject to the child's right on attaining majority to revert to its parent's earlier nationality by a "declaration of alienage."

A wife's nationality follows that of her husband. Hence the wife of a natural-born or naturalized British subject is herself a British subject. She may, however, if he ceases to be a British subject, herself remain one by making a declaration. And the Act of 1918 provides that the British-born wife of an enemy alien may on making a declaration of her desire to resume British nationality be naturalized.

The Act of 1914 repeals section 3 of the Act of Settlement, whereby naturalized aliens are disqualified from holding certain offices.

The British Nationality and Status of Aliens Act, 1918, has restricted the grant and facilitated the revocation of certificates of naturalization: (1) *As to grant*, section 3 provides that no certificate shall for a period of ten years after the war be granted to any subject of a country which at the time of the passing of the Act was at war with his Majesty. Exceptions are, however, made in favour of such persons if they have served in his Majesty's or the Allied forces during the war, or were at birth British subjects, or are members of a community or race known to be opposed to the enemy governments. (2) *As to revocation*. Before the Act of 1914 a certificate of naturalization was irrevocable. That Act enables certificates to be revoked if obtained by fraud or false representations. The 1918 Act, however, provides that certificates may be revoked on a number of additional grounds, *e.g.*, when the Secretary of State is satisfied that the holder of the certificate has shown himself disloyal to his Majesty, or has traded with the enemy during any war, or has been sentenced to not less than twelve months' imprisonment within five years of the grant of the certificate, or was not of good character at the date of the grant—but in the last three cases the Secretary of State must further be satisfied that the continuance of the certificate is not for the public good (section 1, 1918 Act).

The Act also provides (section 3 (i)) that certificates granted during the war to any person who at, or before, the grant was the subject of an enemy power shall be reviewed by a committee and withdrawn if the committee so recommend.

Denizens.—The status of denizens is not affected by the foregoing Acts. By letters of denization the Crown can confer on a foreigner the majority of the rights of citizenship. A denizen can hold land and vote at a parliamentary election (*Solomon's Case* (1869), 2 Peck, 117), but he cannot sit in Parliament or be a privy councillor, or hold any office of trust under the Crown (see Chitty's Prerogatives of the Crown, p. 15). Letters of denization are hardly ever now granted.

Loss of British Nationality.—A British subject could not at common law, but may now, become naturalized in a foreign country, and any person so doing ceases to be a British subject. Naturalization, however, in a country with which his Majesty is at war not only amounts to an overt act of treason but is probably for civil purposes a mere nullity (*Rex* v. *Lynch*, *ante*, p. 73).

A person can also in some cases renounce British nationality by declaration of alienage; *e.g.*—

(1) An infant child of a foreign father, naturalized at the same time as its father and at his request, may do so on attaining majority.

(2) A person who, though born out of his Majesty's dominions, is deemed to be a natural-born British subject can make a declaration of alienage (apparently at any time after majority).

(3) Where a convention to that effect exists between his Majesty and a foreign State, persons of foreign parentage

of alienage.

As to history and status of aliens, see page 32, *ante*.

Extradition.—Certain Acts, called the Extradition Acts, which are now four in number, provide that when the Crown makes a treaty by virtue of these Acts with a foreign State, it (the Crown) may, subject to certain restrictions and formalities, hand over to any given foreign State any persons (whether foreigners or British subjects) who have been found guilty of any offence covered by the Extradition Acts or any of them. The foreign State in return undertakes to surrender to us persons who have committed extradition crimes in British territory.

The English law will not allow a man's surrender for a political offence (Extradition Act, 1870, s. 3), and further provision is made that, subject to certain reservations in the Act specified, no person is to be surrendered or be tried for any crime other than the crime in respect of which his extradition was demanded. The Act of 1870 further enables the Crown to make Orders in Council directing that the Extradition Acts shall apply to any given State. This Order in Council, furthermore, shall be deemed conclusive evidence that the arrangement therein referred to complies with the provisions of the Act, and that the Act applies in the case of the foreign State mentioned in the Order, and the validity of the Order is not to be questioned.

The Act of 1870 provides for the question of surrender being tried by a Bow Street magistrate, who is styled in the Act a "police magistrate."

When extradition is desired, accused can be arrested—

(1) By police magistrate's warrant issued on the order of the Secretary of State.

(2) By warrant of a justice of the peace issued upon information on oath in the ordinary way.

It is the duty of a justice who issues a warrant under the Act of 1870 to send the prisoner before a police magistrate.

When a police magistrate commits a prisoner for surrender, such surrender cannot take place for fifteen days, or such further time as a *habeas corpus* application (if applied for) may occupy (Extradition Act, 1870, s. 11).

Section 12 provides that if a fugitive criminal is not conveyed out of the kingdom within two months after committal for surrender by the police magistrate, or if a writ of *habeas corpus* is issued after the decision thereon, any superior court judge may upon the prisoner's application, and upon proof that the Secretary of State has had reasonable notice of such application, order the discharge of the prisoner from custody.

If the fugitive is not discharged, he is surrendered under the warrant of the Secretary of State.

Foreign jurisdiction.—The foreign jurisdiction of the Crown is not easy to deal with in an elementary treatise. It rests primarily on the fact that when a British subject goes abroad he still remains a British subject, though he may owe temporary allegiance in the country where he is residing.

In the first place, if a British subject commits certain crimes in foreign territory, *e.g.*, murder or manslaughter, he may be tried and punished for them on his return to England, though, in many cases also, he may be tried and punished in the country where he committed the crime.

In the second place, special provision has to be made for the protection of the persons and property of British subjects abroad. As regards civilised countries, this is provided for by the appointment of consuls, whose duty it is to help British subjects who are charged with crime abroad or would otherwise get into difficulties. Of course, if the foreign country persists in doing wrong to a British subject, the only remedy is by way of diplomatic representation. Diplomatic agents and consuls have notarial powers, and under certain restrictions have the power to celebrate marriage between British subjects.

Thirdly, in the case of barbarous countries, or countries where there is no regular government, foreign jurisdiction is exercised on a much more extensive scale, and its exercise is regulated by the Foreign Jurisdiction Act, 1890, which begins by reciting that by treaty, capitulation, grant, usage, sufferance and other lawful means, the Crown has jurisdiction within divers foreign countries. The Act then proceeds to empower persons authorised by warrant from the Crown to send for trial, at some specified British court, persons charged with offences in the particular foreign country named. It also authorises the Crown, by Order in Council, to create courts of civil and criminal jurisdiction in the foreign country and to regulate the procedure of these courts, and to define the persons who should be subject to their jurisdiction. For example, consular courts of civil and criminal jurisdiction have been created in Persia by an Order in Council of 1889. So, too, consular courts have been created in Morocco, with a curious concurrent and appellate jurisdiction in the Supreme Court at Gibraltar.

Fourthly, reference must be made to the Foreign Enlistment Act, 1870, which regulates the conduct of British subjects during the existence of hostilities between foreign States with which his Majesty is at peace. That Act punishes British subjects who accept commissions or engagements in the military or naval service of any foreign State which is at war with any other foreign State with which we are at peace.

The Act further punishes the building of ships for any foreign country which is at war with any friendly State, and penalises any persons who, in British dominions, prepare or fit out any naval or military expeditions to proceed against the dominions of any friendly State.

(As to foreign jurisdiction generally, see Hall's Foreign Jurisdiction of the Crown.)

Fugitive Offenders Act.—As to the surrender of offenders as between the United Kingdom and its colonies, see the Fugitive Offenders Act (44 & 45 Vict. c. 69).

PART III.

The Crown

CHAPTER X.

TITLE TO THE CROWN.

Under the Saxons the title to the Crown was by election, but generally, where he was fit to govern, the eldest son of the deceased King was elected if of full age. Under our common law the title to the Crown may be said to have been hereditary, the nearest male feudal heir being chosen. But (1) where the Throne devolved upon a female the eldest female and her issue was preferred. The first Queen Regnant was Mary, who came to the Throne under Henry's VIII.'s will, sanctioned by an Act of Parliament, and, to allay all possible doubts as to her powers, she being a married woman, a statute (1 Mary I., c. 1) was passed conferring upon her as Queen Regnant all the powers of a King; and (2) the ancient legal rule relative to the exclusion of the half-blood never applied to the title to the Crown (cf. Halsbury, vol. 6, p. 320).

The first four Norman Kings were elected, and Henry II., a grandson of Henry I. in the female line, succeeded owing to a compromise after the civil war in that reign. Richard I. was the eldest surviving son of Henry II. John was the youngest son of Henry II., and is supposed to have murdered Arthur of Brittany—the son of Geoffrey, his elder brother—in order that he might lay claim to the Dukedom of Normandy, then annexed to the English Crown. Hereditary descent was in John's time not strictly recognised, but the idea was growing owing to the close association of the Crown with the land, the Norman kingship, unlike the Saxon, being territorial rather than personal. This may have been the reason for the murder of his nephew attributed by historians to John.

It is a significant fact that Henry III., John's infant son, was chosen as his successor, though at the time of his accession he was only nine years of age. Edward I. was the son of Henry III. and, though abroad in Palestine at his father's death, he was proclaimed King *jure hæreditario.*

Edward II. was the eldest and only son of Edward I., and Edward III. was Edward II.'s eldest son. Richard II. was the grandson of Edward III., being the son of Edward the Black Prince, the eldest son of Edward III.

Richard II. was deposed and was succeeded by Henry IV., the son of John of Gaunt and grandson of Edward III., who succeeded to the Throne under an Act of Parliament entailing the Crown on him and the issue of his body. Henry V. and Henry VI. succeeded under the same parliamentary entail. Edward IV. succeeded by conquest and by pedigree, which was afterwards fortified by statute, and Richard III., Edward IV.'s brother, is credited with usurping the Throne after murdering—a fact which is open to doubt—the two sons of Edward IV.

Richard III. based his right of succession on the fact that an alleged precontract of marriage of Edward IV. rendered his issue by Elizabeth Gray bastards.

Henry VII. had no claim to the Crown whatever save as a descendant of Edward III., but he was the recognised head of the Lancastrian party and the winner of the Battle of Bosworth.

There was, moreover, no legitimate heir of the House of Lancaster, but Henry nevertheless procured from Parliament a statutory entail on himself and the issue of his body.

Henry VIII. was succeeded under a parliamentary entail by Edward VI., his son by Jane Seymour.

Edward VI. died in infancy and was succeeded by his half-sister Mary, and, after her death, by his half-sister Elizabeth, both of them succeeding under a statute of Henry VIII., subject nevertheless to restrictions and conditions made by Henry VIII.'s will. Mary and Elizabeth both died without issue. Henry VIII., acting under a statutory power, had devised the Crown, on failure of issue of his three children, to the heirs of the body of his younger sister Mary, Duchess of Suffolk, ignoring the prior claim of his elder sister Margaret.

James I., having got the ear of Elizabeth's Council, was proclaimed King, though Henry VIII.'s will was indisputable. James I., however, sought a parliamentary title, and got it. Charles I. was the eldest surviving son of James I., and Charles II. and James II., as sons of Charles I., succeeded as lawful heirs. The Declaration of Rights declared that James II. had abdicated and that the Throne had thereby become vacant. The Crown was settled by Parliament on William III. and Mary during their joint lives and on the survivor of them during his or her life, remainder to the Princess Anne of Denmark and her issue, remainder to the issue of William III. In 1700 William III., having no issue, and Anne seeming likely to have no surviving issue, the Act of Settlement was passed settling the Throne on the Electress Sophia and the heirs of her body being Protestants.

The Electress Sophia was a daughter of Elizabeth who married the Elector Palatine of Hanover, and a granddaughter of James I. Sophia's son, George I., succeeded Anne under the Act of Settlement.

From the time of George I. to the present the succession has never failed, the legal heir under the Act of Settlement succeeding. Under the Act of Settlement any successor to the Crown who is a Papist, or who marries a Papist, is incapacitated. The successors to the Crown must also take the Coronation Oath and sign the declaration prescribed by the Bill of Rights. The successor to the Throne is to be in communion with the Church.

The words of the oath as taken before the Accession Declaration Act, 1910, were to the following effect :—

" Will you solemnly swear to govern the people of this realm according to the Statutes of Parliament agreed on and the respective laws and customs of the same?"

" A. I solemnly promise so to do."

" Will you to the best of your power cause law and justice in mercy to be executed in all your judgments?"

" A. I will."

" Will you to the best of your power maintain God's laws, the true profession of the Gospel and the Protestant reformed religion established by law? And will you maintain and preserve inviolably the settlement of the Church of England and the doctrine, worship, discipline, and government thereof as by law established in England, and will you preserve unto the Bishops and Clergy of England and to the Church there committed to their charge all such rights and privileges as by law do or shall appertain to them or any of them?"

The King was also required to make a declaration against transubstantiation either at his first Parliament or at his Coronation (Bodley's Coronation of Edward VII., p. 438).

The form of the declaration, however, which was originally prescribed by the Bill of Rights and Act of Settlement, is now, by virtue of the Accession Declaration Act, 1910, as follows:—

"I do solemnly and sincerely in the presence of God testify and declare that I am a faithful Protestant and that I will according to the true intent of the enactments which secure the Protestant succession to the Throne of my realm uphold and maintain the said enactments to the best of my powers according to law" (Accession Declaration Act, 1910 (10 Edw. VII. & 1 Geo. V. c. 29)).

CHAPTER XI.

THE ROYAL FAMILY.

The King.—The King is the chief officer of the State. He is an essential part of the legislature. Justice is administered in his name, and the process of his own courts, therefore, cannot be directed against him. The executive government of the country is carried on in his name and on his behalf, but what were formerly the personal prerogatives of the Sovereign have now become so largely the privileges of the executive that they can only be dealt with collectively as prerogatives of the Crown. As to purely personal privileges, see further Chitty's Prerogatives of the Crown, pp. 12 and 374; and as to the liability of the King's private estates to rates and taxes, see 25 & 26 Vict. c. 37, ss. 8, 9.

Queen Regnant.—The Queen Regnant has the same powers and status as a King (1 Mary I. c. 1).

Queen Consort.—The life and chastity of the Queen Consort are protected by the Statute of Treasons. The Queen Consort, though married, was always a *feme sole*, and could sue and be sued at common law without her husband being joined. She always could purchase property for herself, convey property, and grant leases, and the reason for this is that the King's time is so much taken up that he ought not to be troubled with his wife's business matters. Mr. Robertson says it is uncertain whether the Queen is bound by the Statute of Limitations. The Queen has her own Attorney and Solicitor-General; she pays no toll, neither can she be amerced in any court (Stephen, vol. 2, p. 459; Robertson's Suits by and against Crown, pp. 5, 6, 7). She is the King's subject, and is thus amenable to criminal process. She was formerly entitled to certain reservations out of the royal demesne lands, and to a perquisite called "Queen's gold."

It rests with the King whether he will have her crowned or not (*Queen Caroline's Case*, 1 St. Tr. N. S. p. 949).

On the King's death the Queen Consort becomes the Queen Dowager, and the statute relating to treason no longer applies to her.

Prince Consort.—There are four instances of Queens Regnant having been married. Philip and William III., who married respectively Mary I. and Mary II. These two enjoyed the title of King. Prince George of Denmark and the late Prince Albert were Prince Consorts. Prince Albert at State functions had a precedence next to the Queen allotted to him. He was accorded the title of Prince Consort by Letters Patent. He was made a British subject on taking the oath of allegiance and the oath of supremacy (Anson, vol. 1, p. 256; Stephen's Coms., vol. 2, p. 461; Todd, vol. 1, p. 195). He was allowed to attend Privy Council meetings, though he was never a Privy Councillor; but cf. Todd, vol. 1., p. 195).

The Prince of Wales.—The life of the King's eldest son is protected by the law of treason (Statute of Treasons).

When the King's eldest son is born he immediately becomes Duke of Cornwall if his father (or mother) is on the Throne. When he succeeds to the Throne, the Duchy of Cornwall immediately vests in his eldest son.

If the King chooses, and when he chooses, he can make his eldest son Prince of Wales and Earl of Chester by Letters Patent. The present Prince of Wales was made Prince of Wales by Letters Patent and a ceremony in addition.

The reigning Sovereign can control the custody and education of the children of his heir, and, according to the better opinion, the custody of all princes and princesses of the blood royal save the issue of princesses who have married into foreign royal families (see May's Const. Hist., vol. 1, p. 264). The chastity and life of the Princess of Wales during marriage are safeguarded by the Statute of Treasons (25 Edw. III. st. 5, c. 2).

Princes and princesses of the blood.—These royal persons take precedence of all peers and public officials. 31 Hen. VIII. c. 10

provides that nobody save the King's descendants shall presume to sit at the side of the Cloth of State in Parliament. This privilege, according to Stephen, extends to the King's brothers, nephews and uncles (Stephen's Coms., vol. 2, p. 463). Princes of the blood, till summoned by the House of Lords, are commoners.

By the Royal Marriage Act (12 Geo. III. c. 11), no descendant of the body of George II. (other than the issue of princesses married into foreign families) can lawfully marry without the royal consent signified under the Great Seal and declared in council, and all other marriages are void. All persons solemnizing such marriages, or who are privy and consenting thereto, are to incur the penalties of a praemunire. A descendant of George II. over twenty-five years of age may marry without the Sovereign's consent on giving twelve months' notice to the Privy Council, provided that no objection be taken by Parliament in the interim (cf. May's Const. Hist., vol. 1, p. 265).

CHAPTER XII.

THE ROYAL PREROGATIVE.

There have been numerous definitions of the word "prerogative." Blackstone says it means that pre-eminence which the King hath above all manner of men and out of the course of the common law in right of his royal dignity. It signifies, he continues, in its etymology from *prae* and *rogo*, something which is required, or demanded, in preference to all others. "It can only be applied to those rights and capacities which the King enjoys alone" (Bl. vol. 3, Chitty Prerog. of Crown, p. 4).

Comyn's definition is as follows: "The King's prerogative comprises" all the liberties, privileges, powers and royalties allowed by the law to the Crown of England (Comyn's Digest, vol. 7, p. 42).

Finch says "it is that law in the case of the King which is no law in the case of the subject" (Finch, L. 85).

The following definitions are also noteworthy:

"It extends to all powers, pre-eminencies and privileges which the law giveth to the Crown" (Coke upon Littleton, 1, 90B).

"The prerogative appears to be both historically and as a matter of actual fact nothing else than the residue of arbitrary authority which at any given time is legally left in the hands of the Crown" (Dicey's Constitutional Law, p. 420) (*g*).

"That advantage which the Crown has over the subject where their interests come into competition by reason of its greater strength" (Hallam).

Bracton, speaking of pre-eminence, says: *Rex est vicarius et minister Dei in terrâ, omnis quidem sub eo est, et ipse sub nullo, nisi tantum sub Deo.* The realm of the King is an empire, and no emperor is greater than the King.

(*g*) Professor Dicey is here alluding to the official powers, as the personal privileges of the King are nowadays of less importance than formerly.

The present position of the King as a person.—In theory and by strict law the King has very extensive powers. The conventions have, however, altered his position. After the Revolution the King was put on an allowance by the nation, out of which he had to pay certain posts, whilst military matters were taken in hand by Parliament. Before the Revolution the King and Council conducted the government, though the King was not bound, as now, to take the advice of his Ministers. Parliament could not prevent, as now, threatened mischief, but could only impeach after the mischief had happened.

After William and Mary's accession the prerogative outwardly remained *in statu quo* (as altered by the Bill of Rights), but care was taken to avoid its abuse.

The result of the Revolution was to establish gradually three main principles upon which our system of government now rests : (1) The Sovereign is irresponsible, but (2) Ministers are responsible to Parliament for the exercise of every prerogative, and (3) it is the right and duty of Parliament to enquire into the way in which Ministers exercise the prerogative and approve or condemn the mode of exercise.

Recognition of these principles implies three duties binding on the three parties to the constitutional arrangement, viz. :—

" It is the King's duty to select Ministers enjoying parliamentary confidence (*i.e.*, majority in the Commons) and to retain them so long as that confidence is continued " (Trail, Central Government, p. 5 *et seq.*).

It is the Ministers' duty to court parliamentary supervision over their public conduct and to submit all the acts of their policy, with no further concealment than the national interests may sometimes demand, to Parliament's judgment, and to accept Parliament's adverse opinion upon any important act of administration as an implied summons to resign (*ibid.*, p. 6).

These principles, which embrace the notion of Party Government, gradually began to assume shape after the Revolution.

By Party Government is meant the wielding of the prerogative by the leading party in the Commons, which is now under Cabinet control. We first hear of Party Government in the days of William III., who yielded to it at times, but kept foreign affairs under his control.

The idea gained more definite shape in Walpole's day, as Walpole retired on a hostile vote, and so did North later, but these were the only two cases of these resignations prior to the Reform Act of 1832.

Walpole was not the first Prime Minister, though he resembled one. He was invited by the King to join the Cabinet as the King's friend; he was not asked to form a Ministry or choose his colleagues. By sheer force of character he gained a leadership over his colleagues.

Pulteney, on being asked by George II. to form a Cabinet, only requested the filling up of three or four posts. The better opinion is that there was no Party Government till Pitt the younger came into power in 1782.

At the present day there are no longer two leading parties in the Commons, but there are groups embracing different views, and the man who can represent most groups has the best claim to be Premier.

The personal influence of the King declined in the reigns of George I. and George II. Neither of them could speak English well; they ceased to attend Cabinet meetings; and since then English Sovereigns have not found it expedient to attend them. The member of the Privy Council who sat in the chair when the King ceased to attend was the forerunner of the present Premier.

Classification of the prerogatives.—Blackstone divides the prerogatives into three kinds:—(1) Those regarding the royal character; (2) those regarding the royal authority; and (3) those regarding the Royal revenue.

The first two of these were called by the feudal writers the *majora regalia*, and the third was called the *minora regalia*.

Blackstone's classification of the prerogatives is now obsolete, and so is his whole treatment of the subject. To read him one would suppose that the King is the main source of power in the State, instead of being a mere figurehead and social leader, or when he is an able man the adviser of his Ministers, whose advice carries weight, but who is not their master.

Professor Maitland gives the following classification:—(1) Those prerogatives relating to the convening, proroguing, and dissolving Parliament and assenting to statutes; (2) powers relating to foreign affairs, war, peace, treaties, &c.; (3) powers of appointing and dismissing officers civil, military, executive, and judicial; (4) powers relative to the collection and expenditure of the revenue; (5) powers relating to the naval and military forces; (6) powers connected with the administration of justice; (7) powers connected with the maintenance of order; (8) powers connected with social and economic affairs, such as public health, education, trade, &c.; (9) powers connected with religion and the national Church.

The following division will, however, prove more simple, *i.e.*, the division of the prerogatives into personal and political, and the subdivision of the political prerogatives into domestic and foreign, and further subdivision of the domestic into administrative, judicial, ecclesiastical, and legislative. In conclusion, we will treat of the *minora regalia* or revenue prerogatives.

I. **Personal prerogatives.**—The personal prerogatives still exist, but often clash with the political, overlapping being inevitable. The principal ones are as follows: (1) the King can do no wrong; (2) the King never dies; (3) *Rex est vicarius et minister Dei in terrâ, omnis quidem sub eo est et ipse sub nullo, nisi tantum sub Deo*; (4) lapse of time does not bar the right of the Crown; (5) where the title of the King and that of the subject clash, the King's title must be preferred; (6) the King is not bound by statutes unless named therein; (7) the King is never an infant.

(1) *The King can do no wrong.*—Professor Dicey says this means that the King is not liable for any act of his Ministers, but Ministers are liable for all royal acts.

No administrative act can be done by the King without the counter-signature of a responsible Minister. No man can plead the royal order as justification of an illegal act (Dicey, p. 26).

This maxim, says Broom, has a double meaning: (a) it means that the King in his personal capacity is not answerable to any earthly tribunal—neither can his blood be corrupted; for instance, if the King were before his accession attainted of treason, he would by succeeding to the throne be purged of all guilt; (b) that the prerogative of the Crown extends not to any injury, because, being created for the benefit of the people, it cannot be exercised to their prejudice: "*ergo*, it is a fundamental rule that the King cannot sanction an act forbidden by law: so from that point of view he is not above the law." The act is invalid if unlawful and the instrument of execution is obnoxious to punishment. As in affairs of State the King's Ministers are responsible for advice tendered to the King, or even for measures which might be known to emanate directly from the King, so may the agents of the Crown be civilly or criminally responsible for acts done by his command (Broom on Legal Maxims, p. 40).

Not only can the King not do wrong, but he cannot think wrong.

When, therefore, by misinformation or inadvertence he invades the rights of a subject, as by granting a franchise (*i.e.*, a royal privilege in the hands of a subject) contrary to reason or prejudicial to the community, the law declares that the King has been deceived in his grant, and such grant is void (*ibid.*, p. 41).

Again, the Crown cannot in derogation of the rights of the public fetter the exercise of the prerogative which is vested in it for the public good. The Crown, again, cannot dispense with anything wherein the subject is interested, or make a grant in opposition to the common law, or which adversely affects the interests of an individual (*ibid.*, p. 41).

Even where the royal grant purports to be made *ex certa scientia et mero motu*, the same will be void where it appears that the King was deceived in his grant (*ibid.*, p. 4).

The King cannot by grant of lands create an estate unknown to the law, neither can he grant a peerage descending in a way unknown to the law, as peerage partakes of the nature of land in most respects (*Wilts Case*, p. 227, *post*; *Buckhurst Case*, p. 227, *post*).

A statute, however, though a royal act, is unimpeachable (*Macormick* v. *Grogan*, L. R. 4 H. L., p. 96).

Where the Crown recalls a grant the grantee from the Crown suffers (*Cumming* v. *Forrester*, 1 Jac. & W. 342). As regards patents, the Crown is said to be deceived where the invention turns out not to be a novelty, and every part of the patent is void. Up to the time of Edward I. it may be that actions lay against the King. There was a rumour that a writ was issued against Henry III. This is discredited by Pollock. Chitty admits that the King could be sued up to the reign of Edward I. —at least, he hints that this was possible.

As to petition of right, see Chapter XIII.

2. *The King never dies.*—The King has the attribute of immortality. "Henry, Edward, and George may die, but the King survives them all. For immediately upon the decease of the reigning prince his kingship by act of law, without any interregnum or interval, vests in the King's heir." (Bl. I., p. 249.)

"It is true that the King never dies, the demise is immediately followed by the succession. There is no interval; the Sovereign always exists, the person only is changed" (*per* Lord Lyndhurst in *Viscount Canterbury* v. *Attorney-General*, 1 Phill., p. 321).

As to the effect of the demise of the Crown on Parliament see p. 209. The title of the Sovereign is regulated by succession as well as descent, and therefore if land be given to the King "and his heirs," the word "heirs" means the successors to the throne.

Hence, if the King dies without issue male, his eldest daughter would take under a grant to the King and his heirs (see Grant on Corporations, p. 127). If land is given to the King and his heirs and a new dynasty succeeds, the first King of the new dynasty will take the land granted (Grant on Corporations, p. 127).

It is a mistake to think that the theory of the continuance of the royal person is blindly obeyed. In the case of *Attorney-General* v. *Kohler* (8 H. L. 634) it was held that a Sovereign could not be held responsible to refund money paid to the Treasury by mistake in the reign of his predecessor.

3. *The King is God's minister on earth.*—Everybody is under him and he is under nobody but God.

The King's realm is an empire and no emperor is greater than the King. The King's blood cannot be corrupted. The King's style and title are as follows: "King of the United Kingdom of Great Britain and Ireland and of the British Dominions beyond the Seas, Defender of the Faith, and Emperor of India" (1 Edward VII., c. 15).

4. *Nullum tempus occurrit regi.*—Lapse of time will not, as a rule, bar the right of the Crown to sue or prosecute, but the

exceptions are now numerous. The right of the Crown to claim real property as against the adverse right of the subject is barred after sixty years (The Nullum Tempus Act (9 Geo. III., c. 16)).

Other statutes have also been passed barring the rights of the Crown to death duties after the period named in the statutes has elapsed.

Informations against usurpers of corporate offices must be exhibited within six years after the usurpation (32 Geo. III., c. 88).

Indictments for treason (cases of attempted assassination of the King excepted) must be found within three years after the committal of the crime (8 William III., c. 3). There are also numerous cases where criminal proceedings must be taken within a limited period.

Complaints on information before courts of summary jurisdiction must, as a rule, be laid within six months of the commission of the offence.

5. *Quando jus domini regis et subditi concurrunt jus regis præferri debet.*—When the right of the King and the subject conflict, the subject's right must give way to the King's. Thus, where the King and a subject are joint owners, the King takes the whole.

Where the subject as judgment creditor has seized goods under a writ of *fieri facias*, and after this a writ of extent has been issued affecting the same property, the claim of the Crown under the writ of extent is preferred (Broom's Legal Maxims).

6. *The King is not bound by statute unless expressly named therein.*—It is said, however, that a statute may bind the King by necessary implication as well as express language. The King is also supposed to be bound, though not named therein, by statutes for the public good, for the preservation of public rights, suppression of public wrong, relief and maintenance of the poor, advancement of learning, religion and justice, the prevention of fraud; statutes tending to perform the will of a grantor, donor or founder (Broom's Legal Maxims).

There is a *primâ facie* inference or presumption that a statute made by the Crown as to other cases is made for the subject and not for the King (*per* Alderson, B., in *Attorney-General* v. *Donaldson*, 10 M. & W. 117).

The King's high officials, who are, so to speak, clothed with the King's mantle, are protected by this maxim. Thus, in *Bainbridge* v. *Postmaster-General* ((1906), 1 K. B., p. 178), it was held that the defendant was not liable for wrongful acts of his subordinates in carrying out the business of the Department.

By the Weights and Measures Act, 1878 (41 & 42 Vict. c. 49) persons having in their possession for use in trade untrue scales were liable to a fine. Nicholls, a baker and also a postmaster, had untrue scales belonging to the Government and used them for the purposes of his trade as a baker. A writ of prohibition was applied for, and the court held that the magistrates had no jurisdiction to hear the case, because the provisions of the Weights and Measures Act did not apply to scales which were Crown property. (See *R.* v. *Kent Justices* (1889), 2 Q. B. D., p. 181.) In *Hornsey Urban District Council* v. *Hennell* ((1902), 2 K. B., p. 73) the court held that where land had been acquired and occupied by a Volunteer Corps for military purposes and held under the Volunteer Act, 1863, and the Military Funds Act, 1892, and vested in the commanding officer of the corps for the time being, it is land owned and occupied for the purposes of the Crown. The commanding officer, therefore, was not liable for expenses incurred by a local body. The question in dispute was whether the defendant had to contribute to the cost of paving the street anew.

7. *The King is never an infant.*—Royal grants and statutes assented to by an infant King are valid. Maitland says no provision is made by the law for the King being a minor, or from any other reason being incapable to fulfil the duties of his office. The law holds the King always capable of transacting business. The custom, however, is to provide beforehand for a royal minority by statute.

These statutes are called Regency Acts, giving as they do a Regent limited powers of doing the work of the King, say till the latter is 18 years of age.

II. Political **prerogatives.**—Domestic.

Administrative prerogatives.—These consist of creation of peers; creation of corporations, a power now scarcely ever exercised; the appointment of Ministers and other government officials; the dismissal of Ministers and government officials; the headship of Army, Navy and Civil Service.

The King's signature is necessary for signing numerous appointments. He also signs numerous Orders in Council. Certain documents bear the Great Seal and the Lord Chancellor is responsible for affixing same.

Numerous documents are under the Royal Sign Manual and in all cases Ministers who countersign are responsible for the royal act.

Judicial prerogatives.—The King is the fountain of justice and general conservator of the peace of the kingdom. By the expression "fountain of justice" the law does not mean the author or originator, but only the distributor, of justice. Justice is not derived from the King as his free gift, but he is the steward of the public to dispense it to whom it is due *ad hoc creatus est, et electus, ut justitiam faciat universis* (*h*).

The King is not the spring, but the reservoir, whence right and equity are conducted by a thousand channels to every individual. The original power of judicature (after the period of self-help—the bloodfeud period—had elapsed) was vested in society at large, but as it would be impracticable to render complete justice by the people in their collective capacity, nations have committed that power to selected magistrates, who, in England, were the kings. The King, therefore, has alone the right of erecting courts of justice, and hence it follows that all jurisdictions of courts are mediately or immediately derived from the Crown. Their proceedings run in the King's name (*i*).

In County Courts and in some other local courts the proceedings are unconnected with the King so far as externals are concerned. In ancient times the Kings dispensed justice in

(*h*) The office of "cyning" was evolved from the office of heretog or war leader of the Teutonic classes mentioned in Tacitus. To stop the bloodfeud the heretog settled disputes when a man was killed, and took his "wite," the relations taking the "wer," according to the market price (wergild) of the deceased, which depended on his position. In cases of injury, to prevent a duel the heretog awarded a bôt (compensation), unless the offence was bôtless. Bôtless offences were the precursors of what were later known as crimes.

(*i*) In criminal proceedings the King nominally prosecutes, and civil proceedings in the Superior Courts are commenced by the King, who summons the defendant.

court, but for centuries they have deputed this duty to their judges, to maintain the independence of whom the Act of Settlement provided that their commissions should be made not *durante placito*, but *quam diu se bene gesserint* (Bl. I. ch. 7).

By 1 George III. c. 23 it was provided that the judges should be continued in their offices during good behaviour, notwithstanding any demise of the Crown (Chitty, p. 83). The King is restricted in his appointment of judges. Judges of the High Court must be barristers of at least ten years' standing. County Court judges must be barristers of seven years' standing; recorders, of five years. As to Lords of Appeal in ordinary see p. 231.

The King cannot determine any cause or proceeding save by the mouth of his judges, whose power, however, is only an emanation of the prerogative (Chitty). Courts of justice have gained a well-known and stated jurisdiction and their decisions must be regulated by certain and established rules of law (*k*).

It necessarily follows that even our Kings themselves cannot, without Parliamentary sanction, grant any addition of jurisdiction to such courts, nor authorise anyone to hold them in a manner dissimilar to that established by the common law or statute law of the land. His Majesty cannot grant a commission to determine any matter of equity, but it ought to be determined in the Court of Chancery (now High Court of Justice), which has immemorially possessed a jurisdiction in such cases. (Chitty, pr. 75 *et seq.*) The King cannot legally authorise any court to proceed contrary to English law.

This would hold good as regards our home courts, but as regards colonial courts it would perhaps be more correct to say that the King cannot create any court contrary to English notions of right and justice, *e.g.*, permitting torture.

'Most indubitably the power of the King to erect new courts was exercised in the Middle Ages. Nothing was commoner. A distinction was drawn between common law and other courts. The King could not create a Court of Equity. "Has the Queen nowadays power to create new courts? I believe we must say

(*k*) Rules of Courts, superior or inferior, are mostly instances of indirect legislation of Parliament, and have the force of statutes.

that it exists" (Maitland, Const. History, p. 419). In the *Bishop of Natal's Case* the Court held as follows :—" Though the Crown by its prerogative may establish courts to proceed according to common law, yet it cannot create any court to administer any other law. It was also decided that, as no ecclesiastical tribunal or jurisdiction is required in a colony or settlement where there is no established Church, the ecclesiastical law of England cannot be treated as part of the law which settlers carry with them from the Mother Country" (*Bishop of Natal's Case* (1864), 3 Moo. N. S., p. 152).

Maitland considers that the prerogative as to the erection of courts is now obsolete, because (1) a court of common law would be so clumsy as to be comparatively useless; (2) the King cannot tax his subjects for the upkeep of courts he chooses to erect (*cf.*, Maitland, Const. History, 420).

Pardon.—Pardon is a part of the judicial prerogative (*l*).

The policy of pardoning public offenders has been questioned by Beccaria on the ground that clemency should shine forth in the laws and not in the execution of them. It is for the King to pardon in the legal sense, and for the Home Secretary, or other royal servant entrusted with the duty,, in the conventional sense. No pardon can be pleaded by way of defence to an impeachment of the Commons (Act of Settlement, 1700 (12 & 13 William III., c. 2), s. 3), but the King may remit penalties resulting from the impeachment. Thus, three lords who were impeached and attainted after the Rebellion of 1715 were subsequently pardoned (Halsbury, vol 6, p. 404).

Where the penalty of a præmunire has been incurred by the sending of a man in custody out of the kingdom contrary to the Habeas Corpus Act, 1879, the King cannot pardon (Halsbury, vol. 6, p. 404; Chitty, p. 92).

Where an offence affects the public only the King can pardon, but in many cases the following maxim applies, *Rex non potest gratiam facere cum injuria et damno aliorum.* Thus the

(*l*) Pardon differs from dispensation, as pardon only relates to past transgressions, whilst dispensation concerns transgressions past and also future (cf. Maitland).

Sovereign is unable to pardon a public nuisance whilst it continues (Bacon's Abridgment, sub tit. "Pardon"). Again, the King cannot pardon a libel or a slander, or remit a recognisance to keep the peace (Halsbury, vol. 6, p. 406 *et seq.*).

When once a common informer had commenced a penal action, the King could not remit the penalty, as this would be calculated to prejudice the common informer, but where no proceedings had been commenced the King could remit the penalty. But owing to the Remission of Penalties Act (22 Vict. c. 32) penalties for offences may be remitted by the Crown, though payable to parties other than the Crown.

By 13 Richard II., stat. 2, c. 1, no pardon for treason, murder, or rape shall be valid unless the offence be particularly specified therein, and particularly in murder it shall be expressed whether it was committed by lying in wait, assault, or malice prepense.

Formerly the pardon of a principal offender enured for the benefit of the accessory, but this is no longer the case. No fee or stamp is chargeable for a pardon. A pardon may be pleaded in bar to an indictment, or after judgment in bar of execution (Archbold, Criminal Pleadings).

It must be pleaded at the first opportunity for pleading it, for if the prisoner, who can plead pardon, pleads "not guilty," he is deemed to have waived the pardon and cannot avail himself thereof in arrest of judgment (*R.* v. *Norris*, 1 Roll Rep., p. 297).

By a statute of Henry VIII.'s reign the power of the Lords was taken away, the right of pardoning being reserved for the King alone. Pardon is actual or conditional, and it is frequently conditional on the enduring of another sentence. Again, where a man has undergone the sentence awarded him by the law he is constructively pardoned. The effect of a pardon is to blot out the offence and to reinstate the person pardoned in his former position.

In *Hay* v. *The Tower Division Justices* ((1890) 24 Q. B. D. p. 561), one Hay was convicted of felony and then pardoned. A statute provided that no convicted man could for ever be licensed to sell spirits. The court held that as Hay had been pardoned he could be licensed and hold a public-house.

Enduring a sentence operates as a pardon. In *Leyman* v. *Latimer* ((1876), 3 Ex. D., p. 15), the plaintiff, who was editor of a paper called *The Advertiser*, sued for libel for being called "a felon editor." Leyman had been guilty of felony and sentenced to twelve months' hard labour, but he had been pardoned. The court held that the defendant had libelled the plaintiff.

Baron Cleasby, however, made the following remark in his judgment, "It is not necessary to decide what would have been the result if defendant had only said of the plaintiff, 'he is a convicted felon'" (*m*).

The reason for the decision in *Leyman* v. *Latimer* was as follows. By 9 George IV. c. 32, s. 3, where any offender shall be convicted of any felony not punishable with death and shall undergo the punishment awarded, such undergoing of punishment shall have the same effects and consequences as a pardon under the Great Seal.

Pardons may now be under the Sign Manual as well as the Great Seal (Halsbury, vol. 6, p. 404, *et seq.*).

The King may pardon a clerical offender, thus absolving him from all consequences of an ecclesiastical offence; and by 55 & 56 Vict. c. 32, s. 1, where a clergyman is convicted of any offence which would render him liable to deprivation or loss of preferment, and such clergyman receives the royal pardon before the institution of another clergyman, the bishop shall, within twenty-one days after receiving notice in writing of such pardon, again institute him and cause him to be inducted into the preferment without any fee (Clergy Discipline Act, 1892 (55 & 56 Vict. c. 32), s. 1, sub-s. 2).

The King as arbiter of commerce.—As protector of commerce the King alone possesses the power of creating markets and fairs, nor can anyone claim them but by royal grant or prescription, which presupposes such grant. This prerogative is now unim-

(*m*) In civil actions good character is presumed, but in cases of defamation and breach of promise the bad character of the plaintiff may be proved in chief in reduction of damages (Phipson's Manual of Evidence, pp. 51 and

portant as statutory legislation is now made use of (Chitty, p. 193).

The King as the fountain of honour.—The Crown alone can create and confer dignities and honours. The King is not only the fountain, but the parent of them. For further information see Chitty, p. 6.

Ecclesiastical prerogatives.—See *post*, p. 129.

Legislative prerogative.—As to the relations of the Crown to Parliament full particulars will be found in Chapter XXV. of this book, but it must be stated that by the Emergency Powers Act, 1919, when a state of emergency is proclaimed Parliament must be summoned, if not sitting, within five days.

The King has legislative powers at common law for conquered and ceded colonies until he, without express reservation of his rights, sanctions a Constitution. He has also statutory powers of legislating for settled colonies (see pages 170-1), and the great bulk of our present legislation by Order in Council and occasionally by proclamation is under statutory powers.

Further legislative powers as to certain mandatory colonies have been handed over to the Crown under the Covenant of the League of Nations and the statute sanctioning it. As to legislative powers of the King as head of the Church, see p. 129.

Foreign prerogative.—Issue of letters of marque and reprisals.—The laws of nature and nations vest in every power a right to make reprisals and adopt a system of fair retaliation for the aggressions of another community. Where a nation manifests general hostility towards another by unauthorised attacks and satisfaction is denied and explanations are evaded, it is for the King alone to adopt the *lex talionis*.

Letters of marque were also granted by the King in old days, but this practice of privateering is not adopted now, as England abandoned the practice by entering into an international convention.

Right to make war and peace.—As representative of his people and as executive magistrate the King possesses the exclusive right to make war or peace, either within or out of his dominions, and the Constitution leaves it to the King's discretion to grant or refuse a capitulation or truce to an enemy (Chitty, p. 43).

In the proclamation of war it was not unusual expressly to permit enemy subjects to remain in British dominions if they behaved peaceably.

As incident to the war prerogative the King has assigned to him the management of the war. *Ergo*, the King, as head of the Army and Navy, can order their movements, regulate their internal arrangements, or diminish or increase their number (Chitty, p. 45). The King is also solely entitled to erect forts and other places of strength. Unless Parliament permits it, the keeping up of a standing army in time of peace is forbidden by the Bill of Rights (1 Will. & M., sess. 1, c. 1). The Army is kept up by annual legislation, and the Army Act permits the trial of military offences by court-martial, according to articles framed by his Majesty. The King has a right to require the personal service of every man able to bear arms in case of a sudden invasion, and the allegiance due from the subject renders it incumbent on him to assist his Sovereign on such occasion (Chitty, p. 47).

As regards seamen and sea faring men the King may even in time of peace compel them to enter the Navy by forcibly impressing them (Chitty, p. 47).

This prerogative is only exercisable over individuals who have voluntarily chosen a sea faring life, and it does not extend to landsmen or fishermen except in certain cases (for particulars see Chitty, p. 47).

Maitland says : " There can be no doubt at all that to press sailors into his service is one of the King's prerogatives. It has never been taken away. I cannot say when last it was used. It is not used in time of peace." Maitland suggests a doubt as to whether the King can use this prerogative in time of peace.

In 1743 Broadfoot was indicted for murdering Calahan, a sailor, on a man-of-war. Broadfoot was being impressed for naval service and he shot Calahan.

The judge directed a verdict of manslaughter and held that " pressing for sea service is legal provided the persons impressed are proper objects of the law and those employed in the service are armed with a proper warrant."

As conductor of war the King can also adopt measures to prevent the egress or ingress of his enemies out of or into his Majesty's dominions. Thus, his Majesty may proclaim blockades; may, during war or threatened hostilities and on occasions of emergency, lay an embargo on all shipping, and thereby prevent anyone from leaving the kingdom. The King may, on the other hand, permit an enemy to come into the country by granting to him letters of safe conduct.

But passports granted by the Foreign Secretary are now more usually obtained (Chitty, p. 49). The King can prevent any alien from coming into the country, whether in time of war or peace (*Musgrove* v. *Chund* (1891), A. C. 272). The King on an emergency can enter on his subjects' lands to make fortifications; he has also a prerogative right in saltpetre and gunpowder; he may also prohibit the exportation of arms or ammunition or other articles of that nature useful in war, called contraband of war, out of the kingdom.

What is termed the war prerogative of the King is created by the perils and exigencies of war, is for the public safety, and by its perils and exigencies is limited (Chitty, p. 50).

Ambassadors.—The rights to receive and send ambassadors from and to foreign countries.

The Sovereign can probably refuse an ambassador who is objectionable to him personally, or is otherwise objectionable.

The right to receive ambassadors is more important than it at first sight appears, as no ambassador (*n*) or any member of his train or any member of his family is liable to civil process, and he is probably not liable to criminal process, though Oliver Cromwell is reported to have sanctioned the execution of an ambassador found guilty of murder. But modern practice is in favour of the complete exterritoriality of diplomatic agents (see Hall's International Law, ed. 3, p. 168).

(*n*) Including in this term all superior diplomatic agents—*e g.*, minister plenipotentiary, &c.

In Queen Anne's reign the ambassador of Peter the Great was arrested for debt. He gave bail in the action and com municated with the Russian Court, and Peter demanded instant execution of all parties concerned. This modest request was not complied with, but an Act was passed which provided that all writs and process whereby the person of any ambassador or his domestics may be arrested or his goods distrained or seized shall be void, and the persons prosecuting and their solicitors, and those who execute such process, shall suffer such penalties and corporal punishment as the Lord Chancellor or the Chief Justice or any two of them shall think fit, but no trader within the description of the bankrupt laws, who shall be in the service of any ambassador, is to be protected by the Act, nor shall anyone be punished for arresting an ambassador's servant unless the name of such servant be registered with the Secretary of State (Stephen, vol. 2, Bk. 4, c. 6, and 7 Anne, c. 12).

As to the extent of this privilege some doubt exists, and it probably does not include detention for *mala in se* (Stephen, vol. 2, Bk. 4, c. 6).

It has been held that where an appearance to an action has been entered, such action cannot be set aside, provided that no interference with liberty or personal property has taken place (*Taylor* v. *Best* (1854), 14 C. B. 487).

It is contrary to law to charge ambassadors with customs duty, and they cannot be rated in respect of premises they occupy (*Parkinson* v. *Potter* (1885), 16 Q. B. D. 152; but see *McCartney* v. *Garbutt* (1890), 24 Q. B. D. 368).

A servant residing outside the embassy is not within the privilege where the comfort of the ambassador does not depend on such servant (*Novello* v. *Toogood* (1823), 25 R. R. 507), and a servant whose duties are nil can be proceeded against, *e.g.*, a chaplain who does not perform service (*Seacombe* v. *Bownley*, 1 Wils. p. 20).

An English servant is within the privilege (*Novello* v. *Toogood*, *supra*).

All the officers of the embassy(*e.g.*, attachés) enjoy the same immunities as the ambassador (*Parkinson* v. *Potter* (1885), 16 Q. B. D. 152) (*o*).

Right of the Crown to take the subject's property.—The common law rights of the Crown to take the subject's property were, and in theory at any rate are, extensive.

The Crown in time of war can enter upon and use the lands of the subject to repel invasion, but cannot disseise the subject, as " since Magna Charta the subject's estate in lands or buildings has been protected against the prerogative of the Crown " (*per* Lord Parmoor in *De Keyser's Case* (*infra*, p. 113)) (*p*).

In the *Saltpetre Case* ((1606), 12 Coke's Rep., p. 12) the court held that "when enemies come against the realm to the sea coast, it is lawful to come upon my land adjoining the same coast to make trenches or bulwarks for the defence of the realm, for every subject hath benefit by it, and therefore by the common law every man (including, of course, the King and those under him) may come on my land for the defence of the realm . . . and in this case the rule is true, *princeps et res publica ex justâ causâ possunt rem meam auferre.* But after the danger is over, the trenches and bulwarks ought to be removed so that the owner shall not have prejudice to his inheritance." In Dyer (36b) there is the following dictum, " Yet we will agree that in some

(*o*) Besides ambassadors, nations have certain functionaries of a subordinate description resident in ports and important towns of foreign countries. These agents are known as consuls, vice-consuls, &c. In semi-civilised countries British consuls exercise judicial functions, both civil and criminal, when the work is not delegated to regular judges Ordinary consuls have certain duties as to the effects of compatriot testators and intestates who die in the country to which they are accredited. They have also to collect trade statistics and forward particulars of same in proper form to the British Foreign Office. They perform marriages. They act as notaries. They succour friendless and destitute British sailors. They can arbitrate in disputes where their compatriots are concerned They render assistance in proper cases where their compatriots get into scrapes. They must keep registers of births, deaths and marriages. They register transactions as to ships. They administer oaths. They exercise the functions of magistrates as regards attestations under the Army Act. They must get an exequatur from the country to which they are accredited (see Ridges' Constitutional Law of England and Encyclopædia of Laws of England, sub tit " Consul ")

(*p*) The land must be required for strictly military, and not administrative, purposes (see *Attorney-General* v. *De Keyser's Royal Hotel, Ltd.* [1920] App Cases, p 508).

cases a man may justify the commission of a tort, and that is so, when it sounds for the public good, as in time of war making fortifications on another's land without licence" (*q*).

St. John, the defender of Hampden in the *Ship Money Case*, made the following admission : "In times of war not only his Majesty, but every man that had power in his hands, may take the goods of any within the realm . . and do all other things that conduce to the safety of the kingdom." In the same case, Buller, J., said : "I do agree that in time of war when there is an enemy in the field the King may take goods from the subject, where there is such a danger as tends to the overthrow of the kingdom."

Mr. Dicey, who is perhaps the greatest living authority on the subject of Constitutional Law, and who here is speaking generally of political emergencies, intimates that, by a constitutional convention, in times of danger it is the duty of Ministers to break the law, trusting to Parliament for indemnity (Dicey, Const. Law, p. 418), but what Mr. Dicey calls convention Mr. Justice Darling appears to treat as law : *Salus populi suprema lex* is a good maxim, and the enforcement of that essential law gives no right of action to whomsoever may be injured by it (*per* Darling, J., in *Shipton, Anderson & Co.* v. *Harrison Brothers* (1915), 3 K. B. p. 684). The unbiased dictum of Mr. Justice Darling appears to tally with the so-called corrupt judgment in *Bate's Case* : "The power of the King is both ordinary and absolute. Ordinary power, what exists for the purpose of civil justice, is unalterable save by consent of Parliament. Absolute power, existing for the nation's safety, varies with the royal wisdom" (*Bate's Case* (1606), 2 St. Tr., p. 371).

In the *Petition of Right Case* ((1915), 3 K. B., p. 649), where land was taken from the suppliant for the purpose of an aerodrome, the Court of Appeal, upholding the judgment of Avory, J., held that naval and military authorities acting under orders from the Crown, both under the prerogative and the Defence of the Realm Consolidation Act, 1914, and regulations made thereunder, might enter into possession of and occupy the lands of

(*q*) Privileges which the Crown shares with its subjects are not prerogatives, but these authorities are inserted for convenience.

the suppliant to defend the realm without paying compensation, and that the prerogative was not limited to a case of actual invasion, rendering immediate occupation necessary.

In the case of *Attorney-General* v. *De Keyser's Royal Hotel Company* the facts were as follows : The company at the commencement of the war got into difficulties and Mr. Whinney was appointed receiver and manager by the debenture-holders. In the spring of 1916 there were negotiations between the War Office and Mr. Whinney for the hotel being taken over by the Government at a rental, but the parties failed to come to terms; and in the end the Crown took possession of the hotel under the Defence of the Realm Act, 1914. Mr. Whinney protested against the taking of the premises. A petition was presented claiming a rent for use and occupation of the hotel, and was, at the hearing, dismissed by Peterson, J., who considered himself bound by the *Petition of Right Case*. On appeal, a majority of the court—Swinfen Eady, M.R., and Warrington, L.J., dissenting—ruled that the respondent was entitled to a fair rent for use and occupation under the Defence Act, 1842.

The case came on for hearing before the House of Lords on May 10th, 1920, when their lordships held that the suppliants were not entitled to a rent for the use of the hotel as there was no consensus on which to found an implied contract; that the regulations under the Defence of the Realm Act, 1914, gave no power generally to take the land, but merely authorised the taking under the Defence Act, 1842; that the Crown could not take under its prerogative : but suppliants could, if they chose, claim compensation under the Defence Act, 1842 ((1920), A. C., p. 508). Their lordships were also of opinion that the Crown could not take the land under the prerogative or by any statute for administrative purposes (*ibid.*). At the hearing a suggestion was made that the alleged prerogative on which the appellant (the Attorney-General) relied merged in the statute. It may be that this was the case, but Lord Atkinson with reference to this question said : " It was suggested that when a statute was passed empowering the Crown to do a certain thing, which it might theretofore have done by virtue of its prerogative, the prerogative was merged in the statute. I do not think that the word "merged" was happily chosen. I would prefer to say that when such a statute, expressing the will of the King and the estates of the realm, is passed, it abridges the royal prerogative *while it is in force* to this extent, that the Crown can only do that particular thing under and in accordance with the statutory provisions and that its prerogative to do that thing is in abeyance" (T. L. R., June 11, 1920, p. 607, col. 1).

Lord Sumner appears inclined to think there was more ground for believing in a complete merger of the prerogative, but he hesitated somewhat to commit himself. He expressly said he did not wish to go into the extent of the prerogative. In another portion of his judgment (T. L. R., June 11, 1920, p. 613, col. 1) he said: "Even the restrictions (such as they were) imposed by the Defence Acts were in no way inconsistent with an intention to abate the prerogative in this respect, if not absolutely" (*New Windsor* v. *Taylor* (1899), A. C., p. 41), "at least for so long as the statute operated. In truth, the introduction of regulations so reasonable only strengthened the substance of the royal authority by removing all semblance of arbitrary power."

Lord Dunedin alluded to the alleged powers of the King as defender of the realm as follows: "The most that could be taken from them" (opinions of judges in the *Saltpetre Case*, etc.) "was that the King, as *suprema potestas* endowed with the right and duty of protecting the realm, was for the purpose of the defence of the realm entitled to take any man's property, and that the texts gave no certain sound whether this right to take was accompanied by an obligation to make compensation to him whose property was taken." He also stated further on that "if the whole ground of something which could be done by the prerogative was covered by a statute it was the statute that ruled."

Their lordships laid stress on what Sir Swinfen Eady said at the hearing in the Appeal Court. What he stated was as follows: "Those powers which the Executive exercises without parliamentary authority are comprised under the comprehensive term of prerogative. Where, however, Parliament has intervened, and has provided by statute for powers previously within the prerogative being exercised in a particular manner, then, subject to the limitations and provisoes, they can only be so exercised. Otherwise what use would there be in imposing limitations if the Crown could disregard them at its pleasure."

It is interesting to note that the following definition of prerogative by Mr. Dicey has been judicially confirmed in the above celebrated case: "The residue of discretionary or arbitrary power which at any given time is legally left in the hands of the Crown."

III. Revenue prerogatives and powers: Ancient revenues.—The Norman and early Plantagenet Kings had ordinary and extraordinary revenues, the former consisting of feudal dues, taxes raised from Jews, *bona vacantia*, whales, sturgeons, waifs, strays, perquisites connected with the judicature, and other miscellaneous sources of income. When money was wanted for war and emergencies extraordinary aids were raised.

Ordinary revenue: Feudal dues.—Under the feudal system the King was lord paramount of all the land in the kingdom. He was the supreme feudal lord and not the mere tribal chieftain of early Saxon times.

The King let out the land to followers of his, or, in other words, his tenants in chief, in exchange for money payments, perquisites, and personal services. The tenants also had their feudatories, and so did tenant's tenants, and so on. The King's tenants held by various tenures, some of them free and others unfree. Those who had free tenures were known as freeholders, and those who had unfree were known as copyholders. These latter rendered unfree and uncertain services to the King or their lords, and in early days they were villeins (*i.e.*, serfs). There were various kinds of free tenures, the most important of which were knight service, grand serjeanty and petty serjeanty (the former of which was a species of knight service), free and common socage, and the clerical tenures of frankalmoign and divine service. Archbishops, bishops, abbots, abbesses, and priors held baronies of the King subject to feudal incidents, but tenants in frankalmoign and divine service held their lands in exchange for prayers and masses.

Knight service.—This was the most honourable tenure, but was subject to burdensome incidents, which were as follows: (a) Aids, which were three in number—(1) Liability to contribute towards the expenses of making the eldest son a knight; (2) a similar contribution towards portioning once the lord's eldest daughter; (3) a contribution towards ransoming the lord from captivity. (Richard I. was ransomed.) (b) Reliefs, or sums payable by a tenant on succeeding to the estate of the ancestor. (c) Fine on alienation, which remotely resembled the *laudemium* paid by the *emphyteuta* to his *dominus*. (d) Primer seisin (a burden peculiar to tenants *in capite*), which was the right of the King to the first year's profits from the "fee" provided the heir was of full age when he succeeded his ancestor. (e) Wardship. This was the right to the custody of the person and the rents and profits of the land of the infant, if a male till twenty-one, and if a female till sixteen, without rendering any account. (f) Marriage, or right of disposing of the hand of infant wards. If a male tenant refused to marry a person of equal rank, he had to forfeit the sum the suitor was willing to pay the lord, and if the ward married without the lord's consent he forfeited twice his market price (*duplicem valorem maritagii*). If a female refused a suitable match the lord could take the rents and profits till she had attained twenty-one, and after she had attained that age until such time as the value of the marriage had been collected. (g) Suit of court, which was attendance at, or payment of a fine for non-attendance at, the Court Baron. (h) Escheat, or right of the lord to take the estate on failure of tenant's heirs (*per defectum sanguinis;* and escheat *per delictum tenentis*) or forfeiture of property for treason, felony, outlawry, or abjuring the realm in certain instances. If the tenant committed felony he forfeited his estate to the mesne lord subject to the King's year, day, and waste; and if he committed treason the King took the estate and the mesne lord took nothing.

Grand serjeanty.—This tenure was subject to the incidents of marriage and wardship, but its main feature was the holding of land subject to rendering the King a special service, *e.g.*, being the King's cup-bearer, such service being valued at £5 a year or upwards; but, according to Littleton, the tenant held of the King by some personal service only (cf. Williams's Real Property, 22nd ed., p. 49).

Petty serjeanty in Littleton's time was a tenure where a man held of the King, yielding him annually some implement of war (*ibid.*, p. 52). According to Williams, it might be a socage tenure. In earlier times the tenant also held his estate in exchange for some trifling service either to the King or a mesne lord (*ibid.*, p. 52).

Socage.—The socager received his estate in exchange for fixed services and afterwards for a fixed annual sum. Like the tenant in knight service, he owed to his lord or the King fealty, aids, reliefs and, occasionally, homage. His lord had rights of escheat, but not of wardship or marriage. By the Statute of Tenures, in the reign of Charles II. knight-service tenure was converted into free and common socage, thus enabling all tenants to devise the whole of their lands by will.

Socage tenure still exists and contributes in a small degree to the revenue.

Ordinary revenue is that revenue which the Crown has had from time immemorial, and extraordinary revenue is such as is contributed by subjects out of their private means for Crown purposes (Stephen, vol. 2).

The ordinary revenues are :—

1. The custody of a bishop's temporalities—*i.e.*, the right of the Crown to take the profits whilst the episcopal see is vacant, but these are held in trust for his successor.
2. The right to annates and tenths. Annates were the first year's profits of a church benefice, formerly paid to the Pope and afterwards to the Crown, and tenths were the tenth part of the annual profits of a Church benefice, which formerly were papal dues also. These profits are now paid to the Governors of Queen Anne's Bounty (see Const. Year Book, 1920, p. 81; see also Stephen, vol. 2, p. 532).
3. The profits derived from Crown lands, which are dealt with by the Commissioners of Woods and Forests and the Board of Agriculture.
4. Right to royal fish, wreck, treasure trove, waifs and estrays.

Whales and sturgeon are royal fish. The Crown cannot claim royal fish unless the same be caught on or near to our coasts. The King is entitled, it is said, to the whale's head and the Queen to its tail (Stephen, vol. 2, c. 7).

Wrecks.—Wrecks, subject to certain restrictions, were Crown property, and no ship was a wreck if there were a human being, or any living creature, on board (see Carter, p. 297).

The whole matter is now regulated by sects. 510—537 of the Merchant Shipping Act, 1894. Owners of wrecked ship, goods and cargo, are now entitled to claim their property as against the Crown within a year. They have, however, to satisfy salvage claims. Finders of wreck must hand same to district receivers of wreck. For the purposes of the statute governing the law on the subject, the following things are wreck, namely, *flotsam* (things found floating near shore); *jetsam* (things thrown overboard to save ship); *ligam* (things tied to a buoy or like object for preservation). Where goods are unclaimed for a year and a day they pass to the Crown, and, subject to payment thereout of salvage claims, go into the Consolidated Fund (Stephen, vol. 2, p. 646) (*r*).

Treasure trove.—This consists of money, coin, bullion, plate, silver, or gold discovered either in the earth or some secret place. The concealment must have been made a long time before its discovery (*vetus depositio pecuniæ*). As treasure trove goes entirely to the Crown, it is a misdemeanour to conceal it. What is treasure trove is determined by a coroner and a jury (Stephen, vol. 2, p. 651).

As a matter of grace, the Crown has in certain recent cases paid the finder the value of the treasure trove.

Estrays.—These are beasts of value belonging to unknown owners which are found wandering at large within the precincts of a manor. These beasts belong to the King or his grantee after a year and a day has elapsed, during which period the owner can have them on payment of expenses for keep.

(*r*) *De prærogativâ regis.* This statute is believed not to be genuine, but from the Statute Book we gather that its supposed date was the seventeenth year of Edward II. It deals with feudal incidents like wardship, marriage, primer seisin, and escheat; the right of the King to present to benefices in the case of a lapse; his right to wreck, whales, and sturgeons; his right of guardianship over *infants*, idiots and lunatics; and other matters.

Waifs (*bona waivata*).—These were goods thrown away by the thief in his flight from justice. The property was confiscated by way of punishing the owner for not prosecuting the thief. The goods of foreign merchants were not waifs, as they were not supposed to know English law (Stephen, vol. 2, c. 7).

Royal mines.—This is connected with the prerogative of coining money, as precious metal from mines constitutes the materials for making money. By the old common law, according to Stephen, the King took possession of mines containing gold and silver, whether they contained base metals or not. People would not sink mines, and it was therefore provided by 1 Will. & Mary, c. 30; 5 Will. & Mary, c. 6; and 55 Geo. III. c. 134, that no base metals are to be forfeited, but that the King shall have the mine on payment for the base metals (Stephen's Coms., vol. 2, p. 655).

Escheat.—Escheat was formerly of two kinds, and we may also say is now of two kinds, viz. :—

(1) Per defectum sanguinis.

(2) Per delictum tenentis.

Escheat per defectum sanguinis exists when a man dies without heirs, and by analogy the Crown now takes personal property of those who die without next of kin in many cases (see Intestate Act, 1884).

Escheat per delictum tenentis formerly ensued whenever a man was convicted or attainted of treason or felony, but though forfeiture and corruption of blood has now been abolished in cases of conviction for treason or felony (see Forfeiture Act, 1870), a right of forfeiture to the Crown or its grantee still applies in theory to all cases of criminal outlawry (*s*).

(*s*) There are several statutes on the Statute Book which state that a person for a given offence shall suffer the penalties of a "præmunire." The penalties of a præmunire entail loss of land and goods, and imprisonment during the royal pleasure. This prerogative right to claim forfeiture is, to say the least of it, very obsolete, and it is questionable whether it now can be said to exist. An outlaw is a person who has escaped from criminal process, and cannot be found at the time final steps in outlawry have been taken against him.

Dues for the custody of the estates of idiots and lunatics.

Extraordinary revenue.—We now come to the extraordinary revenue payable by the subject out of his private means. This extraordinary revenue is (a) permanent, (b) annual.

The annual revenue is kept up by annual taxation. It is revenue for the year, *e.g.*, income tax, and it varies from year to year. It is revenue temporarily imposed. All the revenue of the country which is paid into the Consolidated Fund is classed under one or other of the following heads, viz. :— 1. Customs; 2. Excise; 3. Death duties; 4. Stamps; 5. Land tax; 6. House duty; 7. Income tax; 8. Post Office receipts; 9. Crown lands; 10. Suez Canal shares; 11. Miscellaneous heads of taxation.

All these taxes go into the Consolidated Fund (*i.e.*, to the Government's credit account at the Bank of England), and cannot be paid out save by statutory authority.

Customs are duties leviable on exports (if any) and imports. The reason for the tax was that the King permitted the subject to leave the realm taking his goods with him, and also because the King wanted compensation for the upkeep of the ports, and because it was necessary to protect the merchants from pirates.

Customs duty is payable on (*inter alia*) the following articles, viz., imported beer, mum, spruce, chicory, cocoa, cocoa husks, chocolate, coffee, currants, raisins, dried fruits, foreign and colonial spirits, sugar, saccharine, molasses, tea, tobacco and snuff.

Excise.—This is, strictly speaking, a duty leviable on the manufacture of certain commodities, *e.g.*, beer, spirits, chicory, coffee, mixture labels, but divers luxuries are taxed under the head of excise, and also licences, like a hawker's licence, dog licence, gun licence, &c., and railway passenger duty.

Death duties.—These consist of probate duty and account duty (abolished as to future duties by the Finance Act, 1894), estate duty, succession duty and legacy duty. (See now Finance Act, 1910, Pt. III.)

Stamp duties.—The following documents (*inter alia*) are liable to stamp duty, viz., bills of exchange, promissory notes, cheques, deeds, contract notes on sale and purchase of stock, insurance documents, numerous agreements, patents for inventions, writs and certain other legal documents, and numerous other documents. (See Stamp Act, 1891, and subsequent amendments.)

Court fees, it may be noted, are mainly collected by means of stamps.

Income tax.—A tax upon incomes was first heard of in the early part of the fifteenth century (Stephen's Coms., 16th ed., vol. 2, p. 673), but this fell into desuetude, and its next appearance was the tax imposed by the younger Pitt in 1799. This tax was abolished "in 1802, revived in 1803, and again abolished in 1816" (*ibid.*, p. 673). In 1842 the income tax came to stay, and is now an annual imposition recently much augmented by the Great War.

Unearned income is more heavily taxed than earned income, and the tax is graduated according to the domestic burdens of the taxpayer as well as his income. The married man pays less than the unmarried, and the married man with children pays less than the married man who is childless. Abatements are also allowed with respect to each child, stepchild, or adopted child, and also relatives of the taxpayer or his wife whom he has undertaken to support.

The Civil List.—This is a sum awarded to the King, Queen and certain members of the Royal Family in consideration of the King assigning to the nation his life interest in the hereditary revenues of the Crown.

Formerly the payment of certain official salaries, *e.g.*, the judges', and also certain pensions were charged on the Civil List; but since the reign of William IV. it only includes the sum allowed to the King and certain members of his family. By the present Civil List Act, in consideration of the assignment above referred to, the King receives £470,000 per annum, to be applied as follows, viz., £110,000 for the privy purses of the King and Queen; salaries and pensions of household officers, £125,000 per annum; household expenses, £193,000 per annum; royal bounty, alms and special services, £13,200; unappropriated, £8,000; and provision is made for Queen Mary, the Prince of Wales and the younger children of the Royal Family.

Ministers and the prerogative.—At the present day there is a curious divergence between the law and the practice of the Constitution as regards the prerogative. Prerogative acts are done in the name of the Crown, and the executive government is carried on in the name of the Crown. But the prerogative is no longer the personal prerogative of the King. All public acts are done by the Crown on the advice of the Ministers of the Crown. The privileges arising out of prerogative are therefore the privileges of the executive, and as Ministers are dependent on the House of Commons, that House has now obtained control over what was formerly the peculiar province of the Crown. As Mr. Lowell puts it, with slight exaggeration, "by leaving the prerogative substantially untouched by law, and requiring that it should be wielded by Ministers responsible to them, the Commons have drawn into their own control all the powers of the Sovereign that time has not rendered obsolete" (Government of England, p. 13).

CHAPTER XIII.

PROCEEDINGS AGAINST THE CROWN AND ITS SERVANTS.

It has long been settled law that so far as the United Kingdom is concerned no action lies against the King personally. Perhaps this was not the case in early days, and it was rumoured that there was a writ found in the days of Henry III. or Edward I., where the King was made a defendant, but the genuineness of this writ is doubted by high authorities of the present day. Chitty, however, is doubtful as to whether in the days of Edward I. the King could not be sued. What he says is this: "There can be no doubt that, at all events since the reign of Edward I., the Crown has been free from any action at the suit of its subjects" (Chitty, Prerog. of Crown, c. 13, p. 339).

Chitty mentions a statute, viz., 39 & 40 George III., under which in certain events the property of a deceased King is liable for his debts (Chitty, Prerog. of Crown, p. 242).

He also says that the proper remedies to recover land or personal property from the Crown were by: (a) *Monstrans de droit*; (b) Traverse of office; (c) Petition of right.

Monstrans de droit.—This was a mode of procedure employed when the facts upon which the Crown and the suppliant relied had already been established, whether by commission, inquest of office or otherwise, and the judgment of the court was required as upon a special case. It is now obsolete (Broom's Legal Maxims, p. 50).

Traverse of office.—Traverse of office has long been obsolete. Chitty says it was at common law a very contracted remedy. It only lay in the case of goods and chattels, or where the office did not give a seisin or possession of land to the King, but merely entitled him to an action (Chitty, Prerog. of Crown, p. 356).

Petition of right.—The remedy by petition of right still exists, and it lies (1) to recover lands, goods or moneys which have found their way into the possession of the Crown, where the suppliant demands either restitution or compensation; (2) to recover moneys due under a contract made with the Crown, *e.g.*, goods supplied; (3) to recover unliquidated damages for breach of contract by the Crown; (4) for moneys payable to the suppliant under a grant of the Crown. These remedies, as will be seen, are not universally applicable; *e.g.*, where the suppliant is to blame, he can expect no relief. In *Morgan* v. *Seaward* (2 M. & W. 544) Parke, B., said that " a false suggestion of the grantee avoids a grant of land from the Crown " (Broom's Legal Maxims, p. 42).

The King is not responsible for tortious acts. In *Tobin* v. *The Queen* (33 L. J. C. P., p. 206) the court held that " the notion of making the Sovereign responsible for a supposed wrong tends to consequences which are clearly inconsistent with the duties of the Sovereign." In *Feather* v. *The Queen* ((1865), 6 Best & Smith, p. 257) it was held that the grant of letters patent to Feather, the suppliant in the case, did not preclude the Crown from the use of the invention, even without the assent of or compensation made to the patentee. By 5 Edw. VII. c. 29, s. 29, it is provided that a patent shall have to all intents the like effect as against his Majesty as it has against a subject : provided that any government department or its agents or contractors may, at any time, use the invention for the services of the Crown on such terms as may be agreed upon between the patentee and the department or, in default of agreement, as may be settled by the Treasury after hearing all the parties interested.

The maxim *Qui facit per alium facit per se* does not apply where the King's servants are guilty of tortious acts towards individuals.

If the King commands an act which is unlawful, the courts treat the complaint of the suppliant as if there had been no command at all, so that an action will lie against the King's servant in respect of the unlawful act. Under certain colonial statutes and ordinances the Crown can be sued for tort in certain colonies and dependencies. (See *Attorney-General of Straits Settlements* v. *Wemyss*, 13 App. Ca. 192; *Farnell* v. *Bowman*, 12 App. Ca.,

p. 643; *Hettihewage Simon Appu's Case*, 9 App. Ca., p. 571; Broom's Legal Maxims, pp. 46 *et seq.*). In many instances actions will lie against servants of the Crown for tortious acts done in the course of their official duties.

In *Madrazo* v. *Willes* (24 R. R., p. 422) a naval captain was held responsible for the unlawful destruction of a merchant vessel, though he was acting conscientiously and, as he believed, in accordance with his duty. Again, in *Walker* v. *Baird*, a naval captain was held liable for the destruction of a lobster factory off the coast of Newfoundland, the court holding the defendant responsible because, without the authority of the Legislature, he had interfered with a subject's private rights, and that he could not justify his conduct by showing that he was acting under the provisions of a treaty made between France and England (*Walker* v. *Baird* (1892), A. C., p. 491).

The case of *Ralegh* v. *Goschen* illustrates the liability of a servant of the Crown for a tortious act. It was a case of trespass on land by officials of the Admiralty. The court held that the alleged authority of a department of Government did not justify a trespass, but that only those persons who were actually guilty of the act of trespass, or who authorised the same, were liable. The court exonerated Mr. Goschen, the First Lord of the Admiralty, in the absence of proof that the act of trespass was really his act. The court also held that the defendants could be sued individually, but that they could not be sued as an official body, and that proceedings against them in their official capacity would not lie.

The Crown cannot be a trustee.—This rule has one statutory exception in the case of the Public Trustee, for whose defaults the Treasury is responsible.

The first important case on this point was *Baron de Bode's Case* (8 Q. B., p. 208). Here the petition stated that under a convention made with France the British Government had received moneys for compensating British subjects whose property was confiscated during the wars succeeding the Revolution. Here a statute had been passed providing a mode for distribution of the moneys, and the court held that petitioners' rights depended entirely on the effect of the statute. The question was left open as to whether the Crown was responsible for a breach of trust.

In *Rustomjee* v. *The Queen* (1 Q. B., p. 487) the facts were as follows :—The Chinese Emperor, under the Treaty of Nankin, paid to the Crown certain moneys on account of debts due from Chinese to British subjects trading with China. Cockburn, C.J., held that the action was wild and untenable. In *Kinloch* v. *The Secretary of State for India* (7 App. Cases, p. 619) proceedings were brought to compel the defendant to account as trustee for booty granted by the Queen to the Secretary of State for distribution amongst members of certain forces. It was held that the warrant did not transfer the property or create a trust enforceable in equity, and that no action lay against the defendant, who was merely the agent of the Crown for a specific purpose. In *Gidley* v. *Palmerston* (3 Brod. & B., p. 275), Lord Palmerston was sued as Secretary of State for War by the executor of a War Office clerk for arrears of retired allowance, which defendant was authorised to pay out of moneys provided by Parliament. The court held that an action would not lie against a public agent for any act done by him in his public character, though alleged to be in the particular instance done to carry out his official duties.

Contracts made by civil servants on behalf of the Crown.—The case of *Macbeath* v. *Haldimand* illustrates the immunity of a colonial governor in respect of contracts made on behalf of the Crown, but of late years the most important of these cases have been actions brought against civil servants, who have engaged persons to assist them in Government work with the leave of the Crown. In the absence of statutory legislation to the contrary, all Crown servants, both civil and military, hold office during the royal pleasure. Two very important cases on this subject are Dunn v. *The Queen* and Dunn v. *MacDonald. Dunn* v. *The Queen* ((1896), 1 Q. B., p. 116) was a petition of right, where the suppliant sued the Queen for dismissing him from his post. He alleged that Sir Claud MacDonald had engaged him as consular-agent for three years, and he claimed damages for dismissal before the expiration of that period. The court decided that the suppliant held his appointment during pleasure. Dunn afterwards sued Sir Claud MacDonald, and the court held that where a public servant acting on behalf of the Crown makes a contract with a person he is not responsible for a breach of such contract (*Dunn* v. *MacDonald* (1896), 1 Q. B., p. 401).

In *Gould* v. *Stuart* ((1896), App. Ca., p. 575) it was held that the Crown has by law power to dismiss at pleasure officers, both civil and military, a condition, unless it is otherwise provided by law, to that effect being by implication incorporated into every contract of service.

In *Hales* v. *The King* ((1918), 34 T. L. R., p. 589 C. A.), Avory, J., held that a Crown servant holds office during the royal pleasure, and that even if a special contract could be proved, the Crown will not be bound by the same.

Cases where the title of Crown to property is indirectly questioned.—Cases of this kind comprise suits between subject and subject in which the rights of the Crown may be indirectly involved, *e.g.*, action concerning an outlaw's property; also cases where the Sovereign is interested as *parens patriæ*, and finally cases where the King acts as protector of the rights of his subjects, *e.g.*, provisions in a will for general charitable purposes. In all these instances the Attorney-General must be made a party to the proceedings (Broom's Legal Maxims, p. 50).

Procedure on a petition of right.—This is regulated by the Petition of Right Act, 1860. The petition is prepared by the suppliant and left with the Home Secretary for the King's perusal, and the King, if he thinks fit, may grant his *fiat* that right be done. After the *fiat* has been obtained a copy of the petition and *fiat* endorsed with the prescribed prayer is lodged at the Treasury. The Crown has then twenty-eight days to plead or demur to the petition. The procedure after this resembles that in an ordinary action, with the exception that the Crown may have discovery against the suppliant, but that the suppliant cannot have it from the Crown. In the event of the suppliant winning his case, the methods of execution available between subject and subject are not applicable (Broom's Legal Maxims, pp. 44 *et seq.*).

The right of the Crown to withhold the *fiat* is hardly doubtful, as the Petition of Right Act evidently accords to the King a discretion in the matter. At common law the right to refuse a *fiat* would be contrary to Magna Charta, which says, *Nulli negabimus justitiam et rectum.* In *Ryves* v. *The Duke of Wellington* (9 Beav. 600), Lord Langdale said: "I am far from thinking that it is competent to the King or his advisers to refuse capriciously to allow investigation of any proper question raised on a petition of right." It is now customary for the Home Secretary to endorse "Let right be done" as a matter of course, without referring the case to the Attorney-General (Broom's Legal Maxims, p. 46).

By the Indemnity Act, 1920 (10 & 11 Geo. V. c. 48) it is provided that, with certain exceptions the Act sets forth, no legal proceedings, civil or criminal, in respect of any act done in good faith during the recent war shall be instituted, but in lieu thereof all claims are to be brought before a Tribunal of Arbitration constituted by the Act. This is emergency legislation, which is now of secondary importance.

CHAPTER XIV.

THE CROWN AND THE CHURCH.

Relations between Sovereign and the Established Church.—The Sovereign is the supreme head of the Church of England as by law established (see 1 Eliz. c. 1, reviving the Acts of Henry VIII.). Under the Act of Settlement he must "joyn in communion with the Church of England," abjure the papacy, and must not marry a papist. He appoints, on the recommendation of the Prime Minister, archbishops, bishops, and certain other dignitaries of the Church. The supremacy of the Crown over ecclesiastical courts is recognised by the appeal to the King in Council—*i.e.*, the Judicial Committee.

The Sovereign convokes, prorogues and dissolves the two Houses of Convocation. Till the reign of Henry VIII. the Pope and not the King was the supreme head of the Church. By the Submission of the Clergy Act (25 Hen. VIII. c. 19), it was provided that a review of the existing canons be held, and that no canons repugnant to English law were to bind laymen, and no subsequent canons were to bind laymen. There was no review of the canons, and therefore no canons previous to the Act bind laymen if repugnant to common law, neither do canons passed since the Act (cf. *Bishop of Exeter* v. *Marshall*, L. R. 3 H. L. 17).

Convocation.—The legislative authorities for the Church consist of the Houses of Convocation, and since recent legislation the House of Laymen, but their powers are very limited. There are two Houses of Convocation, viz., the Canterbury and York houses. Each Convocation has an upper and lower chamber. In the upper chamber are the archbishop and bishops, and in the lower are deans, archdeacons, and proctors for cathedral chapters and lower clergy.

When Convocation is summoned, an Order in Council is passed, which enjoins the Lord Chancellor to issue writs to the archbishops. The archbishops then, in accordance with the terms of their writs, issue mandates to cite the bishops, deans, &c., to attend Convocation. Convocation cannot initiate a canon till authorized by the Crown, and a further licence from the Crown is necessary before a canon can be promulged, and it is not in force till promulgation (*Case of Convocations*, 12 Co. Reports).

When Convocation was first originated its sole function was to vote money to the King. When once convoked it began to meddle with legislation, and this usurpation of power appears to have been permitted, as the Submission of the Clergy Act, before referred to, recognised this supposed right partially. After a time there were two Houses of Convocation, but no precise date can be fixed for the creation of the second ecclesiastical synod; after the Submission of the Clergy Act the power of Convocation has been insignificant, as the legislative power of Convocation was further restricted by Acts of Uniformity in the reigns of Elizabeth and Charles II. From the reign of Anne to that of Victoria it was customary to dissolve Convocation almost immediately after its summons, but in 1864 it began to awaken, as it condemned the famous "Essays and Reviews," and again in 1870 it considered the report of the Ritual Commissioners. Towards the end of the nineteenth century the clergy, and also the laity, began to desire the creation of a Church legislative body, and in response to the appeals of devout laymen to participate in Church management, the Primate in 1885 agreed to a House of Laymen debating with his clergy. In 1892 the province of York had a House of Laymen. The final result of all this energy was the passing of the Church of England Assembly (Powers) Act, 1919. This Act established three legislative houses, namely, (1) the House of Bishops, containing the bishops of both provinces; (2) the House of Clergy, consisting of the lower houses of Convocation of York and Canterbury; and (3) a House of Laymen, elected in accordance with the Act, upon a principle of popular representation. The Act provides that the members of the Houses of Bishops and Clergy shall continue to be members of the assembly after the dissolution of the Convocation until the new Convocations come into being (Cripps' Law of Church and Clergy, 7th ed., p. 28).

The three Houses can sit together or separately. By the Act they are to appoint a legislative committee to consider measures voted by both Houses.

On the legislative committee approving a measure they submit the same to the ecclesiastical committee formed by the Act, which consists of fifteen lords and fifteen commoners. This committee, with the sanction of the legislative committee, notifies Parliament and copies of the text of the measure are supplied to both Houses. If both Houses confirm the measure by resolution it is sent up to the King for his assent, and on receipt of same has the power of a statute.

Prayer Book and articles.—All clergy must use the Book of Common Prayer at their services as directed by the Act of Uniformity, and they must also, before ordination, and on taking preferment, assent to the Thirty-nine Articles.

Archbishop of Canterbury.—The Primate is the chief officer in the Church. He ranks before the Archbishop of York, who is not subordinate to him. He is a bishop in his own diocese (Canterbury), and the ecclesiastical superior of all the bishops in his province. Like the Pope did in olden times, he can grant dispensations to marry at any time or place (Stephen's Coms. vol. 2, p. 721). He can permit a clergyman to hold more than one living simultaneously (Stephen's Coms. vol. 2). He can claim to crown the King, but it has been said that the Archbishop of York has the right to crown the Queen.

Both the Archbishops can always sit (if they choose) to hear ecclesiastical appeals in the Judicial Committee of the Privy Council.

The Archbishop of Canterbury can grant Lambeth degrees, and does so now and then, to persons who are of eminent piety, but devoid of scholastic attainments.

Archbishop of York.—This functionary is the ecclesiastical superior of all the bishops in his province, who owe him canonical obedience. His duties are almost precisely similar to those of the Primate of all England. Both archbishops present to livings when the bishop of the diocese omits so to do. They are *ex officio* assessors of the Judical Committee in ecclesiastical appeals.

Bishops.—A bishop has multitudinous duties. He ordains priests and deacons. He helps the archbishop to consecrate other bishops. He licenses curates. He licenses churches and other buildings for public worship. He consecrates churches and graveyards. He confirms persons as a preliminary to receiving the Holy Communion.

No curate can officiate for more than three consecutive weeks in a benefice without the bishop's leave.

The bishop institutes clerks to livings, and collates clerks in cases where he has the right of patronage. Under the Benefices Act, 1898 (61 & 62 Vict. c. 48), the bishop may refuse to institute a clerk nominated by the patron in many cases where he was powerless to do so before. He can now insist on a certain amount of pastoral experience, and refuse to institute where the candidate is physically or mentally unfit, of doubtful moral character, or in serious pecuniary embarrassment, or where there has been within twelve months a simoniacal transfer. As to appeal, see section 3. Irrespective of the Act, it is believed that he can refuse to institute where he has good reason for supposing that doctrinal offences will be committed (*Heywood* v. *Bishop of Manchester*, 12 Q. B. D. 404).

The bishops sit in rotation in the Judicial Committee of the Privy Council to hear Privy Council appeals relative to Church matters (see 39 & 40 Vict. c. 5, s. 14). They have to wait their turn before they can demand a writ of summons to the Lords, unless they become *ex officio* lords of Parliament on becoming bishops, as is the case with the two archbishops and the Bishops of London, Durham, and Winchester.

Bishops can visit all the clergy in their dioceses, and insist on preaching in any diocesan church. With the bishops also rests the decision whether their clergy shall be proceeded against by the Church Courts. They have to examine candidates for orders, or rather to supervise such examinations (cf. Phillimore's Ecclesiastical Law, ed. 2, p. 88).

They can in certain cases impose one or more curates on their clergy.

The making and consecrating and enthronement of bishops.—When a bishop dies or retires the Premier sees the King, and a choice is made of some fit person, who must, according to the Rubric, be over thirty years of age. A document, called a *congé d'élire*, is then sent to the dean and chapter bidding them elect a successor, and the dean and chapter then go through a fictitious form of election, as in point of fact they are bound to elect the person nominated in the letters missive, a document which accompanies the *congé d'élire*. After this fictitious election, the candidate for office assents to his appointment before a notary public. After election the new bishop must have the election of the dean and chapter confirmed in the court of an official called the vicar-general of the province. There, persons who object to the appointment have a right to publicly record such objections before the vicar-general, but as this official is only nominally a judge, they gain nothing for their trouble (*R.* v. *Archbishop of Canterbury*, (1902) 2 K. B. 520). In the newly created bishoprics where there is no dean and chapter, the Crown appoints direct by Letters Patent.

After confirmation the bishop is consecrated, installed in his cathedral, and afterwards, on another day, does homage to the king in respect of his episcopal lands. After all this, he has to wait his turn for a summons to the Lords, unless he is an *ex officio* lord of Parliament.

Deans.—Deans (*decani*) are appointed by Letters Patent, and with the exception of the four Welsh deaneries the patronage of the office belongs to the Premier.

The dean is the head of the chapter (consisting of canons or prebends), which is supposed to be the advisory council of the bishop, but which has no advisory functions. The dean is the superior of the other members of the chapter, and he presides at the election of the bishop. He is the parish clergyman, so to speak, of his own cathedral. He performs the ceremony of enthroning an archbishop and installing a bishop.

The canons and prebends.—These are members of the bishop's advisory council. They have few duties beyond assisting the dean in the cathedral services and signing episcopal leases and grants.

Like the dean, they must reside for a prescribed period in the cathedral city. They have certain duties as to preaching in the cathedral church, and sometimes elsewhere (Phillimore's Ecclesiastical Law).

No person can be appointed a dean till he has been in priest's orders for six years (3 & 4 Vict. c. 113).

Archdeacon.—This official is a kind of ecclesiastical superior in his district, where, like the bishop, he is a visitor of the clergy. He has certain duties as to directing church and parsonage repairs. He is the nominal head of a court with jurisdiction both civil and criminal, presided over by a judge called the official principal, but this court is now obsolete (cf. Phillimore, ed. 2, p. 199).

No person can be made an archdeacon till he has been in priest's orders for six years (3 & 4 Vict. c. 113).

The rural dean is an ecclesiastical superior in respect of his ruri-decanal district. He has certain functions incident to repair of Church property. He has certain duties under the old Church Discipline Act, which is now practically only operative as to cases of simony and non-residence; but where there is any clerical scandal in his district he should report to the bishop. He holds ruri-decanal meetings at which his clergy attend.

The parish clergy.—These consist of rectors, vicars, perpetual curates, and curates. A rector takes all the tithes of the benefice, both great and small, whilst the vicar is only entitled to the smaller tithes.

Incumbents of district churches in towns and other populous places may now by Act of Parliament style themselves vicars.

Privileges and liabilities of the clergyman.—A clerk in holy orders is privileged from civil arrest whilst proceeding to the solemnization of Divine service, whilst performing Divine service.

and on his way home from such performance. He enjoys the like privilege whilst going to, during, and returning from Convocation (6 Henry VI. c. 1). He is subject to the canon law, whether he holds any preferment or not, and he can be ordered to pay the costs of proceedings for immoral conduct, and in default of payment can probably be proceeded against under the writ *de contumace capiendo*. He can be tried for simony and non-residence by the bishop under the old Church Discipline Act; for doctrinal offences under the Public Worship Regulation Act, 1874; and for uncleanness and wickedness of life under the Clergy Discipline Act, 1893.

The bishop can veto the proceedings both under the Clergy Discipline Act and the Public Worship Regulation Act. No clergyman can be a member of the House of Commons or a borough councillor, but he may be a county or district or parish councillor. He cannot farm more than eighty acres of land without the bishop's leave, nor can he engage in any trade for profit where there are more than six partners, or unless he has inherited the business. He may be a company director, buy and sell literary productions, edit periodicals, &c., and may be a schoolmaster, professor, university lecturer, dean, tutor, bursar, &c.

A clerk may become a layman by availing himself of 33 & 34 Vict. c. 91. He must give six months' notice, and conform generally to the directions prescribed by the statute.

Again, the bishop has a power, which is very seldom exercised, of expelling a man from the Church. This can be done when the clerk has been found guilty of uncleanness and wickedness of life, and perhaps also in cases of simony and heresy. The ceremony takes place in the cathedral church, and a full account of what was done in Mr. Piggott's (or Smyth-Piggot) case will be found in *The Times* of March 8th, 1909.

In this case the expelled clerk was absent. The bishop, after pronouncing sentence, offered up a prayer for his erring brother. It entirely rests with the bishop whether he will unfrock a man or not, and it makes no difference whether the clerk holds preferment or not.

Ecclesiastical courts.—The following are the principal Church courts :—

1. The Court of the Archdeacon, presided over by the official principal, appointed by the archdeacon himself (Phillimore, Ecclesiastical Law, vol. 1, p. 200). This tribunal is now obsolete, but there is a supposed right of appeal from its decisions to the Court of the Bishop.

2. The Bishop's Consistory Court, presided over by the bishop's chancellor, who must be a barrister of at least seven years' standing. This court has a jurisdiction both civil and criminal, and this jurisdiction extends to clergy and also to laity. It can try clergy for uncleanness and wickedness of life, but not for doctrinal offences. Stephen tells us it can try laymen for fornication, incest, adultery, and other deadly sin, and Professor Maitland thinks it has still jurisdiction over laymen who are guilty of the crime of heresy. It can punish laymen or clergy for brawling (*i.e.*, gross misbehaviour within the precincts of a church or churchyard). It can punish laymen also by keeping them from entering a church, and by refusing them the Sacrament; and where a clergyman refuses the Sacrament to a parishioner the court has jurisdiction. It can mulct clergy, and probably laity, in costs, the payment of which can be enforced by the writ *de contumace capiendo*. The bishop can veto the prosecution of a clergyman for uncleanness and wickedness of life. When the trial is of a quasi-criminal character, the chancellor is assisted by five assessors, who act as judges of fact (Clergy Discipline Act, 1892).

The criminal jurisdiction over laymen is almost obsolete, save perhaps as to brawling. According to Mr. Eustace Smith, the chancellor can punish laymen by admonition (reprimand only by judge), penance (obsolete), expulsion from the Church (*ab ingressu ecclesiae*), and by excommunication. Excommunication is of two kinds, the less and the greater. The less excludes a man from the services and sacraments, and the greater cuts him off, or is supposed to cut him off, from the fellowship of the faithful (Phillimore, Ecclesiastical Law, vol. 2, p. 1087).

Formerly, the excommunicated man had not the privilege of serving on a jury, neither could he give evidence in court, or bring an action to recover property, but by 55 Geo. III. an imprisonment up to six months could be imposed for the greater excommunication, but the excommunicated man is to labour under no incapacity.

As regards civil jurisdiction, a great deal depends upon the patent to act as judge given by the bishop to his chancellor; but, speaking generally, the chancellor grants faculties for alterations in churches, has a supposed jurisdiction as to mortuary fees or corse presents, and deals with questions of repairs of Church fabric and property, and also with disputed rights to pews.

3. The Court of the Bishop sitting in person to try cases under the Church Discipline Act, *e.g.*, simony and non-residence. This court hardly ever sat, as the bishop had a habit of sending the case for trial before the Dean of Arches by Letters of Request.

4. Arches Court. The judge of this court is the Dean of Arches.

The court has cognizance of ecclesiastical appeals from the Consistory Courts of the Bishops in the province of Canterbury, and has taken over the functions of the old Provincial Court of the Archbishop of Canterbury. The Dean of Arches has jurisdiction *quâ* Dean of Peculiars over the thirteen peculiar parishes in the diocese of London which formerly were within the peculiar jurisdiction of the Archbishop of Canterbury. The dean is also the judge under the Public Worship Regulation Act, 1874, for the trial of doctrinal offences and practices. He is also usually Master of the Faculties to the Archbishop of Canterbury (37 & 38 Vict. c. 85, s. 7).

5. The Provincial Court of the Archbishop of Canterbury still exists in theory, but in practice the Dean of Arches hears all Consistory Court appeals.

6. The Provincial Court of the Province of York. This court takes cognizance of appeals from the Consistory Courts in the diocese, and, as regards York, is a Consistory Court of first instance. The judge is the Dean of Arches.

7. The Court of the Archbishop, presided over by himself or his vicar-general, which can try bishops for ecclesiastical offences and also persons accused of heresy in the province.

8. The Judical Committee of the Privy Council, which is the supreme court of appeal in all matters ecclesiastical.

CHAPTER XV.

ARMY AND NAVY.

Military law.—Soldiers and sailors, like other citizens, are subject to the ordinary law of the land, but, in virtue of their profession, they are also subject to military law. The Navy is a standing force, though the necessary supply must be voted annually. The regular Army is not, in theory, a standing Army. It depends for its existence on the passing of the Army (Annual) Act, which specifies the number of troops and continues for one year the provisions of the Army Act (44 & 45 Vict. c. 58), which provides for the regulation of the force and the maintenance of discipline therein. For the history of our military forces see Anson, vol. 2, pt. 2, pp. 167 *et seq.*, Clode's Military Forces of the Crown, and Manual of Military Law, chap. IX.

The Soldier.—Like the sailor, the soldier can be tried for military offences by court-martial, and when his regiment is out of England he can be tried by court-martial for crimes against civilians where there is no civil court with criminal jurisdiction to try him within 100 miles in a straight line. When a soldier is unfairly sentenced by a court-martial he can get his case reconsidered by the Judge-Advocate General, and where the action of the court-martial is *ultra vires* he can apply, according to circumstances, for a writ of *habeas corpus* or *certiorari*, or where he wishes to stop the proceedings he can apply for a prohibition (Manual of Military Law, chap. VIII.) (*t*). By the Soldiers and Sailors Act, 1918, soldiers and sailors are enabled to make informal wills and, under certain circumstances, these wills are valid even though they are under age.

(t) Any person, however, having cause of action or suit against a soldier of the regular forces may, notwithstanding anything in this section (section 144),

The estate of a soldier falling in battle is not liable to estate duty. A man enlists as a soldier by subscribing to a declaration in the presence of a justice of the peace and taking the statutory oath; and a man becomes an officer by acceptance of his Majesty's commission. When an officer has accepted a commission, he holds it at the royal pleasure, but he cannot resign that commission without leave of the proper authorities (Manual of Military Law, chap. XI.; *Hearson and Churchill* ((1892), 2 Q. B., p. 144).

Military tribunals.—The commanding officer has power to deal with petty offences by fine up to a certain amount, and by imposing imprisonment for a limited number of days. The jurisdiction is explained clearly in section 46 of the Army Act. There are four military courts, viz. :—

The regimental court-martial.—This tribunal must consist of not less than three officers, each of whom must have been a commissioned officer for not less than one year, and, with certain exceptions mentioned in section 47 of the Army Act, the president must not be under the rank of captain. This Court may not award imprisonment beyond forty-two days, nor can it discharge accused with ignominy. It must be convened by a proper convening officer.

District court-martial.—A district court-martial shall be convened by an officer authorised to convene the same (see Army Act, s. 123); and it must consist of not less than three officers, each of whom must have held a commission during not less than two years. A district court-martial cannot try a person subject to military law as an officer, nor award sentence of death or penal servitude, but merely imprisonment up to two years. A general court-martial only may try an officer.

General court-martial.—This tribunal may inflict any sentence, including death or penal servitude. It must consist of not less

after due notice in writing given to the soldier or left at his last quarters, proceed in such action or suit to judgment, and have execution other than against the person, pay, arms, ammunition, equipments, regimental necessaries or clothing of such soldier.

than five officers, who have held commissions for not less than three years, and the president of either a district or general court-martial must be a field officer, except in cases mentioned by the Act (see section 46).

Field court-martial.—This court may be convened on active service or in countries beyond the seas in cases where, in the opinion of the convening officer, a general court-martial is impracticable. (See Manual of Military Law, p. 49.)

General powers of courts-martial.—The jurisdiction of courts-martial and the offences of which they may take cognizance, are dealt with by the Army Act. For reasonable cause shown an accused may challenge a member of a court-martial to whom he objects; but unlike the civil felon or traitor, who has a right of peremptory challenge of his judges of fact (the jury), he must show cause. The members of the court-martial (whether military or naval) are judges of fact as well as of law.

The Army Act provides that where a field officer is placed on his trial, no person below the rank of captain can serve on the court-martial.

The sentences of district, regimental and general courts-martial cannot be carried out unless they are confirmed by the proper authorities mentioned in the Army Act. It is impossible to set out the numerous crimes of which courts-martial can take cognizance, but they can deal with numerous offences which are not *mala in se*—*e.g.*, cowardice before the enemy (death); falling asleep or being drunk whilst acting as sentry in time of war (death); malingering, defiance of the orders of a man's superior, striking an officer (death), &c., &c.

Drunkenness, whether on duty or not, is severely punished, comparatively speaking. One noticeable feature of the military penal code is the severe punishment (death) for mutiny or sedition, concealment of mutiny or sedition, &c. (Army Act, s. 7).

Section 45 of the Army Act provides that the charge made against every person taken into military custody be investigated without unnecessary delay by the proper military authority, but there appears to be now no legal remedy, as there is no time fixed for the trial of a military person accused of a military offence. Where an officer or a soldier has cause to complain of the action of any superior officer, means of redress are afforded to him by sections 42 and 43 of the Act. It may be that a civil judge, when asked to interfere, would, before granting relief, be guided by the fact as to whether the complainant had or had not availed himself of the protection conferred by these sections.

Section 162 of the Army Act, 1909, provides that "where a person is sentenced by a court-martial in pursuance of the Act to punishment for an offence, and is afterwards tried by a civil court for the same offence, that court shall, *in awarding punishment*, have regard to the military punishment he may have already undergone, and that when a person subject to military law has been acquitted or convicted of an offence by a competent civil court, he shall not be liable to be tried by court-martial for that offence. See, too, section 46 (7).

In addition to the prisoner having the benefit of challenging members of courts-martial for cause shown, the members of a court-martial are sworn to try the case fairly. All witnesses are examined on oath, and English rules of evidence are to be observed. Civilians may be called as witnesses and are paid for their attendance, and on refusal to attend or take the oath or affirmation, or answer questions, may be reported to the civil power and dealt with as if they were guilty of a contempt of a civil court (section 126).

Naval courts.—The commanding officer of a ship may administer a short period of imprisonment, viz., three months, for divers offences which are not of a serious character. The constitution of a court-martial varies according to the rank of a person tried, and all naval courts-martial must be general courts-martial with power to award any punishment, including death. All naval courts-martial must be held on board a man-of-war.

A court-martial must consist of not less than five or more than nine members. To secure impartiality no person prosecuting can act as judge. Naval offences are very severely punished, and naval courts-martial have drastic powers over naval persons. Ordinary civilians who have been summoned to give evidence before them, and are guilty of contempt, are dealt with by a civil court of competent jurisdiction.

Justice and procedure at naval courts is regulated by the Naval Discipline Acts, 1866 and 1884, and the Naval Regulations.

Certain offences can be punished by a naval court-martial which are punishable by naval custom.

Naval courts-martial, like military courts, take cognizance of several offences which are not *mala in se*.

Sailors and soldiers are primarily bound to obey the civil law, even though such obedience may render them liable to trial by court-martial.

Enlistment.—In the Regular Army the terms for enlistment vary, and in the new Territorial Force enlistment may be for a fixed period, which must not exceed four years, though the territorialist may re-enlist. Any territorialist may retire on giving three months' notice and payment of a fine not exceeding £5.

A private in the regulars may purchase his discharge within three months after enlistment by paying £10. His Majesty may in times of danger retain the services of the soldier though the time for which he enlisted has expired. By section 96 of the Army Act the master of an apprentice may, subject to certain reservations, by adopting certain police court procedure, claim from the military authorities his apprentice.

The apprentice must be bound by a regular indenture for four years, and have been under sixteen when bound apprentice.

Ordinary sailors join the Navy by enlistment, impressment being now obsolete, though never formally abolished. (See May's Const. Hist., vol. 3, p. 21.)

History of the armed forces.—Prior to the Conquest all freemen between fifteen and sixty who were capable of bearing arms had to serve in the fyrd or general levy, and those who evaded service had to pay a fyrd-wite, a penalty which might extend to entire forfeiture of land. There was a levy for each county, presided over by the earldorman or earl. The general levy was a civil as well as a military force, and in its civil capacity it was used to suppress riots and known as the sheriff's *posse comitatus*.

As a military force it could be used to resist insurrections or foreign invasion. It was not bound to serve outside England—Scotland and Wales perhaps excepted. In the reign of Edward VI. we find the lord lieutenant of each county commanding the fyrd, or the militia as it was afterwards called, instead of the earldorman (Military Handbook, p. 147). After the Conquest came the feudal levy, which could be called upon to fight out of England for forty days, and when forty days was not sufficient the Kings were to pay them. All military tenants served at their own expense. Service in the feudal levy was supposed to be personal, but the clerical baron, *e.g.*, the bishop, paid a composition in lieu of personal service.

Henry I. is reported to have invented scutage (shield money), also called escuage, whereby personal service was dispensed with and the military tenant, instead of serving forty days, had to equip and maintain a knight to serve for longer than forty days.

Scutage formed one of the grievances of Magna Charta, and after 1215 A.D. it was supposed not to be levied without the consent of the Great Council and afterwards of Parliament.

In the reign of Edward I. we hear of commissions of array, which were a form of compulsory military service for wars, both foreign and domestic. Compulsory service was much resorted to during the Wars of the Roses, and also in Tudor times. Impressment for military service was declared illegal by 16 Charles I. c. 28. After the Restoration military tenures were abolished and, with them, scutage. The militia was retained, and the King had also a bodyguard. Charles II. raised a certain number of regiments by voluntary enlistment, and James II. raised an army in the same way, which caused such apprehension that a standing army was forbidden by the Bill of Rights. It was, however, soon found that a standing army was necessary, and this form was kept up by Annual Mutiny Acts. These statutes were called Mutiny Acts till 1881, when the Army Act—forming to a large extent a military code—was passed. This Act is annually renewed by a short statute known as the Annual Army Act.

For the Great War military service was made compulsory, but up to 1914 the Army was composed of regular troops, militia, territorials and reservists. Reservists were divided into two classes, viz., the army reserve and the militia reserve, enlistment in which closed after April, 1901. The militia reserve was known as the special reserve.

The Territorial Army.—By the Territorial and Reserve Forces Act, 1907, the auxiliary military forces of the Crown (militia, yeomanry and volunteers) were reorganised. County associations were created, and power was given to the Army Council to prepare schemes for the internal management, incorporation and constitution of the Territorial forces. The proper functions of a county association (section 2) are to master the directions of the Army Council as to the particular county force and to make a study of all statistics and county resources in order to advise the Army Council as to same.

Though the Army Council pay the expenses of the county association, the latter body is practically entrusted, subject to the supervision of the former body, with the entire management of the county Territorial force.

It has to recruit fresh soldiers, provide camps and rifle ranges and also land for military manœuvres.

It can, and ought, to establish battalions of cadets and rifle clubs, but no public money must be spent upon boys under sixteen.

All orders and regulations made by the Army Council must be laid before Parliament.

The force is only liable to serve in the United Kingdom, but it may offer to serve abroad. It has to undergo an annual training of not more than fifteen days or less than eight days. The Crown can embody the force by a proclamation which calls out the Army Reserve, unless the two Houses present an address to veto such embodiment. If Parliament be not sitting when such embodiment takes place, the Crown must convene it within ten days of embodiment.

Territorialists can be tried by court-martial when they do not attend on embodiment of the force and where they neglect to carry out conditions as to training. Whilst under training, or when embodied, they are subject to military discipline.

Part III. of the Territorial Army Act deals with a new force of reserves called special reservists, which is to consist of reservists who have not served in the Regular Army.

By the Territorial Army and Militia Act, 1921 (11 & 12 Geo. V. c. 37), the Territorial Force, created by the Territorial and Reserve Forces Act, 1907, is to be called the Territorial Army.

Section 2 provides that that portion of the army reserve known as the special reserve shall be called the militia.

Section 4 provides that the power to raise a militia force and a yeomanry force shall cease.

CHAPTER XVI.

THE COUNCILS OF THE CROWN.

The three councils.—The King has three councils, viz., the House of Lords, the Privy Council, and the Cabinet. The right of the House of Lords to style itself a council is practically non-existent, as the last instance of the Sovereign convening it was in 1688. Any lord of Parliament may, however, demand access to the King to tender him counsel (*u*).

The Privy Council has at present no deliberative functions, but is to all intents and purposes a constitutional machine for carrying into effect the deliberations of the Cabinet.

According to Sir William Anson every council goes through certain processes. It first increases in numbers, and then a kernel or nucleus forms inside it, and, gradually getting bigger, eats it up. Then the kernel or nucleus gets bigger, another kernel forms inside the first kernel, and the same process is repeated.

The King's continual council was the *nucleus* which formed inside the *Magnum Concilium*, and this continual council got larger; and another council (now known as the Cabinet) formed inside it.

History of the Cabinet.—We know nothing definite about the Inner Council of State, out of which the Cabinet was gradually evolved, till the reign of Henry VIII.; but according to Langmead there were indications of such a council before the time of Henry VII. The Privy Council was, *tempore* Henry VIII., known as *Concilium Privatum*, and besides this there was a small *coterie* of permanent advisers of the Sovereign called by some authorities the *Concilium Ordinarium*. (The subject is fully discussed in Anson, vol. 1, pp. 65—68, and in Fielden's

(*u*) Professor Lowell says that the peer desiring access for this purpose must obtain an appointment with the Sovereign through the Home Secretary.

Constitutional History, pp. 42—46, and pp. 48 *et seq.*) The members of the *Concilium Ordinarium*, however, were in no sense members of a Cabinet as we understand it, though a little later on Bacon describes them as the Cabinet; and though he sums up their merits as well as their demerits, comments upon them in somewhat slighting terms.

According to Mr. Trail, what we now call the Cabinet has gone through four phases, and the effect of what he says is as follows :—

In the first phase it was a small, irregular *camarilla*, consisting of persons of the King's choice. These men had to agree with the King in everything. They gave the Sovereign private advice, but performed no executive functions. During this phase the inner council had no particular name.

In the second stage, this inner body of councillors is called the Cabinet, "but it did not displace the Privy Council from its position as *de jure* as well as *de facto* adviser to the King."

"The third phase commenced with the reign of William III. In this stage the Cabinet was unknown to the law, but it became the *de facto* adviser to the Crown vice the Privy Council, though not the adviser *de jure*."

"In the fourth phase (the present one) the Cabinet is still unknown to the law, though it has displaced the Privy Council as the executive authority in the State. It consists of a body of men known only to the law as Privy Councillors. It is indirectly chosen by the predominating party in the Commons, and consists of men who, though in many respects their political views may be divergent, have agreed to a definite political programme."

We do not notice the Cabinet much as a body till the time of Charles II. This monarch was somewhat secretive as to politics, and many little intrigues were made with France. Previons to matters being introduced to the Privy Council, Charles sought the advice of a few *confidantes*, who were members thereof. Sir William Temple did not appreciate this *modus operandi*, and he at length persuaded Charles to agree to a new plan, which was to reduce the size of the Privy Council from fifty to thirty members. It was hoped that the reduced council would form an efficient working body, but Temple frustrated his own scheme by forming a clique inside the council. The Cabinets both of William and Anne were chosen from both parties frequently, though William had occasionally to recognise that there was such a thing as Party Government (cf. Todd, vol. 2, p. 71; Anson, vol. 2, chap. 25).

It was not, as before stated, till the advent of Mr. Pitt's Ministry in 1783 that the idea of a Cabinet consisting of persons willing to adhere to a definite programme was deemed in any way a necessity (cf. Todd, vol. 1, p. 58).

The Premier and Cabinet.—The present Cabinet consists of persons who are willing to work under a chief called the Premier or Prime Minister. The Premier is an official unknown to the law. The only capacity in which the law recognises him is as First Lord of the Treasury, or holder of some other Cabinet office, and a member of the Privy Council (*x*).

All members of the Cabinet are by convention members of the Privy Council. The entire Cabinet, again, is collectively responsible to Parliament for the policy pursued (collective responsibility). They are, in theory, obliged to stand or fall together, and when the policy pursued does not meet with the approval of the majority in the Commons, they are in duty bound to resign *en bloc* (cf. Todd, vol. 2, pp. 141—143).

The King can, if he chooses, dismiss the Cabinet, but this conduct, though legal, would on most occasions be considered unconstitutional. All members of the Cabinet must, in theory, defer to the Premier, and when they disagree with him on a serious question of principle they ought in strictness to resign. In the event of a split the question becomes serious, and the Premier, after trying every expedient to bring his colleagues into agreement, as a last resource seeks an interview with the King.

Mere departmental errors may or may not be the causes of the resignation of a Cabinet Minister, but they do not generally necessitate the resignation of the Cabinet.

Nearly all the members of the Cabinet are heads of departments, but one or two old experienced Ministers are often placed

(*x*) The Premier has now a definite precedence allotted to him.

there for the sake of the valuable advice they can give, holding some such office as Lord Privy Seal or Chancellor of the Duchy of Lancaster. The following Ministers must be in the Cabinet, viz., the six Secretaries of State, the First Lord of the Treasury, the Chancellor of the Exchequer, the Lord Chancellor, the President of the Council, either the Lord Lieutenant of Ireland or his Chief Secretary (the Irish Secretary). Neither the Secretary for Scotland nor the Irish Secretary is a Secretary of State, but lately the former has had a seat in the Cabinet, and so had the Presidents of the Board of Trade and Local Government Board. It is the duty of the Premier to support his colleagues and to smooth over the difficulties (if any) which may occur with the King.

The King and the Cabinet.—The King is constitutionally bound to take the Cabinet's advice and support it socially. By convention the King is also bound to say nothing against the Cabinet, lend it his moral support, and to dismiss high government officials who oppose it.

On a Ministry resigning, the King is supposed to take the advice of the outgoing Premier as to who shall be summoned and asked to form a Ministry. There is generally, however, no choice, and when there is a choice it is only between two or three at the most. The leading man of the party, whether he be a commoner or lord, has a right to be Premier, and the King is obliged to send for him, and should he send for anyone else, it is supposed to be the duty of the person thus sent for to urge the claims of the leader of the party, as was the case when Lord Granville was sent for and not the late Mr. W. E. Gladstone (Bagehot's English Constitution, 2nd ed., p. 13) (*y*).

When the King chooses his Premier, the Premier, on the formation of a new Ministry, chooses his colleagues. He can undoubtedly select whom he likes, but etiquette does not permit him to exclude ex-ministers of the Crown belonging to his party, as a rule (Bagehot's English Constitution, 2nd ed., p. 12).

The Cabinet deliberate secretly, but the results arrived at are communicated to the Sovereign (Todd, vol. 2, p. 201).

(*y*) Professor Lowell says it is not the King's constitutional duty to consult the outgoing Premier; but Sir William Anson thinks otherwise.

The Premier has an exclusive right to approach the Sovereign on all important matters of State, but other Ministers have a right to discuss with him matters which are merely departmental (Todd, vol. 2, p. 208).

The Sovereign in his dealings with the Cabinet has three rights, viz.: 1. To be consulted; 2. To warn; 3. To encourage (Bagehot's English Constitution, 2nd ed., p. 75).

It is necessary to consult the Sovereign before any definite step is taken, even though that step takes the direction of legislation. It may be mentioned that at present legislation is perhaps the chief duty of the Cabinet, who, owing to certain new rules of procedure, have a monopoly in this respect (Bagehot's English Constitution, 2nd ed., p. 75).

The King.—The King, though he is now, as Mr. Trail says (see Central Government, p. 3), but the visible symbol of power, is by no means a *quantité négligeable* in the Constitution.

Owing to his peculiar position, he has a unique experience of the inner workings of ministry after ministry. He has been the receptacle of many State secrets, and can say to a Minister : " In such and such a case the course you suggest was pursued and it failed." As to foreign matters, it would be presumptuous, and frequently most inexpedient, to ignore the warnings of the King. He is related to several reigning heads, and enjoys the respect and confidence, perhaps, also of several European and Asiatic statesmen; and, granting this to be the case, he has a greater knowledge of the inner workings of foreign Cabinets than anybody else in the kingdom. In the reign of her late Majesty Queen Victoria this point cropped up. Lord Palmerston was Foreign Secretary and Lord John Russell Premier. Lord Palmerston answered important despatches without consulting Queen Victoria or his chief; and, on complaint being made to the Queen, the rule was made that all letters coming from abroad and drafts of replies thereto (not being matter of ordinary routine) be submitted to the Sovereign for approval, and also draft letters written to foreign ministers. (For further particulars, Todd, vol. 2, pp. 213 *et seq.*, and McCarthy's History of Our Own Times).

The King is obliged to be in the confidence of his Cabinet. He is supposed to see his Ministers in private. The question came up after the marriage of Queen Victoria. Ministers did not like the presence of the Prince Consort at audiences. Mr. Gladstone in his "Gleanings of Past Years" defined the true position of the late Prince Albert when he remarked that the Sovereign may take counsel with anyone, subject only to the condition that the relationship existing with Ministers is not disturbed. Though the Sovereign cannot take counsel with the Opposition, he may speak freely with others. As to letters from foreign potentates, the rule now is that all correspondence must pass through a Minister where the foreign ruler is not the Sovereign's relative (*z*).

Working majority.—No Cabinet can either take office or retain it without a working majority, and such majority must be more or less substantial, though it is difficult to state precisely what would constitute one.

(*z*) Lowell, "Government of England," I., p. 37.

CHAPTER XVII.

THE PRESENT PRIVY COUNCIL—COUNCIL OF DEFENCE.

The present Privy Council.—This Council is now, as Sir William Anson points out, the machinery by which the Cabinet expresses the royal pleasure, which is signified for the most part in two ways :—

1. By Proclamation;
2. By Order in Council.

When it is desired that the entire country should know the will of the Executive, a Proclamation is resorted to, and in other cases an Order in Council is usually made.

Orders in Council.—Apart from the King's regulations for the Army and Navy, and legislation for Crown colonies and protectorates, Orders in Council are now largely made in pursuance of express statutory powers. Very numerous statutes authorize what may be called subordinate legislation by Order in Council. They authorise the making of schemes, or the introduction of postponed provisions, or the temporary application of certain statutory provisions to special areas. The provisions of the Extradition Acts are applied by Orders in Council to the States with which treaties have been made, and courts for the trial of British subjects in barbarous countries are created by this machinery under powers given by the Foreign Jurisdiction Act, 1890.

Most of the business formerly transacted by the Privy Council has now been transferred to other departments of government.

The Judicial Committee of the Privy Council.—This committee sits as a court, and hears colonial and Indian appeal cases, also ecclesiastical appeals and appeals from prize courts. It also grants extensions of time for patents. As the laws differ in English colonies this tribunal, which largely consists of the same judges as hear appeals in the House of Lords, has a very difficult task, and it has to be versed in all kinds of law. It does not pronounce judgment, but advises the Sovereign to give judgment in a particular way. If its members differ, the difference does not appear in the opinion of the Board, and it is the duty of members not to disclose this difference. In ecclesiastical cases provision is made for the attendance of prelates as assessors. Since the constitution of the Judicial Committee by the 3 & 4 Will. IV. c. 41, it has been strengthened by the addition of Indian and Colonial judges and judges of the Court of Appeal who are Privy Councillors.

Position of Privy Councillor.—Privy Councillors are nominated by the Sovereign, and on appointment they attend and kiss the King's hand, and also take the Privy Councillor's oath.

Privy Councillors are in the commission of the peace for every county in England, and hold office during the life of the King, though, as a matter of course, the new Sovereign continues them in office, and he must conventionally continue in office such of them as belong to the Cabinet at the time of the demise of the Crown. A man is dismissed from the Privy Council by the Sovereign erasing his name from the roll of Privy Councillors. Persons are now frequently appointed Privy Councillors because they have distinguished themselves in some walk of life, and not because the King wants their assistance, and they probably never exercise the functions of a Privy Councillor. The head of the Privy Council is the president of the Council, who is generally an old parliamentary hand whose advice is required. The duties of the post are not onerous. All Cabinet Ministers must not only be members of the Privy Council, but also members of the Lords or the Commons; but Sir William Anson says an exception was once made in the case of the late Mr. W. E. Gladstone, who held office for three or four months without having a seat. There has been at least one other instance since then, namely, in the case of Mr. Winston Churchill.

The Council of Defence.—Its proper designation is the Committee of Imperial Defence. When Lord Salisbury came into power in 1895, a Committee of National Defence was created, and this committee was composed of members of the then Cabinet.

Since 1904, however, the constitution of this body has undergone alteration, as it now consists not only of Cabinet Ministers but also others. The idea is to create a council with a continuous policy independent of party politics, combined with full recognition of Cabinet control (*a*).

The council at present consists of the following persons, viz., the Prime Minister, who is chairman, the War and Indian Secretaries, the First Lord of the Admiralty, Lord Esher, Viscount French, and certain naval and military experts (*b*).

(*a*) This council, in its present state, cannot in any way be considered an inner council within the Cabinet, though at one time it perhaps was.

(*b*) See "Constitutional Year Book," p 63.

CHAPTER XVIII.

SECRETARIES OF STATE AND THEIR UNDER-SECRETARIES.

History of office of Secretary of State.—Secretaries of State are channels of communication between the Crown and subject. There was a King's clerk in the time of John, and in the reign of Henry III., when the Chancellor (*i.e.*, the progenitor of the present Lord Chancellor) became too busy to do clerical drudgery, a confidential clerk was appointed (*secretarius*). In the reign of Henry VI. there were two King's clerks, and in the reign of Edward IV. one of these was known as head clerk or chief secretary. When the Crown work was in after times very heavy, three secretaries were necessary, but, strange to say, there were two only in the year 1794. According to Professor Maitland, there were three in 1801, viz., one for home affairs, one for foreign matters, and a third for war and colonial work. In 1854 there was a Secretary for War appointed, and in 1858 the office of Secretary of State for India was created after the suppression of the Mutiny.

The Secretary of State did not become the great executive officer he now is until the business formerly transacted by the Privy Council committees was transferred to Government departments.

Henry VIII. allotted to his secretaries precedence at court functions, but notwithstanding this, they were on one or two occasions treated as common clerks by the Lords of the Council in the reign of William III. Secretaries of State, if commoners, now come in the table of precedence next after the Vice-Chamberlain of the Household.

Present Secretaries of State.—As will be seen above, the Secretaries of State are now six in number, viz., the Foreign Secretary, the Home Secretary, the War Secretary, the Colonial and Indian Secretaries, and the Secretary of State for Air (Air Force Constitution Act, 1917 (7 & 8 Geo. V., c. 51).

They can all do each other's work. Prof. Maitland quotes one exception, and tells us that it is the Home Secretary alone who can deal with the Act to amend petitions of right (Petition of Right Act, 1860). But there appear to be other exceptions created by statute: see, for example, the provisions of the Government of India Act, 1858, as to the Indian Secretary. It is doubtful whether the Secretary for Scotland and the Secretaries of State can interact.

Each Secretary of State is assisted by a Parliamentary Under-Secretary and by a Permanent Under-Secretary and official staff.

The Secretary of State is appointed by delivery to him of the seals of office. Only five Secretaries of State can sit in the Commons.

Under-Secretaries.—Each Secretary of State is assisted by a Parliamentary Under-Secretary, appointed by himself. The Parliamentary Under-Secretary is a subordinate member of the Government, changing with the Ministry. Only five Under-Secretaries can sit in the House of Commons (see 27 & 28 Vict. c. 34); consequently one Under-Secretary at least must be in the House of Lords. An Under-Secretary does not vacate his seat in the Commons by acceptance of office (see 21 & 22 Vict. c. 106) (*c*).

Prof. Maitland further tells us that Secretaries of State have extensive common law and statutory powers, and he says "it seems certain that they may commit persons to prison for treason or treasonable offences," though he admits the power is now never exercised. He quotes the prosecution of the editor of the *North Briton* newspaper (see Maitland's Constitutional History, p. 410).

(*c*) For a detailed account of the history of the office of Secretary of State and his duties, see "Trail on Central Government," pp. 55 *et seq.*

CHAPTER XIX.

THE PERMANENT CIVIL SERVICE.

Each important department of the Executive has a Parliamentary head who controls the general policy of that department, but who is necessarily assisted by a large subordinate staff. The Parliamentary Chief, of course, can only deal with matters of importance, but all the business of the department is conducted in his name, and he is responsible for it to Parliament. The staff of the executive departments constitute the Civil Service. Judicial officers hold their appointments during good behaviour, and their salaries are charged on the Consolidated Fund. Civil servants, on the other hand, hold their posts "during pleasure" (cf. *Young* v. *Weller*, (1898) A. C. 661), and their salaries are charged on the annual votes. Though technically a civil servant holds during pleasure, practically he has security of tenure, and the service is known as the permanent Civil Service. If an office is reorganised, and the services of a civil servant are dispensed with in consequence, provision is made for compensation. A civil servant is entitled to a pension at 60, and he must retire on pension at 65, unless for special reasons he receives an extension not exceeding five years. A civil servant is not disqualified from voting at a parliamentary election, but if he wishes to stand for Parliament he must resign his appointment. With the exception of the Foreign Office the entry into either the First or Second Division of the Civil Service is by competitive examination. But certain of the higher appointments, and the appointments requiring professional qualifications, are exempted from the examination rule, the Minister making the appointment direct. The office of a Secretary of State may be taken as a type. The Secretary of State is a member of the Cabinet, and, of course, goes out with the Government. He is assisted in his parliamentary work by a Parliamentary Under-Secretary, who, in addition to his parliamentary duties, does such office work as may be arranged for by his chief. If both Secretary of State and the Parliamentary Under-Secretary sit in the House of Commons, some peer is selected, who answers for the department in the House of Lords. At the head of the office is the Permanent Under-Secretary of State, who sometimes has risen in the office itself, but who is generally chosen from the outside. There are, as the case may be, two or three Assistant Secretaries, and under them a sufficient number of clerks of different grades. The subordinate departments of the Government are for the most part placed under the general control of one of the great departments. The proceedings of the subordinate departments or boards are conducted in the name of that department, but all matters of importance have to be referred to the higher authority. For example, many orders would be made in the name and under the authority of the Commissioners of Metropolitan Police or of the Prison Commissioners, but these departments are under the supervision and control of the Home Secretary, and all matters of first-rate importance must be referred to him. (See, further, Lowell's Government of England, Chap. VII.)

Executive appointments generally are held " during pleasure." But certain officers, who perhaps might be classed as civil servants, by the terms of their appointments hold during good behaviour, *e.g.*, the Comptroller and Auditor-General and the Charity Commissioners.

CHAPTER XX.

IMPORTANT DEPARTMENTS OF STATE.

The Foreign Secretary and his staff.—This appointment is generally given to a member of the House of Lords. He is assisted by the Parliamentary Under-Secretary, who, like himself, goes out with the Government, a Permanent Under-Secretary, and three Assistant Under-Secretaries.

This great functionary conducts negotiations with foreign Powers, and, as far as is consistent with our national interests, cultivates amicable relations with them. He recommends the appointment of ambassadors to foreign courts; he receives new ambassadors, and introduces them to the King. He hears the representations of foreign ambassadors resident in England as to their privileges and otherwise. He appoints numerous diplomatic officials, and also consuls, vice-consuls, &c. He superintends the preparation of trade statistics collected from British agents abroad, which he then has published and distributed amongst various chambers of commerce. He interviews foreign ambassadors here as to foreign affairs, and advises our ambassadors abroad. He grants passports, and often acts as the protector of British subjects abroad who have sustained injury whilst abroad. He, in concert, as a rule, with the rest of the Cabinet, carries into execution the treaty-making prerogative of the Crown, and he must bear the principal brunt of any treaty which is concluded, and which either clashes with the rights of the subject, or for any grave reason necessitates the sanction of the Legislature (see *Parlement Belge Case* (1878), 4 P. D., p. 129). (As to functions of office, see Const. Yr. Bk. 1910, p. 64; Todd, vol. 2, p. 504.)

He is allowed considerable latitude as to the answering of questions put in either House, as it would be frequently inexpedient to prematurely publish delicate negotiations with foreign Governments.

Home Office.—The powers and duties of the Home Secretary are very varied. As regards home affairs, he is the authorized channel of communication between the King and his subjects; petitions or addresses to the King should go through the Home Secretary. He advises the Crown as to the exercise of the prerogative of mercy, which includes both pardons and commutation or reduction of criminal sentences. He can license prisoners under sentence of penal servitude, either conditionally or unconditionally, though in certain cases the licence has to be laid before Parliament. He has the general superintendence and control over prisons, criminal lunatic asylums, juvenile reformatories, and industrial schools and inebriate reformatories. The Metropolitan Police are under him, as the police authority for the Metropolitan district. He inspects the country police forces, and exercises a certain amount of control over them, and if he finds them inefficient he can advise a withdrawal of the Treasury contribution. He appoints recorders and stipendiary magistrates, and fixes the salary of magistrates' clerks. He prescribes scales of costs in criminal matters, and supervises, to some extent, the proceedings in magistrates' courts, though any misconduct on the part of a magistrate is a matter for the Lord Chancellor. He can require the Director of Public Prosecutions to take up a case, though this is a procedure seldom adopted. Formal proceedings in the case of the bestowal of honours pass through his office. He administers the provisions of the Aliens Act and the Naturalization Acts, and he can refuse a certificate of naturalization without giving reasons. All extradition proceedings pass through the Home Office, and the Home Secretary makes the final order. Commissions from foreign courts (*commissions rogatoires*) to take evidence in England are referred by the Foreign Office to the Home Office. He administers various Acts of Parliament and has other miscellaneous duties.

War Office.—At the head of the War Department is the Secretary of State for War, who is the Minister responsible to Parliament for military matters. To assist the Parliamentary head, an Army Council was created in 1904, and its functions are particularised in an Order in Council dated August 10th in the said year; but the Secretary of State can reserve certain functions for himself.

The council consists of six members besides the War Secretary, and these are the first military member (Chief of General Staff), the second military member (Adjutant-General), the third military member (Quartermaster-General), and the fourth military member (Master-General of Ordnance). These four members are to be answerable for the due performance of such business relating to organization, disposition, personnel, armament, and maintenance of the Army as shall be assigned to them, or each of them, by the War Secretary.

The fifth member is called the Finance Member, who looks after monetary affairs and such other business as may be from time to time assigned to him.

The sixth member is the Civil Member, who looks after non-effective votes, and has certain other duties from time to time assigned to him. The seventh member is the Secretary of the War Office, and upon him devolves all the secretarial work of the Army Council, and he is charged with the preparation of official communications to that council, and has to see to the interior economy of the War Office, besides other duties (Constitutional Year Book, 1920).

The Old Admiralty.—Up to the reign of Queen Anne Admiralty work was presided over by an official called the Lord High Admiral, but since that period the office has been placed in commission (*i.e.*, Royal Commissioners were appointed to do the work of one man).

The Board of Commissioners now consists of eight persons—to wit, the First Lord of the Admiralty, four Sea Lords, one Civil Lord, a Parliamentary Secretary, and the Permanent Secretary. The First Lord, who is in the Cabinet, is responsible to Parliament for all naval matters. Though in theory merely *primus inter pares*, he is the head of the Admiralty. Each of the seven other members of the board has special duties attached to him, besides attending the board meetings (see Constitutional Year Book, 1920).

The Parliamentary Secretary has duties analogous to those of the Under-Secretaries of State.

The Treasury and its history.—The First Lord of the Treasury is almost invariably the Premier, though Lord Salisbury was Premier and Foreign Secretary. He is only, however, the titular head, because the duties of Premier are too important to secure the efficient discharge of departmental work in addition.

In the days of the Plantagenets the present Treasury was known as the *Scaccarium* (Exchequer), and it was so named because the committee of the continual council of the King sitting for revenue purposes occupied an apartment called the *Scaccarium.*

This Scaccarium, or Exchequer, was divided into two departments, viz., the Upper Exchequer, or Exchequer of Account, and the Lower Exchequer, or Exchequer of Receipt. The former department "recorded and checked payments made for the service of the Sovereign and the State," and the latter "received payment of royal dues payable by local officers appointed for collection of the same" (Trail, Central Government, p. 32). At the head of the Scaccarium was a personage called the Treasurer, who was inferior in point of rank to the Justiciar and Chancellor (as to these officials, see Carter, pp. 118 *et seq.*).

When the Chancellor became a person of weight and importance and his duties onerous, the Treasurer gradually became prominent, and in the time of Elizabeth Burleigh styled himself Lord High Treasurer.

The Treasurer had certain colleagues known as Barons of the Exchequer, and these persons probably sat at meetings of the Exchequer of Account. In the year 1612 A.D. the Treasury was placed in commission, and is in commission now, though its real head is an official called the Chancellor of the Exchequer.

The Chancellor of the Exchequer.—We first hear of this office in the 18th year of Henry III., as in that year "John Maunsell was appointed by writ directed to the then treasurer." "He was to reside at the Exchequer of Receipt, and to have a counter-roll of all things pertaining to the said receipt." (Trail, Central Government, p. 34.)

Maunsell was probably the first *Cancellarius de Scaccario*, and that office is mentioned in a later record of the reign of Henry III. (see Trail, p. 34).

Present Chancellor of the Exchequer.—This official is now of necessity a Cabinet Minister. He is appointed by letters patent under the Great Seal and personal delivery of certain seals of office.

He is one of the Treasury commissioners (the commissioners for executing the offices of Treasurer of the Exchequer of Great Britain and Lord High Treasurer of Ireland); but in reality he is the head man of that great department, the other commissioners having little or nothing to do with the policy of the office.

The present nominal commission consists of the First Lord of the Treasury (who has large political patronage, but does not concern himself with the work of the office; the First Lord is usually the Prime Minister), the Chancellor of the Exchequer, and three members of the Government who are not members of the Cabinet, but who go out with the Cabinet, viz., three Lords of the Treasury. For the most part their office duties are of a formal character.

It is supposed to be the chief function of the Chancellor of the Exchequer to protect the taxpayer and prevent waste in all directions, and to this end he has to overhaul the estimates of other departments, which are annually submitted to him for the purpose. When the estimates are presented, the Treasury officials cut them down to the smallest possible compass compatible with the national requirements, and from these estimates thus cut down the Chancellor prepares the annual Budget, and to meet the requirements of the nation as disclosed thereby he submits to Parliament the necessary measures of taxation, either imposing new taxes or taking off old ones. The Chancellor represents all the revenue offices in Parliament (Todd, vol. 2, pp. 434 *et seq.*).

The Financial Secretary.—This official has a seat in Parliament, and his work, both at the Treasury, and in Parliament, is to master financial details and assist generally the Chancellor of the Exchequer in this respect (cf. Laws of England, vol. 7, p. 101).

The Patronage Secretary.—This gentleman is Chief Government Whip, with important Parliamentary duties, and he has also extensive duties as to the awarding of patronage in various ways at the instigation of Members of Parliament, and otherwise (Todd, vol. 2, p. 592).

The Treasury Solicitor.—This functionary is generally a barrister. He is the legal adviser to the Government departments, and defends actions brought against Ministers and, in some cases, other public functionaries. He has to do with the estates of intestates when the Crown succeeds. As King's Proctor he intervenes to stop decrees nisi in divorce being made absolute in cases of collusion and other instances where it would be contrary to morality to sever the marriage bond. He can demand to see briefs, letters and other documents in divorce cases, whether the same be privileged or not (Constitutional Year Book, 1910, p. 76).

Director of Public Prosecutions.—This office was formerly combined with the office of Solicitor to the Treasury, but the offices have been severed by the 8 Edw. VII. c. 3. Regulations made under the Prosecution of Offences Act, 1879, provide for his taking action in criminal cases which appear to be of importance or difficulty, or which from other reasons require his intervention.

Parliamentary Counsel to the Treasury.—Two barristers are appointed to this office. Their duties are to draft all Government Bills, and occasionally important Orders in Council, and also to advise on matters connected with legislation.

Public Trustee.—The Public Trustee is a State functionary empowered by statute to take over trusts of private individuals subject to certain unimportant statutory restrictions. He is a source of public convenience and of profit to the Revenue. From a Constitutional standpoint the office is of interest as affording an exception to the maxim, "The King can do no wrong," since a remedy exists against the Consolidated Fund in respect of certain torts committed by him, *e.g.*, negligence (see 6 Edw. VII. c. 55, s. 7).

Ministry of Health.—This Department was created by the Ministry of Health Act, 1919 (9 & 10 Geo. V. c. 21) to supervise the public health and to do the work formerly allotted to the Local Government Board, which has been abolished.

Its head is the Minister of Health, who has a seat in the Cabinet and is assisted by a Parliamentary Secretary. The permanent officials consist of two first secretaries and the first, being the senior, chooses under-secretaries and a clerical staff.

The functions of this department consist of (a) the former Local Government Board work; (b) the powers and duties of the Insurance Commissioners; (c) certain functions formerly appertaining to the Education Board and relating to the health of certain women before confinement, the medical supervision of very young children, supervision of the health of children at Board schools, supervision of midwives, certain duties under the Children Act as to protection of infant life, and other matters concerning the health of the community.

Ministry of Labour.—This Department was created by the New Ministries and Secretaries Act, 1916 (6 & 7 Geo. V. c. 68). Its head is the Minister of Labour, who has a seat in the Cabinet.

There is also an Under-Secretary, with a seat in Parliament, and a Permanent Secretary, assisted by a large clerical staff. Its functions are to relieve the Board of Trade of its duties under the Labour Exchanges Act, 1909, the Conciliation Act, 1896, the National Insurance (Unemployment) Acts, 1911 to 1918. Power was also reserved for the Crown to assign to it other duties by Order in Council.

Board of Trade.—The Board of Trade has had various temporary duties assigned to it connected with the late war. Owing to the numerous changes in the work of the Departments, it is increasingly difficult to describe the functions of the Board of

Trade. It is nominally a board, but its effective head is the President of the Board, who changes with the Ministry, and is assisted by a Parliamentary Secretary and Permanent Secretary and a clerical staff. It is still in a state of reconstruction. In its main department it registers ships and seamen. There is a commercial department, which has duties with reference to commercial treaties and commercial intercourse with other States.

It has also inland commercial duties. It controls patents, bankruptcy proceedings, and matters connected with insolvent companies. It also supervises pilots, has duties with reference to solicitors, prepares commercial statistics and has miscellaneous work (Constitutional Year Book).

Ministry of Pensions.—This Department was created by the Ministry of Pensions Act, 1916 (6 & 7 Geo. V. c. 65), which transferred to it the functions formerly discharged in relation to pensions by the Army Council, the Admiralty, and the Commissioners of Chelsea Hospital. Its head is the Minister of Pensions, assisted by a Parliamentary Under-Secretary.

The Law Officers.—These officers are the heads of the Bar in their respective countries, and they change with the Government, and as a rule are not in the Cabinet. They consist of the Attorneys and Solicitors-General for England and Ireland, and the Lord Advocate and Solicitor-General for Scotland. The English Attorney-General is appointed by letters patent under the Great Seal, and must be in the House of Commons. In civil work he represents the Crown, and in criminal proceedings he or the Solicitor-General, or their deputies, prosecute in cases of importance. He is the head of the Bar and general referee as to points of etiquette. He advises the Government departments in legal cases, and he has certain judicial functions connected with committees of privilege in the Lords. His *fiat* is necessary in certain legal proceedings where the public are concerned, and he can in certain other cases intervene on behalf of the public personally or by deputy. He deals with certain matters relating to patents. The Solicitor-General is in a sense a subordinate of the Attorney-General, and frequently gives a joint opinion with the former on legal matters when required so to do by the Government departments. He usually succeeds to the post of Attorney-General when it is vacant. He changes with the Ministry, and must be a member of the Commons. His duties are similar to those of the Attorney-General, save as to one or two matters. Both the law officers are precluded from private practice during tenure of office. The Irish law officers have duties very similar to those in England, and so have the Scotch.

The Colonial *Office* is presided over by a Secretary of State, who is assisted by a Permanent and a Parliamentary Under-Secretary. The Secretaryship for the Colonies was separated from the War Secretaryship in 1854. The office is divided into three departments : (1) The Dominion department, which deals with self-governing colonies and the Imperial Conference when it assembles; (2) The Crown Colony department, which deals with Crown colonies and protectorates; and (3) the general and legal department. Colonial governors are appointed by the Crown on the recommendation of the Secretary of State, who makes judicial and executive appointments in the Crown colonies and protectorates, except in the case of minor appointments, which are made by the governor. He speaks for the colonies on all matters arising in Parliament in relation to them.

CHAPTER XXI.

COLONIES.

The term British Islands means the United Kingdom, the Channel Islands, and Isle of Man (Interpretation Act, 1889, (52 & 53 Vict. c. 163), s. 18) (*d*).

A British possession is any part of his Majesty's dominions, exclusive of the United Kingdom (*id.*).

A colony is any part of his Majesty's dominions exclusive of the British Islands and British India, and the expression British India means all territories governed by his Majesty through the Governor-General of India, and India means India together with the adjacent territories under the Suzerainty of his Majesty (*id.*).

A British Settlement or Settled Colony means any British possession which has not been acquired by cession or conquest, and is not for the time being within the jurisdiction of a Legislature constituted otherwise than by virtue of the British Settlements Act, 1887 (50 & 51 Vict. c. 54).

Dominions are colonies possessing responsible government, *i.e.*, the Ministers are responsible to the Legislature of the colony in question.

A Protectorate is a place outside his Majesty's dominions placed under the protection of the British Sovereign, who

(*d*) *The United Kingdom.*—England, Scotland, and Ireland are governed in many respects by different laws, but for most constitutional purposes they form a single entity known as the United Kingdom of Great Britain and Ireland. The Crown and Parliament are supreme over them all. The operation of an Act of Parliament is a good test of this constitutional doctrine. Parliament can legislate for all the dominions of the Crown, and for British subjects everywhere. But, unless a contrary intention is expressed, an Act of Parliament extends to the whole of the United Kingdom, and does not extend beyond. For example, if an Act is intended to apply to England only, the regular form of the extent clause runs: "This Act shall not extend to Scotland or Ireland." It should be noted that the Channel Islands and the Isle of Man do not form part of the United Kingdom, and also that the expression "England" in an Act of Parliament includes Wales and Berwick-on-Tweed (see 20 Geo. II. c. 42, s. 3).

regulates its foreign relations. Where a protectorate at the time of protection has an adequate settled Government it is assumed the British Government allows it to legislate, subject to a veto on legislation; otherwise the protectorate is managed like a Crown colony, though the dignity of the native ruler is placated.

Protectorates are mainly regulated by the Foreign Jurisdiction Act, 1890 (*e*). Their affairs are administered by the Crown in a more or less paternal fashion suited to native races not far advanced in civilisation. Our control tightens or slackens according to circumstances. In many cases they are governed through native chiefs, the Crown retaining the ultimate and supreme control. The expression "protectorate" is used somewhat indefinitely. On the one hand it includes what are practically Crown colonies, whilst on the other it shades off into what is called a sphere of influence (*i.e.*, a place over which another country has bound itself by treaty not to exercise influence, as, for instance, in Persia before the war). A native State is also said to be within our sphere of influence when we leave its internal affairs alone, but exercise a greater or less degree of control over its foreign relations in order to protect our interests.

For further particulars as to protectorates and spheres of influence, see Hall's Foreign Jurisdiction of the Crown. The Crown controls the public officers who govern the protectorate. The Crown has power under the Foreign Jurisdiction Act, 1890, to legislate for protectorates by Orders in Council.

Sometimes the control of a group of protectorates is delegated to a High Commissioner, and at other times to an administrator, who is nominally assisting the native sovereign, thus preserving the dignity of the latter. Sometimes the protectorate has a Legislative Council, and occasionally its legislation is in the hands of an adjoining colony.

The main object of establishing a protectorate is to take care of English residents and English interests therein, but in certain protectorates laws may be made affecting the natives : thus, it

(*e*) Under the Covenant of the League of Nations England is given certain protectorates to administer.

has been held that when a Commissioner had been appointed to do what was lawful in a protectorate for maintenance of order and good government he could detain a person—a tribal chief—in custody. Here a habeas corpus was applied for and the legality of the detention upheld—*R.* v. *Crewe; ex parte Segrome* ((1910) 2 K. B. 577).

Great Britain is entrusted by the League of Nations with mandatory colonies of which our King is not the sovereign, and of which the League may be the sovereign.

These territories are of three kinds—(1) Nations under Turkish rule, which will require only administrative advice and assistance till they can stand alone. (2) Certain Central African colonies which are not in such an advanced state as the first class. Here the mandatory will be responsible for administration under conditions guaranteeing freedom of religion subject to maintenance of public order, prevention of slavery, restriction of traffic in arms and liquor, and of the formation of armies and navies. (3) A third class, like certain South-West African territories, which will be administered under the laws of the mandatory subject to the safeguards above mentioned.

It will be the duty of all mandatories to furnish annual reports to the League touching their administration.

Acquisition of Colonies.—Colonies have been acquired by (i) occupancy; (ii) conquest; (iii) cession; (iv) mandate.

The position of the mandatory colony is doubtful and depends on who is its sovereign.

(i) A *Settled Colony* is a place to which British settlers have resorted, and which at the time of settlement was either uninhabited (*e.g.*, Pitcairn Islands) or had no civilised government. The British Settlements Act, 1887 (50 & 51 Vict. c. 54), defines it as "any British possession which has not been acquired by cession or conquest and is not for the time being within the jurisdiction of a legislature constituted otherwise than by virtue of this Act or any Act repealed thereby of any British possession."

Section 2 of the Act provides that "it shall be lawful for his Majesty in Council to establish all such laws and institutions, and constitute such courts and officers and to make such arrangements for administration of justice as may appear expedient to his Majesty for the peace, order, and good government of his Majesty's subjects and others within the Settlement."

Section 3 empowers the Sovereign to delegate to any three or more persons within the settlement all powers of legislation by His Majesty in Council either absolutely or conditionally.

Section 4 enables the Sovereign to confer jurisdiction as to matters arising within the settlement on any court of any other British possession.

As to settled colonies, the settlers take with them (a) the common law of England so far as the same is applicable to an infant community; (b) existing English statute law so far as the same is applicable to an infant community. The Statutes of Mortmain, for instance, would not be so applicable.

Settlers are not bound by statutes made after the foundation of the settlement unless the statute in question contains an express direction that it is to apply.

(ii) *Conquered Colonies.*—When a country is conquered the following changes take place :—

(1) The conquered territory belongs to our King and becomes subject to the legislation of the Imperial Parliament.

(2) The conquered inhabitants become our King's subjects and cease to be alien enemies.

(3) The laws of the conquered colony continue to exist till altered by the conqueror so far as they are consonant with our principles of right and justice, and if there are no laws those entrusted with the management of the colony must govern in accordance with right and justice. When a country has been conquered all laws connected with allegiance to the former Sovereign cease, and also all laws relating to the administration of the law in its original and appellate jurisdictions, and, in addition, all laws connected with the exercise of the sovereign authority (Broom's Cons. Law, 2nd ed., p. 49).

(4) Royal ordinances are subordinate to the Parliament of Great Britain.

In the case of *R.* v. *Picton* (30 St. Tr. 225) the court held that torture allowed by the law of Spain could not be permitted in a British colony taken from the Spaniards.

When the King grants a Legislature to a conquered or ceded

colony his power of legislation by Order in Council ceases unless his power so to legislate has been reserved (*Campbell* v. *Hall* (1774), 20 St. Tr.).

(iii) *Ceded Colonies.*—There is no practical difference between a ceded colony and a conquered colony except this, that the treaty of cession may perhaps place the inhabitants in a better position than if they had been conquered.

(iv) As to *Mandatory Colonies*, see *ante*, p. 170. They are colonies placed or to be placed under English protection either by the League of Nations or a treaty, the terms of which will have to be observed.

Classification of colonies.—From a different standpoint colonies may be classified as follows : (a) Those not possessing responsible government. (b) Those possessing responsible government. Class (a) may be sub-divided into (i) colonies possessing an elected house of assembly and a Crown-nominated legislative council, *e.g.*, Bahamas, Barbadoes, Bermuda (Colonial Office List, 1918, p. 719); (ii) colonies possessing a partly elected legislative council, the constitution of which does not provide for an official majority, *e.g.*, British Guiana, Cyprus (*ibid.*); (iii) colonies possessing a partly elected legislative council, the constitution of which provides for an official majority, *e.g.*, Fiji, Jamaica, Leeward Islands, Malta, Mauritius (*ibid.*); (iv) colonies and protectorates possessing a Crown-nominated legislative council, *e.g.*, British Honduras, Ceylon, East African Protectorate, Falkland Islands, Gambia, Gold Coast, Grenada, Hong Kong, Nyassaland Protectorate, St. Lucia, St. Vincent, Seychelles, Sierra Leone, South Nigeria, Straits Settlements, Trinidad. In all the above except British Honduras the Crown provides for an official majority. The legislative councils of Gambia, Sierra Leone and Southern Nigeria have power respectively to legislate for the Gambia Protectorate, Sierra Leone Protectorate, and South Nigeria Protectorate; (v) colonies and protectorates without a legislative council, *e.g.*, Ashanti, Basutoland, Bechuanaland Protectorate, Gibraltar, North Nigeria, Northern Territories of the Gold Coast, St. Helena, Somaliland, Swaziland, Uganda, and Islands in the Western Pacific. In all these colonies and protectorates the Crown can legislate by Order in Council with the exception of British Honduras and the Leeward Islands (*ibid.*).

The Crown can legislate for colonies with non-representative assemblies, *i.e.*, assemblies in which, whether they are partly elective or otherwise, the Crown can secure half of the votes.

The Imperial Parliament can tax any colony, but it is inexpedient, as well as unconstitutional, to do so. What would be done if our colonies became federal States is at present difficult to forecast. Where there is an elective representative legislature in a colony the tendency is gradually to give it responsible government, as is being done in India. The governor would, in such a case, be given instructions to develop any germs of a party system existing in the colony, and responsible government might follow if this experiment were successful.

(b) *Self-governing Colonies.*—In all these colonies there is a governor-general or, at any rate, a governor, who acts more or less as a constitutional sovereign, and there are also, as a rule, two legislative chambers. The Executive is, moreover, selected by the predominating party in the lower house.

The legislative powers of a self-governing colony, though controllable by the Imperial Parliament, are unrestricted within their areas (*Powell* v. *Apollo Candle Co.* (1885), 10 A. C., p. 282).

In *Riel* v. *Regina*, 10 App. Cas., p. 675, the Judicial Committee of the Privy Council held that they would not grant leave to appeal in any criminal case except where the requirements of justice were very clearly departed from, and that the trial of a man for treason before two magistrates and a jury of six men was not such a departure. The court also held that 34 & 35 Vict. c. 38, which authorised the Dominion Government of Canada to provide for the administration, peace, order and good government of any territory not for the time being within any Canadian province, gave to the Dominion Parliament the utmost discretion to effect those objects, and that 43 Vict. c. 25 (a Canadian statute) which prescribed a definite procedure for the trial of criminal cases (impliedly including treason) was not *ultra vires*.

All self-governing colonies can legislate for the peace, order and good government of the colony, but extra-territorial legislation is not, as a rule, conceded.

In the case of *Macleod* v. *Attorney-General for New South Wales* ((1891), A. C., p. 455) the appellant had committed bigamy in the United States. The New South Wales Criminal Law Amendment Act, 1883, punished bigamy, wherever committed, with penal servitude; but the Privy Council (Judicial Committee) held that the Act above mentioned was *ultra vires* so far as concerned legislation against bigamy committed outside the territorial limits of the legislating body. But where extra-territorial legislation is passed the Privy Council, as far as possible, acts on the maxim *Ut res magis valeat quam pereat*, and gives to the colonial enactment an extra-territorial application whenever it can. In *Attorney-General* v. *Cain* the Privy Council held that a Canadian Act which impliedly authorised the personal restraint of an alien outside the territorial limits for the purpose of expelling him from Canadian territory was not *ultra vires* (*Attorney-General for Canada* v. *Cain* (1906), A. C., p. 542). Again, in the case of *Peninsular and Oriental Company* v. *Kingston* ((1903), A. C., p. 471) it was held impliedly that a colonial Act may have an extra-territorial application and that the breaking of Custom House seals on the high seas was punishable within the limits of the colony.

In *Tilonko* v. *Attorney-General of Natal* ((1907), A. C., p. 93) it was held that an English court could not enter into the propriety or impropriety of a colonial statute.

Colonial governor.—Every colony has a head—its governor, administrator, high commissioner, or governor-general—and with this office is united that of commander-in-chief of the military forces.

All colonial bills before they become statutes must receive the governor's assent. The governor has, as a rule, a discretion as to assenting to bills, but as to certain bills he is required by his commission or instructions to reserve them for the signification of his Majesty's pleasure, or assent to them only where they contain a clause suspending their operation until they are confirmed by the Crown, *e.g.*, bills which might militate against Imperial interests (such as bills restraining immigration of certain aliens, which were for a long time vetoed).

It may be said that in a colony with responsible government

the governor is the connecting link between the Crown and the colony. As regards internal administration, he is a constitutional sovereign, so far as a man can be called a sovereign who has to take orders from political superiors. As to such administration, he interferes but little, if at all.

But directly the interests of the Mother Country are involved, he must see that they sustain no detriment, and he may have to act in opposition to his ministers by vetoing an Act (Todd, Parliamentary Government in the Colonies, 2nd ed., p. 806).

As to his personal position, the colonial governor is hardly a sovereign, unless perhaps he be a viceroy. This functionary, it appears, can commit in his official capacity certain wrongs with impunity for which ordinary governors could be penalised (*Luby* v. *Lord Wodehouse* (1865), 17 Ir. C. L. Rep. 618; *Sullivan* v. *Lord Spencer* (Ir. 6, C. L., p. 173); and *Tandy* v. *Lord Westmorland* (27 St. Tr., p. 1246), cited and critically commented on in *Musgrave* v. *Pulido* (1879), 5 App. Cas., 111).

With governors other than governors of self-governing colonies the case is somewhat different. Though they more resemble autocrats than constitutional sovereigns, they can be tried in England under the joint operation of the Governors Act of William III. (*f*) and 42 Geo. III. c. 85, for an official crime committed in the colony. In 1802 Governor Wall was tried at the Old Bailey, convicted, sentenced and executed for causing the death of one Benjamin Armstrong by the infliction of excessive corporal punishment.

In *R.* v. *Picton* (*supra*) Governor Picton was tried at the Old Bailey for torturing Luisa Calderon, the law of Spain, which partly prevailed in the colony, permitting torture. He was tried twice, but not found guilty, and the prosecution was dropped.

In *R.* v. *Eyre* (L. R. 3 Q. B. 487) it was held that where a colonial governor has been found guilty of crime in his official capacity, the Court of King's Bench, either upon information by the Attorney-General, or indictment found by the grand jury, may try such crime, and such crime may be said to have been

(*f*) Probably these Acts extend to all kinds of governors

committed in Middlesex. It was also held that the magistrate could examine Mr. Eyre and commit him for trial.

In *Phillips* v. *Eyre* ((1867), L. R. 4 Q. B., p. 225), a civil case, it was held : (1) That where a colonial legislature with plenary powers has been established in an English colony the comity of nations is to apply to its legislation; (2) that a colonial governor could legally assent to a bill in which he is personally interested, *e.g.*, a bill of indemnity for official acts.

In *Musgrave* v. *Pulido* ((1879), 5 A. C., p. 102) the governor was sued for damages respecting the detention of a vessel. He pleaded that what he did was an act of State (cf. *Buron* v. *Denman* (1859), 2 Ex. Rep. 167). The court held that a colonial tribunal could try the question whether a given official act of a governor was or was not an act of State ((1880), 5 App. Cas., 102 Thomas, p. 87).

In *Hill* v. *Bigg* it was held that a colonial court could try an action of debt to which the governor was a party ((1841), 3 Moo. P. C. C., p. 465; Thomas, p. 85), but that the person of the governor cannot be attached in a civil court whilst he is acting as governor (*ibid.*).

In *Mostyn* v. *Fabrigas* a petition of an alleged mutinous character was presented to the Governor of Minorca by one Fabrigas and was followed up by imprisonment, and it was held that the Court of King's Bench in England could entertain an action of tort committed by a colonial governor in a colony (I. S. L. C. 591).

In *Cameron* v. *Kyte* it was held that a governor has not *virtute officii* a delegated authority to do any act unauthorised by his commission or the accompanying instructions (Brooms, Const. Law, p. 64).

Status of governors.—They are appointed under the Royal Sign Manual, and represent the Crown in their colonies. The extent of their powers and duties varies with the constitution of the colony. In self-governing colonies they are, as has been said above, practically constitutional sovereigns acting on the advice of responsible Ministers, whilst in Crown colonies of the strict type they are practically autocrats who, subject to the control of the Colonial Office, exercise legislative and executive powers.

Subject to any modification introduced by the constitution of the colony, the status of the governor may be described as follows :—

He is entitled to obedience and assistance from all civil and military officers. He has no authority over his Majesty's ships, and if he requires their assistance he must communicate first with the Colonial Office, unless the lives of British subjects be in urgent danger, when he may practically order the Navy to assist.

He exercises the prerogative of mercy and issues warrants for the expenditure of public money. He appoints and dismisses public servants, including judges, the latter having a right of appeal as a rule to the judicial committee. He assents to or withholds assent from bills, if there be a legislative body, or in certain cases reserves bills for the assent of the Crown at home. He must not leave the colony without his Majesty's permission (Colonial Regulations, s. 2, published in Colonial Office List, 1921).

Alteration of constitutions.—Not only all self-governing colonies, but also all colonies with representative legislatures can, if these are constituent assemblies, alter their constitutions. A constituent assembly is a body within a country which can alter the constitution of that country.

When a constitutional law is altered the machinery directed by the Constitution must be employed (*e.g.*, where a second legislature, or, rather, extraordinary legislature, has to be created for the purpose, any alteration of the Constitution is null and void unless effected by such extraordinary legislature. Most federal States have two legislatures, and a strictly federal system demands them for the protection of State interests.

The Dominion Government of Canada is not a constituent assembly.

The Colonial Laws Validity Act, 1865, s. 2, provides that a colonial law which is in any way repugnant to any Imperial statute applying to the colony to which such law may relate, or repugnant to any order or regulation made under any such statute, or having in the colony the force and effect of such statute, shall not be void altogether, but shall be read subject to such statute, order, or regulation, and shall only be void to the extent of the repugnancy.

Section 3. No colonial law shall be deemed to be void on the ground of repugnancy to English law unless the same be repugnant to such statute, order, or regulation as aforesaid.

Section 4. No colonial law passed with the concurrence of, or assented to by, the governor of any colony shall be void by reason only of instructions with reference to such law or the subject thereof which may have been given to the governor by, or on behalf of, his Majesty by any instrument other than the Letters Patent or instrument authorising such governor to concur in passing, or to assent to, laws for the peace, order, or good government of such colony, even though instructions may be referred to in such Letters Patent or last-mentioned instrument.

Section 5. Every colonial legislature shall be deemed at all times to have had full power within its jurisdiction to establish courts of justice and to abolish and reconstitute such courts, and to alter the constitution thereof, and to provide for administration of justice therein, and every representative legislature shall be deemed at all times to have had power to make laws respecting the constitution, powers, and procedure of such legislature, provided that such laws have been passed in such manner and form as may from time to time be required by any statute, Letters Patent, Order in Council, or colonial law for the time being in force in the said colony.

Privileges of colonial legislatures.—Unless (1) The statute of the Imperial Parliament which confers upon it a constitution confers upon it the full privileges of the Imperial Parliament, or (2) it has adopted by statute the privileges of the British House of Commons, a colonial legislature has only limited privileges.

It can protect the assembly from disorder, but it is unable to punish disorderly persons. The point arose in the case of *Kielley* v. *Carson* ((1884), 4 Moo. P. C. 63), where it was held that a legislative assembly *did not possess as a legal right the power of arrest prior to adjudicating on a contempt outside the House, but only such powers as were reasonably necessary for the proper exercise of its functions and duties as a local legislature.*

In *Barton* v. *Taylor* ((1886), R. 11 App. Cas., p. 197) it was held that punitive action was not justified, neither was the unconditional suspension of a member during the pleasure of the House, but that he could only be suspended during the sitting; and in *Doyle* v. *Falconer* ((1866), 4 Moo. P. C. N. S., p. 203) it was held that a member could not be committed to prison merely for disorderly conduct in a colonial legislative assembly.

In the case of certain dominions of the Crown, Imperial statutes have expressly provided that such dominions may, in their own legislatures, pass statutes conferring on themselves the privileges of the English House of Commons.

The Colonial Laws Validity Act, by section 5, confers the like indulgence on every representative legislature, but express statutes have been passed notwithstanding this section of the Colonial Laws Validity Act (cf. the Australian Commonwealth Act).

In *Dill* v. *Murphy* ((1864), Moo. P. C. N. S., p. 487), an old case arising under an old Act authorising the Victoria Parliament to adopt the English House of Commons privileges, the committal of a man for contempt for publishing a libel on a member of the Victoria Legislature was allowed. In the important case of *Speaker of Victorian Legislative Assembly* v. *Glass* ((1871), L. R. 3 P. C., p. 560) it was held that where an Imperial statute had given to the Victorian Legislature legislative power to pass a statute conferring on itself the privileges of the English House of Commons it was competent for the Victorian Assembly to commit a man for contempt under a warrant which did not specify the grounds of commitment, and that the Supreme Court of Victoria had acted illegally in releasing Glass from custody. Special leave to appeal was granted though the captive had been released, on the ground that the case being one of public interest the opinion of the Judicial Committee would be a valuable precedent.

Treaties.—Before the war the colonies could not, as a general rule, conclude treaties without the consent of the Imperial Government, though, as a matter of policy, such consent was rarely withheld. The war has altered this position, and it is a noteworthy fact that not only were colonial delegates consulted as to the recent Treaty of Versailles, but they were actually signatories of that treaty.

Up till very recently the colonies were consulted as to treaties made by the Imperial Government and their wishes were studied, but the Home Government reserved to itself full freedom of action, especially in cases where Imperial interests were vitally concerned, as in the recent Treaty of Peace.

As a rule, it has been the custom for the Colonial Secretary to negotiate direct with foreign nations through agents of the Home Government. This rule, however, was occasionally departed from and Canada has been allowed to negotiate treaties from beginning to end with Indian chiefs, and also with the United States where Canadian interests only were involved.

Appeals from the colonies to the Privy Council.—From the days of Henry VII. all appeals from the colonies, or plantations, as they were then called, lay to the King in Council, and these appeals were heard in the Star Chamber, which may or may not have been a Committee of the Privy Council (*g*).

The statute which abolished the Star Chamber in 1641 did not, at any rate, do away with colonial appeals, and these appeals were heard by the King in Council, in virtue of the royal prerogative.

In *Fryer* v. *Bernard* ((1734), Peter Williams) it was laid down by Lord Macclesfield that "appeals from the courts in the plantations lay to the King in Council alone."

The prerogative right still remains, but has to a certain extent been restricted by statutes. The Sovereign can hear appeals from superior as well as inferior courts in the colonies and the right of the Crown to hear these appeals cannot be taken away save by express words. Thus, in the case of *Cushing* v. *Dupuy* ((1880), 5 App. Cas., p. 409), where the Canadian Insolvent Act provided that the judgment of the court shall be final, it was held that an appeal still lay to the King in Council.

Criminal appeals are not, as a rule, encouraged by the Judicial Committee, nor are civil appeals unless the case is of

(*g*) There has been much academic discussion as to whether this Court was a Committee of the Privy Council or a distinct Court. Maitland says it was a Committee of the Privy Council (Constitutional History, p. 460).

great importance, or property of a considerable amount is affected, or the issue vitally affects the public interest (*Prince* v. *Gagnon* (1882), 8 App. Cas., p. 1031), and this principle is applied throughout all our colonies.

Appeals to the Privy Council are either: (1) Appeals as of right; (2) Appeals by special leave.

"It is a general rule of law that an appeal to the King in Council does not lie as of right unless given by express enactment or express grant" (Safford and Wheeler's Privy Council Practice, 1st ed., p. 710).

Appeals by special leave.—Where no appeal lies as of right, a petition must be addressed to the Crown for leave to appeal. In most cases leave to appeal will be confined to cases where such leave is in accord with the rules in force in the colony (Ridge's Const. Law, 2nd ed., p. 453), or to cases where the prerogative is existent and has not been parted with (*R.* v. *Bertrand* (1867), L. R. 1 P. C., p. 520).

In criminal cases the Judicial Committee will not give leave to appeal unless there has been a gross miscarriage of justice (*Ex parte Deeming* (1892), A. C. 422) or where issues of importance are involved (*R.* v. *Bertrand*, *supra*).

Where the court below does not possess the power to grant leave to appeal the appellant can petition the King in Council for leave to appeal (Safford's P. C. Practice, p. 738).

Whatever the amount in dispute, an appeal to the Privy Council will generally be allowed where the rights of a colonial legislative assembly are involved (*Speaker of Victoria* v. *Glass*, *supra*).

It should be noted that the King can hear appeals from inferior courts, but leave will as a rule be refused where there is a competent court on the spot able to deal with the case. Appeals will probably be refused where appellant has chosen the Supreme Court as his forum of appeal (Halsbury, vol. 10, p. 583).

Colonial judges.—Colonial judges in colonies which are not self-governing are appointed by Letters Patent under the Royal Sign Manual. They hold office during good behaviour and they are dismissible by the governor acting in conjunction with his council, but they can appeal to the Judicial Committee (22 Geo. III., c. 76, ss. 2 and 3, and Todd's Parliamentary Government in the Colonies, 2nd ed., pp. 827 and 829).

In self-governing colonies a statute frequently provides that judges are to be removable on an address from both Houses to the governor. "All legislative assemblies have a right to petition the Crown as to removal of a judge" (Todd, 2nd ed., p. 19).

Statutes binding on the colonies.—No statute binds the colonies unless it expressly states that it is to bind them.

PART IV.

Judicature

CHAPTER XXII.

COURTS OF JUSTICE.

History of the courts.—In William I.'s reign there were eight courts: (1) The Curia Regis, or Great Council of Tenants *in capite*, which discharged legislative, judicial, and executive functions. (2) The King's Court, composed of those councillors who were from time to time with the King temporarily or permanently (Carter's English Legal History, p. 25). (3) The Exchequer Court, a fiscal committee of the "Curia," which acted judicially as to matters concerning the royal revenue. (4) The County Court (Shire Moot), which in Saxon days sat twice annually, and in Norman times at more frequent intervals. Its nominal judges were the county freeholders, its presidents being the earl and bishop, and latterly the sheriff or *vice-comes*. It had a jurisdiction civil and criminal. (5) The Hundred Court, with the freeholders of the hundred as judges, under a president known as hundred's elder, or *ballivus*. It had a similar jurisdiction to the County Court and there may have been an appeal from its decisions to the County Court. (6) The Manor Court, a court of varied jurisdiction depending probably on the particular grant from the King of "sac and soc" (right to hold court and take profits thereof). (7) The Burgh Moot or court of a borough, almost precisely similar to the County Court. (8) The Forest Court, regulating the royal forests and awarding punishments to the extent of death.

In the reign of Henry II. we hear of the "Court of judges of the Bench," five in number (which may have been an evolution from the King's Court), Glanvil, the justiciar and supposed author of the Commentaries bearing his name, being one of them. John's Magna Charta (1215) provided that Common Pleas should not follow the King, but be held in a fixed place, and this was the origin of the Common Pleas or Common Bench, which for centuries thereafter sat at Westminster to try causes between subject and subject.

In the reign of Edward I. the justiciar, that great political and judicial officer, and viceroy when the King was abroad, was dispensed with and Edward created chief justices of the King's Bench and Common Pleas and a Chief Baron of the Exchequer, and assigned (1) to the King's Bench the function of protecting the King's peace; (2) to the Exchequer the protection of the royal revenue; (3) to the Common Pleas cases between subject and subject.

In spite of this regulation, the King's Bench judges encroached on the Common Pleas, which was wealthy as regards business, by a process called a Bill of Middlesex. The plaintiff falsely but collusively, to give the Court of King's Bench an excuse, averred that the defendant had invaded his close with force and arms—whereas the defendant probably owed him money only. The defendant was arrested at the beginning of the action and placed in the custody of the marshal of the King's Bench, and this fact alone gave the King's Bench jurisdiction. In the time of the Stuarts it was thought advisable to acquaint the defendant with the real cause of his detention and a clause called the *ac etiam* was added. If defendant could not be found in Middlesex—the county for which the bill was obtained—a writ of *latitat* was sued out, which enabled defendant to be arrested in the county where he sought refuge.

The Exchequer obtained jurisdiction over subject and subject cases by a writ of *Quominus*, the plaintiff averring that defendant would not pay him, "by which the less" he, the plaintiff, was able to pay the King what he owed him *qua* tax, farmer or debtor. Henry II. was the inventor of the circuit system (*a*).

(*a*) When a judge went on circuit he held four royal commissions: (1) "Oyer and Terminer," to hear and determine all treasons, felonies, and misdemeanours; (2) "Gaol Delivery," to clear the county gaol of all prisoners; (3) "Assize," to determine questions relating to real property; (4) "Nisi

Thus, the three great courts of common law at the time of the Judicature Acts exercised jurisdictions almost parallel—at all events, as regards personal actions.

By the Uniformity of Process Act the co-ordinate jurisdiction of the three courts was formally recognised and variety and multiplicity of process put an end to (see Carter's English Legal History, p. 67).

The common law procedure was simplified, and still further improvements were effected, by the Common Law Procedure Acts and the Judicature Acts, 1873 and 1875.

History of the Chancellor.—In old days the Chancellor was the King's chief chaplain, and his confessor, and keeper of his conscience. He was a sort of secretary, who sealed the royal writs. At first the Chancellor was probably the most learned man in the King's Council, and in the reign of Henry III. he must have been a very important man. The Provisions of Oxford, however, ordained that he was not to make new law by sealing novel writs and that he was only to seal writs for which there was an exact precedent on the register.

These provisions were very short-lived, and in the reign of Edward I. the statute *in consimili casu* (one of the Statutes of Westminster) provided that the Chancellor might seal a writ where there was one resembling it on the register. In the reign of Edward III. matters of grace were referred to the Chancellor for consideration, and from that period his duties became more judicial.

We hear of his sitting sometimes alone, but frequently with other members of the council and the common law judges, and with the latter, though at times there were differences, he preserved in the main friendly relations.

In the reign of Henry VI. we find the Chancellor granting injunctions, and some of these injunctions prevented litigants from enforcing judgments obtained at common law. Wolsey was a powerful Chancellor. He procured the establishment of four Equity Courts, only one of which, viz., the Court of the Master

Prius," to determine cases of debt and injury. This commission derived its name from the fact that the sheriff had to summon twelve men to Westminster at a given date, "nisi prius judices in comitatem venerint."

of the Rolls, then head clerk of the chancellors, survived his downfall.

The chancellorship of Lord Ellesmere was conspicuous for his dispute with Coke as to whether a litigant who had obtained a judgment in a common law court by fraud could be restrained by injunction from enforcing it. Ellesmere prevailed. Under Hardwicke and Nottingham equity was systematised. In 1813 one vice-chancellor was appointed, and in 1842 two more vice-chancellors, to take over the equity work of the Courts of Exchequer.

Equity had three jurisdictions at the time of the Judicature Acts : (a) exclusive jurisdiction in cases where common law gave no relief; (b) concurrent jurisdiction where common law gave inadequate relief; (c) auxiliary jurisdiction where common law courts were assisted by equity : *e.g.*, equity would grant discovery from a litigant to help on a common law action. The work assigned to the Chancery Division by the Judicature Acts is the administration of the estates of testators and intestates, the taking of partnership or other accounts, redemption and foreclosure of mortgages, raising of portions or other charges on land, sale and distribution of proceeds of property subject to any lien or charges, execution of trusts charitable or private, rectification or cancellation of written instruments, specific performance of contracts as to real and leasehold estates, partition sales of real estates, wardship of infants and care of their estates.

Admiralty.—The word "admiral" is of Arabic origin. "Emir" or "Amir" meant rulers, and "al" meant "of." Amir al Bahr meant a prince of the sea. The first use of the word "admiral" as to English matters was in 1285 or thereabouts, and in the reign of Edward I. an admiral of the Bayonne (Baion) fleet was appointed (Carter, English Legal History, p. 135).

At the commencement of the 14th century we hear of an Admiral of the Cinque Ports. There was no Admiralty Court—except local courts perhaps—till the middle of the 14th century (cf. Carter, p. 136), when, to check piracy, an admiral was appointed by Edward III. to deal with maritime crimes. By

13 Richard II. c. 3 the admiral or his deputy was not to meddle with anything save such as was done upon the sea, and by 15 Richard II., st. 1, c. 5, the admiral was to have no cognizance of contracts or other things done or transpiring inside a country, whether on land or water, nor of any wreck, but he might have jurisdiction over flotsam, jetsam, and ligan. The admiral, again, might enquire into deaths of persons and acts of mayhem in great ships in the main stream of great rivers below the bridges [or points] of the same rivers nigh to the sea and nowhere else.

The admiral in the reign of Edward III. took certain civil cases as well as criminal mercantile and maritime cases.

Towards the end of the fifteenth century a judge was appointed to assist the admiral. Henry VIII. by statute gave the admiral various civil functions, including a jurisdiction in respect of bills of exchange and contracts made abroad, but may be said, though other statutes contributed, to have abolished the criminal jurisdiction by providing that treason, murder and felonies within the purview of the admiral be tried before the admiral or his deputy and three or four other substantial persons, who were invariably common law judges. By the Central Criminal Court Act, 1834, sea crimes were made triable in the Central Criminal Court, and by a more recent statute these offences can be tried at the Assize Courts therein mentioned. In the reign of Elizabeth there were disputes between the admiral and the common law judges as to prohibitions and an agreement was arrived at. The judges considered that they could issue these prohibitions as the Admiralty, in their opinion, was not a court of record.

According to Blackstone, the common law judges encroached on the Admiralty as to contracts made abroad by conniving at a fiction that these contracts were made at the Royal Exchange (Bl. Comms., vol. 3, p. 107).

By the combined effects of Admiralty Courts Acts the court gained control of all necessary jurisdiction, its procedure was rendered more rapid and effective, and machinery was provided for transferring certain admiralty business to certain convenient county courts.

As to appeals : Henry VIII. constituted the Court of Delegates to take over appeals from the Courts Christian and Admiralty

Commissioners, which appeals were afterwards transferred to the Privy Council. This accounts for the grouping together of probate, divorce, and admiralty in the present High Court of Justice. By the Vice Admiral Courts Act, 1863, and the Colonial Courts of Admiralty Act, 1890, Colonial Courts of Admiralty were created with full civil powers. At the time of the Judicature Acts appeals from the British Admiralty Court and the secular Courts of Probate and Divorce established in 1857 lay to the Privy Council, and, by virtue of the Judicature Acts, these appeals now lie first to the Court of Appeal and ultimately to the House of Lords.

Admiralty business relates to such topics as bottomry and respondentia bonds, flotsam, jetsam, ligan, towage, salvage, collisions and negligent navigation, transactions giving rights *in rem* against a ship, and other maritime matters.

Probate and Divorce.—William I., by severing the lay and clerical jurisdictions, urged into activity clerical courts with special procedure over clergy and laity. The clergy took charge of wills of personalty, and their control continued till 1857, when a secular Court of Probate was created. The Churchmen also concerned themselves as to lay immorality, punishing adultery, fornication and other deadly sin criminally, and this they are still supposed to be able to do, though such jurisdiction is obsolete. Up to 1857 they gave decrees of judicial separation and administered relief in other matrimonial cases. After the creation of the secular Divorce Court in 1857 divorce *a vinculo matrimonii* became obtainable.

The Judicature Acts created a Court of Appeal and a High Court of Justice. The High Court contained the following divisions : the King's Bench Division, the Common Pleas, and the Exche er Division (the last two being merged in the King's Bench Division in 1880), the Chancery Division, the Probate, Divorce, and Admiralty Division.

The common law work of the County Palatine of Lancaster was also transferred to the High Court (*b*).

(*b*) There were from medieval days three Courts called Courts Palatine—viz., the Courts of Lancaster, Durham, and Chester, that of Chester dating from the reign of William I. The powers of the grantees of these palatinates

Present courts.—The constitution of the higher courts of justice has been so fully dealt with by many writers, that only the briefest description of them is given here for the sake of completeness. The Supreme Court of Judicature consists of two branches, namely, the Court of Appeal and the High Court of Justice. The High Court of Justice is composed of twenty-five judges (the two additional judges recently appointed to the King's Bench Division are not to be regarded as necessarily constituting a permanent increase), and is divided into three divisions, namely, the Chancery Division, the King's Bench Division, and the Probate, Divorce, and Admiralty Division. It exercises the consolidated jurisdictions of the old Courts of Chancery, King's Bench, Common Pleas, Exchequer, Admiralty, Probate, Divorce and Matrimonial Causes Courts, and also of the London Court of Bankruptcy—but bankruptcy jurisdiction outside London is vested in the county courts. Bankruptcy and Winding-up work, and the judicial functions of the Railway Commission, are assigned to particular judges of the High Court. Every judge of the High Court can exercise all the powers of the Court, and can act in any division, but for the sake of convenience special classes of business are assigned to special divisions. The judges of the Court of Criminal Appeal are selected from the judges of the King's Bench Division, and for the most part appeals from inferior courts are heard by the divisional courts of the King's Bench Division.

The Court of Appeal consists of six regular judges, and sits in two divisions, one of which is presided over by the Master of the Rolls. The Lord Chief Justice, who is the head of the King's Bench Division, the President of the Probate, &c., Division, who is the head of that division, and the Lord Chancellor, who is the titular head of the Chancery Division, are *ex officio* qualified to sit in the Court of Appeal. An ex-Lord Chancellor can sit also, and provision is made for calling in a judge of the High Court

were almost royal They selected their own judges and lower magistrates, processes ran in their name, and they could pardon offences. About the middle of the fifteenth century the Palatinate of Lancaster passed to the Crown, and that of Durham in the reign of William IV. After 1830, there were no local judges for Chester; and since that date the Chester judicial work passed to the judges of Assize and other functionaries.

to reinforce the Court of Appeal when necessary. Subject to certain exceptions, an appeal lies from the High Court to the Court of Appeal from every judgment or order of the High Court, but no appeal lies in criminal matters, and in the case of an appeal from an inferior court, only by leave.

The sittings of the Supreme Court are in London, but provision is made for administration of justice in the country by commissions of assize, and for this purpose the country is mapped out into circuits. The judges of the King's Bench are the only judges who go on circuit, and as sometimes, owing to press of business or illness, the judges cannot get through their circuit work within the prescribed limits of time, provision is made for supplementing them by other commissioners. Any king's counsel on the circuit is qualified to act as a commissioner of assize, and county court judges also may be included in the commission.

Special provision is made for the administration of criminal justice in the metropolis by the Central Criminal Court, which was created in 1834. The lord mayor and aldermen are titular judges of the Central Criminal Court, but the regular judges thereof are the Recorder of London, the Common Serjeant, and the two judges of the City of London Court. The sessions are held monthly, and a judge of the High Court attends at each session to try murder cases and other cases of great importance.

Besides the county courts and the courts of quarter sessions, which, as inferior courts, exercise general civil and criminal jurisdiction throughout the country, there are certain local courts of civil jurisdiction which must be noted. The most important is the Chancery Court of the County Palatine of Lancaster, which, within its local limits, has similar powers to those of the Chancery Division. There are also a few courts having full common law jurisdiction within their local limits, such as the Mayor's Court of London, the Passage Court of Liverpool, and the Salford Hundred Court.

The county court.—In old days the claims of poor suitors were somewhat inefficiently dealt with by courts of request and a few scattered local courts.

In the year 1846 our present county courts were established, the main functions of which were to afford relief to poor suitors. Latterly, however, the duties of county court judges have been materially increased. Most of these judges have full jurisdiction as judges in bankruptcy. As to ordinary cases, they have jurisdiction up to £100 under the County Court Acts, 1888 and 1903. They are judges of equity as well as of common law. They alone take cognizance of cases under the Employers' Liability and Workmen's Compensation Acts. They have jurisdiction as to winding-up companies when the capital is under £10,000. As to suits for administration of estates of deceased persons, actions for the execution of trusts, actions for the redemption and foreclosure of mortgages, for specific performance of contracts relating to the sale of freehold or leasehold estates, and as to certain other causes of actions of an equitable kind, these courts have jurisdiction up to £500. When the subject-matter of the dispute does not exceed £5, neither litigant can demand a jury, but in other cases the privilege can be claimed. Again, when the subject-matter of the dispute does not exceed £20, no appeal lies to the High Court, except by leave of the judge.

Cases of large amounts are often remitted to the county court for decision, either by consent or where the plaintiff is adjudged too poor to pay the defendant's costs if the defendant should win the case. By consent of both sides a county court judge may decide any common law action. They also take cognizance of interpleader cases sent to them by the High Court, and by the rules of the High Court they hear judgment summonses in High Court cases as well as in their own. These summonses have for their ultimate object the committal of debtors to prison for neglecting to pay judgment debts when since the judgment they have had the means so to do. They have also certain functions which they share with justices of the peace under the Lunacy Act, 1890.

CHAPTER XXIII.

THE MAGISTRACY.

History of the office of justice of the peace.—Up to the time of Richard I. frankpledge was resorted to for maintaining public order, but, by a decree of Richard I.'s justiciar made in 1195 A.D., knights were assigned to receive oaths for the preservation of the peace. These knights were probably the precursors of the conservators of the peace, who were afterwards known as justices of the peace, and whom we first hear of in the reign of Edward III.

In 1253 A.D. and 1264 A.D. we hear of *custodes pacis*, who were occasionally chosen by the landowners of the shire but afterwards appointed by royal writ (Langmead, Const. Hist., p. 172).

By 1 Edward III. st. 2, c. 16, it was ordained that for the better maintaining of the peace good and lawful men be assigned to keep it, and by 34 Edward III. c. 1 these men received the power of trying felonies and also obtained the title of justices of the peace (*ibid.*).

Blackstone, however, states that the justices "seldom if ever try any greater offence than small felonies within the benefit of clergy; their commission providing that if any case of difficulty arises, they shall not proceed to judgment but in the presence of one of the justices of the King's Bench or Common Pleas or one of the judges of assize" (Bl., vol. 4, p. 271). They cannot try any newly-created offence without express power given them by the statute which creates it (*ibid.*).

"These justices," says Blackstone, "are appointed by the King's special commission under the Great Seal, the form of which was settled by all the judges in 1590." Numerous statutes have conferred on justices jurisdiction both civil and criminal.

County justices.—For a long time prior to the Local Government Act, 1888, all the administrative work of the county fell to the lot of the justices, but that Act, though it left religiously alone their judicial work, took away the bulk of the administrative functions formerly exercised by county magistrates. It may be mentioned, however, that by means of a joint committee the magistrates and the county council jointly superintend the county police.

A man is appointed a county magistrate by the Lord Chancellor, who usually selects a person recommended by the Lord Lieutenant. The Lord Chancellor, however, it is believed, can appoint county justices independently of the Lord Lieutenant (Report of Royal Commission on Selection of Justices, 1910). The post has no salary attached to it, and since the Act of 1907 came into force, no property qualification is necessary.

Borough justices.—Dr. Odgers, in his work on local government, gives a very diverting account of borough magistrates prior to the passing of the Municipal Corporations Act, 1835. He discusses the fact not only of their legal ignorance, but says also that they were in many instances practically destitute of any educational attainments at all. He tells us of abuses in the shape of recorders who were laymen, and of borough coroners who were small tradesmen with small businesses. He informs us that aldermen were frequently *ex officio* magistrates.

The Municipal Corporations Act, 1835, cleaned up the Augean Stable, by substituting magistrates appointed by the Lord Chancellor in the place of ignorant and undesirable persons who had contrived to get elected as members of the corporation. That Act is now repealed, being superseded by the Municipal Corporations Act, 1882.

The mayor is a magistrate *ex officio* during his year of office and the year after.

Boroughs can petition the Crown for the appointment of a stipendiary magistrate, who is then appointed by the Home Secretary. He must be a barrister of at least seven years' standing. This functionary, sitting alone, has the same powers as a petty sessional court of two or more justices.

Powers of magistrates generally.—One magistrate acting alone has very limited powers, but he can hear a case prior to committing for trial, bail the prisoner, take his recognizances to appear, and discharge him when the evidence is insufficient to send him for trial. A petty sessional court has far more power of acting judicially than one ordinary justice sitting alone, and this rule of law applies to county magistrates as well as borough magistrates.

Numerous civil judicial powers have more or less recently been conferred on magistrates. They can make orders in bastardy cases; they can grant judicial separations between husband and wife; they can make maintenance orders against a husband in favour of his wife up to £2 per week; they have a limited jurisdiction as to ejectment; besides other powers. They can license places for sale of intoxicants. They have many duties purely ministerial (Report of Royal Commission on Selection of Justices, 1910).

Court of quarter sessions.—This court is a court of first instance and of appeal. It must meet once a quarter. Two or more justices make a quorum, and one of them, the chairman, acts as judge, deciding questions of evidence and summing up to the jury, though both or all are judges in reality. Two or more courts may sit when the work is heavy. The court can try all indictable offences save treason, murder, and capital offences, or any felony (burglary excepted) which, when committed by a person not previously convicted of felony, is punishable with penal servitude for life, misprision of treason, offences against the royal title, prerogative of government or either House of Parliament, offences punishable by a praemunire, blasphemy, perjury and subornation of perjury, making or being privy to the making of false oaths, administering of unlawful oaths, forgery, burning corn, grain, wood, &c., bigamy, abduction, concealment of birth, bribery, certain conspiracies, theft of records, stealing bills, &c. and documents relating to real property, frauds by trustees, factors, &c. punishable under the Larceny Act of 1864 (Stephen, vol. 4, p. 249 *et seq.*).

This court exercises appellate jurisdiction on the merits from decisions of magistrates, and an appeal lies from its original decisions to the Court of Criminal Appeal as to points of law, law and fact, fact alone, and sentences. Though justices in quarter sessions can impose very heavy sentences, no legal qualification is necessary either for the members of the court or the chairman. They entertain appeals as to questions of rating (Local Government Act, 1888, s. 8).

Borough quarter sessions.—Where a borough has a court of quarter sessions the court sits four times a year, and its judicial functions are identical with the county court of quarter sessions. Its judge is the recorder, who then becomes a borough magistrate *virtute officii*. He must be a barrister of at least five years' standing. He is not eligible to stand for his borough in the House of Commons, neither can he be elected a member of the corporation. When necessary, he may appoint a deputy, similarly qualified, to do his work. He has no powers of granting licences to sellers of alcohol, neither can he take cognizance of rating appeals (Odgers' Local Government, pp. 97, 98).

The Lord Lieutenant.—This functionary first appears in the Tudor period. He is appointed by the Crown from amongst the county nobility or rich squirearchy. In process of time he relieved the sheriff of the county of the control of the militia, and he retained nominal control over that force till the year 1871, and he is now usually president of the county association under the Territorial and Reserve Forces Act, 1907. He is *ex officio* a magistrate for the county, and on his recommendation county magistrates are appointed, and also *Custos Rotulorum* (custodian of the county records).

Clerk of the Peace.—This functionary is now appointed by a joint committee of quarter sessions and the county council. He is usually paid fees for what he does instead of a salary. He has various duties. He is clerk to the county council; he issues precepts to overseers (see *post*, Chap. XXXVIII.); he has certain duties *re* quarter sessions juries and jury lists in general; he keeps the records of quarter sessions and justices out of session; he or his deputy usually attends the justices in quarter sessions and advises them as to law matters. He is almost always a solicitor by profession. When he devotes his entire time to county duties he, like other county officials, cannot sit in Parliament. He has certain other functions.

Clerks to magistrates.—These officials or their deputies usually attend the magistrates at petty sessions, write down the depositions and give legal advice to the magistrates. The post is a salaried one, and is almost invariably given to a solicitor. They are paid by the county council (Local Government Act, 1888, s. 84) or borough council (*c*).

(*c*) As to their appointment and removal, see 40 & 41 Vict. c. 43, ss. 5, 7.

CHAPTER XXIV.

THE CORONER.

Office of coroner.—According to Maitland the office of coroner dates from 1194. Three knights and one clerk were to be elected in the County Court to keep the pleas of the Crown (Maitland's Const. Hist., p. 44).

The duties of the ancient coroner resembled in many respects his duties at the present day, but amongst other things he had to keep a roll of suspected persons, to act as a check not only on the sheriff but on the jury of presentment.

Again, when a man who was suspected of a crime fled to the nearest church for safety the coroner was sent for. The coroner talked with the refugee, giving him the option of abjuring the realm or throwing himself on his country. If the prisoner chose the first alternative he was taken to the nearest available port and shipped, and if he returned was executed. Abjuring the realm in this instance entailed forfeiture of property. Finally, when a man desired to appeal another of felony, the coroner was approached.

The ancient coroner had also jurisdiction as to wreck, whales, sturgeons, and deodands.

Coroners of present day.—The coroner has still jurisdiction in cases of treasure trove, and where the sheriff is personally interested in a case the coroner acts as his substitute, but his chief duty is, with the aid of a jury, to inquire into the deaths of persons who have died suddenly, by violence, under suspicious circumstances, in prison, or at the hands of the hangman. The inquest is held *super visum corporis*. The jury must be composed of at least twelve men, and the number must not exceed twenty-three. The witnesses are examined on oath, the coroner discharging the office of judge. The coroner can enforce a post *mortem* examination, and insist on the attendance of medical and other witnesses. He can order exhumation, though in cases of doubt—as, for instance, where other graves would be interfered with—he usually gets the Home Secretary's order. The finding of the jury in cases of murder or manslaughter must be attested by the hands and seals of the jury and also the coroner. The coroner can commit the accused for trial, and in manslaughter cases admit him to bail.

The signed and sealed inquisition is a sufficient warranty to try the accused without the necessity of the grand jury finding a true bill for murder or manslaughter. It is the practice, however, for the case to be heard before the magistrate in the usual way and then for the grand jury to find a true bill. The depositions taken before the coroner and those taken before the magistrate are sent to the assize court where the trial is to take place.

The coroner for the City of London, under a local Act, may inquire into the outbreak of fires, holding an inquest, which may result in a verdict of arson (51 & 52 Vict. c. 38).

Various kinds of coroners.—There are 200 county coroners, who are chosen by the county council, and 76 borough coroners, who are chosen by the borough council, and 54 franchise coroners, chosen according to the charter of prescription. For example, the coroner for Westminster is chosen by the dean and chapter. Borough councils cannot elect a coroner unless they possess more than 10,000 in population and in addition possess a bench of borough magistrates. A county coroner must be a freeholder in the county. A High Court judge is a coroner *virtute officii*, but no instance is recorded of judges holding inquests (Home Office Committee on Law relating to Coroners, 1910).

Removal of coroner.—The Lord Chancellor can dismiss the coroner for inability or misbehaviour, and where he misbehaves by omission or commission he is generally guilty of a misdemeanour.

CHAPTER XXV

THE SHERIFF.

The sheriff (*vice-comes*) was formerly the deputy of the earl or ealdorman of the shire, and when the bishop and earl gradually desisted from judicial work at the county court the sheriff took upon himself their functions. When in the reign of Henry II. King's justice began to override local justice, it frequently fell to the lot of the sheriff to execute the King's writs. To this circumstance can be attributed the present function of the sheriff in executing writs of *fieri facias*, *elegit*, *capias*, &c.

There are two kinds of sheriffs, viz., sheriffs of counties and sheriffs of certain ancient cities and boroughs, chosen by those towns (as to these localities, see Odgers on Local Government, 1st ed., pp. 95 and 96).

The county sheriff is elected in the following manner :—The Chancellor of the Exchequer and certain judges of the High Court meet at the Royal Palace of Justice, the Strand, Middlesex, on November 12th in each year, and choose three men of sufficient means from each county. The Sovereign pricks the name of one of these three men, who is then duly constituted sheriff of the county for the year. The sheriff is bound to serve without salary, but he is consoled by the fact that he takes precedence over the entire county, the Lord-Lieutenant excepted. If he refuses his services he can be fined. His duties are to execute High Court writs, summon juries, supervise executions of persons sentenced to death, and perform the duty of returning officer at a Parliamentary election. Since the passing of the Prisons Act, 1877, the sheriff has no longer control over prisoners in his county. He has to wait upon the judges at the assizes, and to pay liberally for their entertainment. Though almost all the duties of the sheriff are undertaken by his deputy, the under-sheriff, the former is responsible for the acts of the under-sheriff and all persons engaged under him, *e.g.*, bailiffs who execute writs of execution. Where the sheriff's underlings commit tortious acts in the course of their employment, the sheriff is responsible, *e.g.*, trespassing in a man's house.

When judgment has been entered in the High Court for an unliquidated amount (interlocutory judgment), it often falls to the lot of the sheriff to assess the damages. On these occasions the under-sheriff sits in court as judge and hears both sides on the question of damages and all matters relevant thereto. A jury of twelve men then fix the damages. He has similar functions in compensation cases where land is compulsorily taken.

PART V.

Parliament.

CHAPTER XXVI.

THE HIGH COURT OF PARLIAMENT.

The distant precursor of what we now call the High Court of Parliament was the Curia Regis, its remotest ancestor being the Witan, which was a national court, a national executive, and in a minor degree a legislature (*a*).

Within the Curia Regis there were noteworthy cleavages. (1) In 1215 A.D. when the new Court of Common Pleas, in obedience to Magna Charta, took up its quarters in a fixed place, viz., Westminster. The provision prescribed *at communia placita non sequantur personam domini regis*, but *assignentur in aliquo certe loco*. (2) When, after the fall of the Justiciar (*b*), the three great courts of common law split off from the council. (3) When the council separated from Parliament in the reign of Richard II.

After the second cleavage appellate jurisdiction passed to the Lords. When we speak now of the High Court of Parliament we mean the judicial functions claimed by our Legislature, viz.: (1) The appellate jurisdiction of the Lords, both civil and

(*a*) The expression "Curia Regis" had various meanings, to wit: (1) The Great Council of the Realm; (2) The King's Court—i.e., the Court held by the King's continual councillors; (3) The County Court, at which royal justices periodically attended; (4) Those great assemblies at Easter, Whitsuntide, and Christmas when the King wore his crown.

(*b*) The Justiciar, or "Justiciarius capitalis totius Angliæ," was a great political, fiscal, and judicial functionary, who acted as the King's chief assistant whilst he was in England, and as Regent when the Sovereign was abroad. The office was abolished in the reign of Edward I.

criminal. (2) The joint judicial and quasi-judicial functions of the Lords and Commons as to impeachments and bills of attainder. (3) The judicial functions of the Lords and Commons within the orbits of their respective privileges. (4) The jurisdiction of the Lords and the Commons in their respective committees as to private bills. The primary function of the High Court of Parliament was probably judicature and the primary function of the Model Parliament was judicature. In the statutes of the Lords ordainers (*tempore* Edward II.) we come across the following passage : " Whereas many folk are delayed in the King's Court because defendants allege that the plaintiffs ought not to be answering in the absence of the King, and many also are wronged by Ministers, which wrong they cannot get redressed without Parliament : we order that the King hold a Parliament once a year or twice if need be, and that in a convenient place and in the same Parliament state pleas which have been delayed, and pleas about which the judges differ be recorded and determined " (Pollard, Evolution of Parliament, p. 35). (5) The judicial functions of the Lords as to determining claims to ancient peerages provided that the King (as he has done for over two hundred years) refers such claim to them. (6) The judicial function of the Speaker and certain members of the Chairman's panel when they decide whether any given bill is a money bill. (7) The right of the Lords as a court of first instance to try peers by blood of England, Scotland, or Ireland for treason or felony, and also peeresses of the three kingdoms by blood or marriage.

The most ancient of these judical functions is probably the right of the Lords to try peers for crime, as the Witan was a court for the trial of great offenders and so was the feudalised Witan of the Normans.

Up to the reign of Edward I. the Court of King's Bench, or Coram Rege Court, was the supreme Court of Appeal as regarded civil matters, but Fleta (*c*) writes as follows : *Habet rex curiam*

(*c*) Fleta was not the name of this author, who wrote from the Fleet Prison, and was believed to be a degraded judge who lived in the reign of Edward I. The work ascribed to him is a Commentary, insignificant beside that of Bracton, written in Latin, and of some note because Fleta was the last commentator to write in that tongue.

suam in concilio suo in Parliamentis suis ubi terminatæ sunt dubitationes judiciorum novisque injuriis emersis nova constituuntur remedia et unicuique justitia prout meruit retribuetur ibidem (Fleta, Bk. II., c. 2, De Differentiis Curiarum).

This court, which settled judicial doubts and devised new remedies for injuries as they arose, will strike the reader at first sight as being the precursor of the House of Lords, regarded as an Appellate Civil Court, in which aspect it was afterwards known as "the High Court of Parliament," though in reality appellate civil jurisdiction was only one judicial function of that court.

This court was held in the presence of prelates (who were forbidden by the Constitutions of Clarendon to give a verdict of "guilty" in any case involving loss of life or limb), earls, barons, the "proceres"—whoever they were (*d*)—and other skilled men.

According to some views, when the Curia Regis split up into the courts of justice the King in Council remained the final Court of Appeal, but no mention is made of this by Bracton, who wrote in the reign of Henry III. and treated the King's Bench as the Appellate Court.

The Commons never, except on two occasions, laid claim to exercise criminal jurisdiction, or indeed any purely judicial function outside their privileges, and in 1399 both Houses passed resolutions that the judicial power of Parliament was not vested in the Lower House.

On two separate occasions they usurped criminal judicial functions. The first instance was in the case of Floyd in 1621, and the second was the case of Mist in 1721. Edward Floyd was a barrister and a Roman Catholic, who wrote slightingly of the Elector Palatine, and the Commons, animated by Protestant zeal, sentenced Floyd to the pillory and ordered a whipping and a fine of £1,000, with imprisonment for life thrown in. The Lords remonstrated, and in the end the Commons allowed Floyd to be tried in the Lords. The Lords inflicted a punishment still more severe on Floyd, though the whipping was remitted. Here

(d) The proceres have been identified by some with the ancient order of Vavasours, of whom little is known.

both Houses illegally usurped criminal judicial functions (cf. Langmead, p. 426 and note).

In 1721 Mist, a printer, was committed to Newgate by the Commons for printing a Jacobite newspaper which the Commons deemed a traitorous libel. This was an extension of privilege so called, but it was not within the true ambit of their privileges and therefore illegal.

At the present day the privilege committee of the Lords universally tries claims to ancient peerages, though in strictness the King has a prerogative right to refer these claims to any court he selects. As, however, the Sovereign has not attempted to exercise this prerogative for over two hundred years, it is probably obsolete.

The House of Lords considered that it possessed original jurisdiction to try civil cases; and a controversy arose in the case of *Skinner* v. *The East India Company*, the final result being that the Lords abandoned their contention.

In the case of *Shirley* v. *Fagg* the Commons contested the right of the Lords to hear equity appeals, but were unsuccessful.

By the Judicature Acts, 1873-1875, the appellate jurisdiction of the Lords was taken away, but was revived by the Appellate Jurisdiction Act, 1876.

By the above Act this court is to try all English, Irish and Scotch appeals. Though all the Lords may act as judges, by convention the lay peers absent themselves, and the statute provides that no appeal can be heard unless there be present three at least of the following persons : (1) the Lord Chancellor; (2) a Lord or Lords of Appeal in ordinary; (3) Lords of Parliament who have held high judicial office.

The court can sit during a prorogation and after a dissolution of Parliament, and in cases of difficulty their lordships may call to their assistance the King's Bench Division judges. The House of Lords is now a court of final appeal in criminal cases by virtue of the Criminal Appeal Act, 1907. They can hear appeals as to all cases cognisable by the Court of Criminal Appeal, which comprise appeals from the verdicts of juries and, presumably, also from the convictions by magistrates of persons as incorrigible rogues, and from sentences of magistrates of persons to Borstal treatment (see Criminal Justice Administration Act, 1914). For further particulars see Odger's Common Law, vol. 2, 2nd ed., where the whole matter is fully discussed.

The Lords have for centuries tried all peers by blood for treason or felony, and peeresses by blood or marriage, under a statute of Henry VI.

The accused is summoned or arrested in the ordinary way and committed for trial by justices of the peace.

The case then goes before a grand jury. If the grand jury find a true bill the accused may plead peerage, but whether he does so or not the case is removed to the House of Lords by writ of *certiorari*.

If Parliament is sitting the accused is tried before the Lords themselves as judges of law and fact, a judge appointed by the King as lord high steward presiding. Each peer then gives his verdict, commencing with the youngest peer.

If Parliament is not sitting the King appoints a lord high steward, who acts as judge as to law, and a minimum of twelve peers—though all have a right to attend—act as judges of fact.

Spiritual peers have a right to be present until the time for delivering a verdict arrives, and then, in obedience to the Constitutions of Clarendon, they retire after protesting.

Irish and Scotch peers and peeresses are triable before the Lords, but not bishops or their wives.

Impeachment.—An impeachment is a judicial proceeding against a lord or a commoner who is accused of a high crime or misdemeanour, or of treason or felony.

The first recorded case of impeachment occurred in 1376 A.D., when Lords Latimer and Neville and four commoners—viz., Lyons, Ellys, Peachey, and Bury—were charged with: (1) removal of the staple from Calais; (2) lending the King money at usurious interest; (3) buying Crown debts for small sums and then paying themselves in full out of the Treasury.

In 1386 Michael de la Pole, the Chancellor, was dismissed for official misconduct after impeachment. William de la Pole was impeached in the reign of Henry VI. and after this there was no impeachment till the reign of James I., bills of attainder taking their place. A bill of attainder amounts simply to trying, convicting and sentencing a man by Act of Parliament, but in some cases at any rate the proceedings were not unfair and the prisoner could be heard in his own defence, *e.g.*, *Case of the Regicides.*

In 1621 Lord Bacon and Sir Giles Mompesson were impeached, and down to the Revolution there were forty cases of impeachment.

From the accession of William III. to the death of George I. there were fifteen cases. There was one case during the reign of George II. The case of FitzHarris was noteworthy, as the question arose whether a commoner could be impeached for a capital offence. The real object of this impeachment was to manipulate the exclusion of James II. from the throne. To stop this Charles II. directed the prosecution of FitzHarris in the King's Bench, as the Lords had stated that they could not try a commoner for a capital offence.

The Commons resolved that the action of the Lords in refusing to try the accused was a denial of justice and as violation of the constitution of Parliament, and that if any inferior court tried FitzHarris, it would be guilty of a breach of the privileges of the Commons. Charles II. dissolved Parliament, and afterwards FitzHarris was tried in the King's Bench and then condemned and executed.

In the case of Sir Adam Blair and four others, who were impeached for treason in 1689 for publishing a proclamation of James II., the Lords proceeded with the impeachment, and now it is fairly settled law that the Lords can try a commoner in a capital case.

The last two cases of impeachment were : (1) The impeachment of Warren Hastings (1786) and Lord Melville (1804), and at these trials the question arose whether a prorogation or dissolution stopped an impeachment; though it was held that neither did so, yet in both cases statutes were passed legalising the continuance of the trials. This contention was raised in *Danby's Case.*

Impeachments may, perhaps, be said to be now practically obsolete, though it has been talked about in the House comparatively recently and might still be applicable to a case, say, of clear corruption which was not discovered in time. But in these days many kinds of misconduct for which impeachment was once the only remedy have been made ordinary criminal offences.

Section 8 of the Act of Settlement provides that a pardon under the Great Seal cannot be pleaded by way of defence to an impeachment of the Commons. The King can, however, pardon after the Lords have passed sentence, and this was done in the case of three lords who were impeached and sentenced after the Rebellion of 1715.

This section in the Act of Settlement arose out of the case of Danby, who was impeached for the high misdemeanour of writing a letter to the English ambassador at Versailles at the express command of Charles II., who wrote on the letter : "This letter is writ by my Order.—C. R." (*f*).

The proceedings on a private bill are partly legislative and partly judicial. Private bills involve hearings by committees of both Houses at which counsel can be heard and witnesses may be examined. Again, where public legislation is contemplated, *e.g.*, in the case of the Moneylenders Act, 1900, a commission consisting of a committee of the Commons or the Lords may be appointed to which witnesses can be summoned and made to answer questions on pain of contempt, another exercise by Parliament of functions resembling those of a court of law.

Again, on the contemplated removal of a judge or, say, the Comptroller and Auditor-General, when an address is to be presented to the Crown by both Houses of Parliament, the duties of either House are semi-judicial.

When either House is considering a proposed committal for contempt they exercise a function purely judicial. Perhaps, also, the functions of the Speaker alone, or the Speaker aided by members of the Chairman's panel under the Parliament Act, 1911, are also purely judicial.

(*f*) *Danby's Case* involved the following constitutional questions: (1) Whether a Minister of the Crown can shield himself by pleading the express command of his Sovereign; (2) Whether the Lords can deny justice when a man is impeached; (3) The right of pleading the royal pardon by way of defence; (4) The right of the bishops to be present at the trial before the Lords of a capital offence provided they retire before verdict given. The Commons objected to the presence of the bishops on the ground that final judgment frequently depends on preliminary proceedings

CHAPTER XXVII.

PARLIAMENT AND THE CROWN.

The King's prerogatives as to Parliament.—It is the prerogative of the Crown to summon Parliament, to prorogue Parliament, and to dissolve Parliament. The Royal Proclamation which dissolves one Parliament summons another (Anson, vol. 1, p. 51; Todd, vol. 1, p. 57).

On the accession of a new Sovereign, Parliament is to assemble without delay (see May, Parl. Practice, p. 41, 11th ed.; 6 Anne, c. 7, s. 4).

In mediæval times, as we have seen, certain Sovereigns pleased themselves as to whether they would convene Parliament, though as early as Edward III.'s reign, a statute provided that Parliament be convened annually, or oftener if need be.

In the reign of Charles I. the Long Parliament passed an Act (repealed *temp.* Charles II.) enabling the Lords to convene Parliament should the King omit so to do for three years. If the Lords, moreover, omitted to call Parliament the constituencies were to be at liberty to summon it (Langmead, p. 457).

In the reign of Charles II. a statute passed to the effect that the sitting of Parliament should not be discontinued for over three years, and in the reign of William III. another statute was passed to the same purport and effect. The Bill of Rights states that Parliament is to be summoned frequently, but the real security of the nation consists in the following facts : (1) that the Army Act would no longer exist, and (2) that the levying of certain taxes would be illegal.

It is necessary to keep Parliament in almost constant session in order to cope with increasing demands for fresh laws.

The existence of Parliament is terminated by—

(A) Effluxion of time, to wit, five years, under the provisions of the Parliament Act, 1911.

(B) By a dissolution.

A dissolution brings a Parliament to an end, and prorogation terminates a session.

Bills in progress have their careers checked by a prorogation, and must be commenced *de novo* in the next session or else abandoned. Impeachments and appeals to the House of Lords are not affected (see May, ed. 10, p. 43) (*g*).

Parliament and the demise of the Crown.—In old days Parliament died when the King died. By 7 & 8 Will. III. c. 15, Parliament was not to die till the King had been dead six months, unless the new King chose to dissolve it. By the Representation of the People Act, 1867, the death of the King is not to affect the existence of Parliament at all. As to demise of the Crown during a general election, see 37 Geo. III. c. 127.

Dissolution.—Though the King can dissolve Parliament when he likes, his conduct, though legal, would be unconstitutional if he did so without taking the Cabinet into his confidence. As to when it is constitutional to dissolve, see Anson, vol. 1, p. 293. Parliament is dissolved by a Royal Proclamation issued with the advice of the Privy Council (Ilbert's Manual of Procedure, p. 4).

Adjournments.—Either House may adjourn its sittings for any given number of hours, days, weeks, or even (in modern times) months, but the Crown possesses a statutory power to order resumption of business when both Houses stand adjourned for more than six days (37 Geo. III. c. 127, amended by 33 & 34 Vict. c. 81).

King's visits to Parliament.—The King is not supposed to visit Parliament officially save on stated solemn occasions. He

(*g*) Under the Triennial Act of William III., Parliament was to last for three years, unless sooner dissolved by the Crown.

attends at the commencement and close of Parliament and a parliamentary session. He can also personally attend Parliament to assent to laws. The Speech from the Throne at the opening of the session, after dealing with foreign relations and other matters of national importance, indicates the Government programme of legislation, while the Speech when Parliament is prorogued sums up the legislative results of the session.

Modes of giving the Royal assent.—The royal assent is now almost universally given by royal commission under 33 Hen. VIII. c. 21. Should the King chance to refuse his assent, the words "*Le Roy s'avisera*" would be used. When the King assents to a public bill the words "*Le Roy le veult*" are used. For a private bill the words "*Soit fait comme il est désiré*" are used, and for a money bill the following, "*Le Roy remercie ses bons sujets, accepte leur bénévolence, et ainsi le veult*" (Anson, vol. 1, p. 313; May, p. 512, 11th ed.).

It is contrary to parliamentary etiquette to *drag the name of the Sovereign into debate* in order to influence either House· neither is a member permitted to speak in slighting terms of his Sovereign (Ilbert's Manual of Procedure, p. 127).

CHAPTER XXVIII.

CONVENTION OF A NEW PARLIAMENT—OPENING OF A NEW SESSION.

When a dissolution is contemplated by the Crown a Cabinet meeting finally settles the matter, together with a Proclamation dissolving the existing Parliament; after which come the Order in Council (heralded by the Proclamation) enjoining the issuing of writs to the temporal and spiritual peers and returning officers, and a separate Proclamation directing the election of sixteen representative peers of Scotland to serve during the ensuing Parliament. The Clerk of the Crown in Chancery then prepares writs, which on being sealed are sent to the following persons, viz. :—

1. Temporal peers of the United Kingdom, who are summoned on their faith and allegiance.

2. The twenty-six spiritual peers, who are summoned on their faith and love, and whose writs contain a "praemunientes clause," bidding them bring also archdeacons, deans and representatives of their clergy, which they are not supposed to do.

3. The twenty-eight Irish peers, elected for life.

4. The judges, the Attorney-General, the Solicitor-General, and the King's ancient Serjeant. These functionaries take no part in the debates of the Lords, but merely give advice. They are summoned to treat and give counsel.

5. Returning officers. The returning officer of a county is the sheriff, and of a borough is the mayor (cf. Anson, vol. 1, p. 53; Encyc. Laws of Eng. vol. 12, p. 707).

Meeting of new Parliament.—On the appointed day each House assembles in its own chamber until the Gentleman Usher of the Black Rod requires attendance of the Commons at the bar of the Lords. As many members as can squeeze in then proceed with the Under-Clerk of Parliament (Clerk to the House of Commons) to the bar. The commission for opening Parliament is then read, unless the Sovereign is present, which would render a commission unnecessary (see May, ed. 11, p. 146).

When this has been done by the Lord Chancellor, the Commons are bidden by him to retire and proceed to the election of a Speaker. The Clerk of the House then takes the chair and a Speaker is elected, and this ends the day. (*Ibid.*, p. 197.)

After the election the new Speaker proceeds with the Commons to the bar of the Lords. He announces his election, which is confirmed by the Lord Chancellor in the name of the Sovereign. After this the Speaker claims certain ancient privileges of the House (see *post*, pp. 241 *et seq.*). The King, if present, reads his speech, but if absent his speech may be read for him by the Lord Chancellor, unless he chooses to read it himself on a future day. After this the Commons retire, and each member of either House proves his right to membership, and then members of both Houses either take the statutory oath or affirmation, as the case may be, of allegiance (as to oath, see Parliamentary Oaths Act, 1866, and as to affirmation, see Parliamentary Oaths Act, 1888).

New session.—At the beginning of each session (including, of course, the first), on the return of the Speaker from the Lords, the usual sessional orders are moved and a bill is read formally the first time. The Speaker then reads a copy of the King's Speech to the House, and an address of thanks to the Crown for the speech is moved and seconded. On that question amendments may be moved, and a general debate on the address takes place, in which the Government programme is discussed and criticised (May's Parl. Practice (ed. 11), p. 149 *et seq.*; Anson, pp. 42—67; Ilbert's Manual of Procedure, Chaps. I. and II).

Parliamentary oaths.—The passing of the Parliamentary Oaths Act, 1888, was due to the efforts of Mr. Bradlaugh.

This gentleman, in 1880, was returned as member for Northampton. He avowed his disbelief in God, and claimed the right to affirm instead of taking an oath which would not bind his conscience. He was permitted to affirm by a provisional order, subject to the risk of an action, and was then sued by one Clarke, a common informer, for £500, because he sat and voted without having taken the oath of allegiance. The court held that the law had been broken (*Clarke* v. *Bradlaugh*, 7 Q. B. D. 38, C. A.). Mr. Bradlaugh then tried to take the oath (Anson, vol. 1), but this was not permitted by the House, which passed a resolution to that effect.

In February, 1884, Mr. Bradlaugh administered the oath to himself in the House, and then voted at a division.

This was followed by an action by the Attorney-General, when the penalty of £500 was recovered, and the court decided that as Mr. Bradlaugh was an atheist the self-administered oath was no oath (*Attorney-General* v. *Bradlaugh*, 14 Q. B. D. 667, C. A.).

In January, 1886, Mr. Bradlaugh was returned a member at the new Parliament; and on a motion being made that he should not be permitted to take the oath, the Speaker held that the old resolution of a former Parliament did not bind the new one, and the second motion was not carried. In 1888 the Parliamentary Oaths Act was passed, which permitted an affirmation as regards Parliament instead of an oath (Anson, vol. 1, pp. 87 *et seq.*; May, 11th ed., p. 160 *et seq.*).

The removal of tests in the case of Members of Parliament has been a slow process. Formerly a member had to take the oath of supremacy, the oath of abjuration, the oath of allegiance, and also to make a declaration against transubstantiation. Quakers were the first persons to get relief, then came the Catholic Emancipation Act of 1829, and finally provision was made for Jews in 1858. In 1866 the Parliamentary Oaths Act of that year substituted a simple oath of allegiance for the three oaths, and now, under the legislation of 1888, there is no necessity for any religious belief.

Professor Maitland contends that Nonconformist Protestants were never actually excluded from the House (Maitland's Const. Hist., p. 364).

Evidence of right to membership.—In the Lords, Garter King-at-Arms produces a roll of peers entitled to be summoned as lords of Parliament. Each peer places his writ on the table of the House, and a new peer hands his patent of nobility to the Lord Chancellor, kneeling as he does so. An hereditary peer does not require an introduction, nor does an elected Irish peer, but a newly-created peer must be proposed and seconded (May,

Chap. VII.). The certificate of the Lord Clerk Register's return of Scotch peers is evidence of a Scotch peer's right to sit in the House.

The book of returns of elected commoners entitled to sit in the lower House, which is made out by the Clerk to the Crown in Chancery, is evidence of the right of each commoner to sit (May, pp. 150 *et seq.*).

Where a member, new or old, is elected at a by-election, he must be introduced by two other members (May, p. 176) (*h*).

All members of both Houses must take the oath of allegiance to the new Sovereign on the demise of the Crown.

(*h*) In Dr. Kenealy's case introduction was dispensed with (May, p. 171, note).

CHAPTER XXIX.

OFFICERS OF PARLIAMENT.

House of Lords.

Speaker of Lords.—The Speaker of the House of Lords is usually the Lord Chancellor of England, who occupies a seat on the Woolsack, but though the course is most unusual, a functionary called the Lord Keeper (a commoner) can be Speaker in the Lords.

Neither the Lord Chancellor nor the Lord Keeper have the powers of the Speaker for maintaining order in the House. Questions of order are settled by the House itself, and in debate peers address the House and not the occupant of the Woolsack.

On a division the Lord Chancellor votes first, and he has no casting vote.

Chairman of Committees.—This officer takes the chair when the House is in committee. He holds office during the whole Parliament. He also superintends all matters relating to private Bills.

Gentleman Usher of the Black Rod.—This functionary is appointed by Letters Patent under the Great Seal. He is a member of the Royal Household, and sits within the Bar. He executes warrants of commitment, and desires attendance of Commons when necessary. He is assisted by the Yeoman Usher of the Black Rod. The Gentleman Usher is an officer of the Order of the Garter. He derives his name from the black wand, surmounted by a golden lion, which is used as the Mace of the Lords. Black Rod has in his custody all persons detained for trial by the Lords, either as peers or as the result of an impeachment. He also assists at the introduction of new peers (Encyc. Laws of Eng., vol. 2, p. 284; May, 11th ed., p. 199).

The Serjeant-at-Arms.—This official's duties are not arduous. He carries the Mace when the Lord Chancellor enters and leaves Houses (May, 11th ed., p. 199).

Clerk of Parliament.—This functionary keeps the journals of the Lords.

Officers of Commons.

The Speaker.—The Speaker is elected at a new Parliament, though the old Speaker is generally chosen if his behaviour gives satisfaction, and if he can retain his seat. The King may refuse to accept the choice of the Commons as to electing a Speaker, but by convention he never does so. When the House is not in Committee, and sometimes on other occasions, *e.g.*, when a royal message is expected or a message from the Lords, the Speaker occupies the chair. When in the chair he maintains order and names members guilty of disorder. He gives rulings as to procedure. He signs warrants of committal for contempt and reprimands members and others when necessary. He signs warrants for by-election writs, and when he is absent certain other selected members do this duty for him. On all State occasions he can claim the escort of a life-guardsman, and when he attends a levée he can drive in the centre of the Mall. He is the first Commoner in the land. He has an official residence and a salary of £5,000 per annum. He can claim from the royal forests a buck and a doe twice a year. On retirement it is customary to bestow on him a peerage and a pension (Encyclopædia of the Laws of England, sub tit. "Speaker"; see also May, pp. 191-195).

Under-Clerk of Parliament.—This office is worth £2,000 per annum, and the appointment is by Letters Patent under the Great Seal. When the Commons retire to elect a Speaker, the Clerk of the House occupies the chair. He makes entries of what transpires in the House, and from these materials prepares the journals. He endorses bills sent up to the Lords.

The **Serjeant-at-Arms** is appointed by Letters Patent under the Great Seal. During session he attends the Speaker when the latter enters and leaves the House. His duty is to carry out directions for maintaining order, and arrest strangers who have no business in the House. He executes warrants for contempt, and when ordered to do so brings persons in custody before the Bar of the House. He or his assistants serve processes of House. When a person is arrested by order of the House he keeps the prisoner in his custody till arrangements are made elsewhere (Encyclop. Laws of Eng., sub tit. "Serjeant-at-Arms"; cf. May, p. 204).

Chairman of Ways and Means.—This official, who has a salary of £2,500 a year, takes the chair when the House is in committee, and acts as Deputy-Speaker when necessary. He maintains order in committee, and can name members; but where a suspension is necessary the Speaker reoccupies the chair. The closure can be applied by the chairman in committee. He has important duties in conjunction with the chairman of committees of the Lords as to private bills. There is a deputy-chairman, with a salary of £1,000 a year (cf. May, p. 604).

Government and Opposition Whips.—The Government Whips consist of (1) the patronage secretary, who interviews members as to patronage in Premier's gift, and acts as a kind of intercessor on occasion; (2) the junior whips, who are junior Lords of the Treasury, but who do only routine work there.

It is the duty of the recognised whips, whether acting for the Government or not, to see that their party is duly represented at a division. They must know their men by sight, and when a division comes on see that a majority is safe, and keep all their members within sound of the division bell. When an important debate is pending, the whips have to do with the order of the speeches, and sometimes have to get a member to continue speaking till they can bring up their forces. The whips are supposed to know all the members of the party, and to keep the leaders posted with the necessary information about them. They also act as intermediaries between the leaders of the party and the local organisations, and can pass the word down that the candidature of a given person is or is not to be supported (for further particulars about local organisations of a party, see Lowell's Government of England, vol. 1, pp. 466 *et seq.*).

CHAPTER XXX.

THE HOUSE OF LORDS.

Origin of the Peerage; Powers of King to create Peers.—The Saxon Witan was not a council of wise men, but of the chief men of the State.

It was not so much an assembly of nobles by blood (eorls), as of thanes; the word "thane" comes from "thegnan," to serve, and denoted those great men who were useful to the King in war or otherwise.

With the Conquest the personal monarchy gave way to the territorial, and the chief men of the kingdom were among the number of tenants *in capite*, and were known as the greater barons. All the land for the most part in England belonged to the King in a more marked degree after the Conquest.

According to Magna Charta, the greater barons (*majores barones*) were summoned to the council or the army by a special writ of summons, whilst the lesser barons were summoned in batches (*in generali*) through the various sheriffs of counties.

Both greater barons and lesser were tenants in chief of the King, and all the King's tenants had a supposed right to attend the Magnum Concilium, as the feudalised Witan of the Norman and early Plantagenet Sovereigns was called. There are various theories extant as to what entitled a man to a special writ of summons.

The lesser baron was in the ancient sense a baron also, the word "baro" originally meaning man, and the King's tenants being known as King's men; but by degrees only the holder of a baronia—*i.e.*, 13⅓ knights' fees—was considered as a baron. Barony, in early times, depended on tenure and nothing else; and long after this ceased to be the case this old notion was adhered to. When barony ceased to depend on tenure has formed the subject-matter of much academic discussion.

There are several theories as to this. Camden, judging from his "Britannia," appears to think that Henry III., owing to the turbulence of his barons, summoned to his Great Council only the more worthy of this class. He says: "Ad summum honorem ex quo Henricus III. ex tantâ multitudine quae seditiosa et turbulenta fuit optimos quosque rescripto ad comitia Parliamentaria evocaverit—Ille eum (ex satis antiquo scriptore loquor) post magnus perturbationes et enormes vexationes inter ipsum regem Simonen de Monteforti et alios barones motas et susceptas statuit et ordinavit quod omnes illi comites et barones Angliae quibus ipse rex dignatus est brevia summonitionis dirigere, venirent ad Parliamentum suum et non alii nisi forte dominus rex alia vel similia brevia eis dirigere voluisset" (Camden's Britannia; Cruise on Dignities, p. 15).

Selden, according to Cruise, disparages this explanation; but considers that even in the time of John tenure *in capite* of a baronia might not have entitled the holder to a summons as a matter of course (see Cruise on Dignities, p. 15).

Maitland remarks that the holder of a "baronia" had a supposed right to be summoned, and had to go if summoned; but that the King did not observe the rule rigidly, one of the results being that barons had to go whose estates did not amount in value to a baronia; and Pollard says that the receipt of summons depended on the discretion and caprice of the King; to the Parliament of 1295, he adds, forty-one barons only were summoued, to that of 1300 ninety-nine barons were summoned, and to that of 1322 Edward II. summoned fifty-two barons (Pollard's Evolution of Parliament, p. 99).

Stubbs thinks that any tenant *in capite* could be specially summoned; whilst Anson thinks that anyone could be summoned, baron or no baron, and his view is supported by the authors of the report on "The Dignity of a Peer," and also by Hallam (see also Pollard, Evolution of Parliament, p. 99).

Whatever the qualification was for a special writ before the middle of Edward I.'s reign, it is probable that at the date of Edward I.'s Model Parliament (1295 A.D.)—

(1) The King could not refuse a summons to a man who had once received one (Stubbs, vol. 2, p. 182).

(2) That if a man was summoned to Parliament by special writ, his heir had a right to a summons after his death (*ibid.*, p. 182).

(3) The making of the status of the peer depended on the hereditary reception of the writ rather than on the tenure, which had been the hereditary qualification of the summons (*ibid.*, p. 182), before a man could attend Parliament.

(4) A royal summons was necessary (Cruise, p. 40). The peerage, like the Crown, became hereditary owing to close association with land, and when once the hereditary principle was established, it was continued, the King's opposition to an hereditary nobility being overcome. Pollard is doubtful as to when it was established.

In the *Clifton Case* it was held that where a man receives a summons, and takes his seat, his blood becomes ennobled, and he acquires an hereditary peerage (Palmer's Peerage Law in England, p. 189).

The taking of the seat in obedience to the summons was, however, an essential. In 1677 Lord Freschville claimed a more ancient peerage than he then possessed, alleging that he was the heir of the body of Ralph de Freschville of Staveley, but he failed in his contention, as there was no evidence that Ralph de Freschville had ever taken his seat. The above case shows that lapse of centuries does not prevent a man claiming a peerage.

Mr. Round states that the *Freschville Case* broke down because the claimant's ancestor was not summoned to a proper Parliament (Round's Peerage and Pedigree, p. 193).

The taking of the seat may, perhaps, be made by proxy, as the following case shows. Thomas Howard, second son of the then Duke of Norfolk, was summoned to Parliament in 1597, and he was unable, owing to sickness, to attend, and Lord Scrope attended as his proxy (Cruise, quoting Camden, p. 72).

Lapse of time is no bar to a peerage claim, and when a man proves that he is the heir of a man who sat as a baron *in pleno parliamento* as a member of the Lords, even so early as the reign of Edward I., he is entitled to the peerage as of right (cf. *Hasting's Case*, p. 144). In the above case the claimant proved that his ancestor sat in a full Parliament (*in pleno parliamento*) on May 29th, 1290, and won his case. Yet in the *St. John Case* the claimant, who proved that his ancestor sat in the same Parliament of 1290, lost his case on the ground of its not being a full Parliament, since the knights of the shire did not attend till the following July (*St. John Case* (1915), App. Cas., p. 282). These two cases are conflicting, and they are both of equal rank, though the *St. John Case* will probably be followed. They illustrate the fact that a decision of the Committee of Privileges need not be followed on future occasions like a decision of the House of Lords on appeal.

Though there is ground for supposing that the King could, in early times at least, refuse a writ of summons to certain of his greater barons, it is doubtful when he acquired the right to summon anybody he chose, baron or no baron, or, rather, tenant or no tenant.

We notice, however, that after the year 1373 peers were summoned *fide et ligeantia*, and not *fide et homagio*, and this shows that a right to be summoned to the Great Council was independent of holding land of the King (cf. Anson, p. 197). Peers, however, were sometimes summoned *fide et ligeantia* from the reign of Edward III. downwards (*ibid.*, p. 197). The epochs in the history of the peerage are as follows :—

(1) Epoch of barony by tenure. (2) Epoch when baronies depended on a summons to Parliament by individual writ. (3) Creation of peerages by charters and, later on, by patents. (There was only a mere formal difference between a charter and a patent.)

It is clear that barony by writ was an offshoot of barony by tenure. If once the hereditary principle be accepted, we must discard barony by tenure.

Again, the theory of barony by tenure involves the consequence that the holders of land, who acquire it by an ordinary purchase, can claim a given title.

In the *Berkeley Case* (Palmer, p. 183) it was held that barony by tenure cannot exist, and this is now considered the ruling case on the subject.

According to Prynne, a peerage could be acquired by alienation, and his opinion is practically borne out by Lord Coke, who, with some reservations, gives an instance of a peerage being granted by deed to an alienee, but states that Parliament adjudged the grant to be void because the King's licence was not obtained (Cruise, p. 111); but whether peerages were originally alienable or not, the power of alienation ceased before the reign of Henry VI. (Cruise, p. 111); as it was by that time clear "that a dignity could not be created by the mere conveyance of a baronial estate" (Cruise, p. 111). In the *Ruthyn Case* the Lords held that no person that hath any honour in him may alien or transfer that honour to any other person.

In 1640 the Lords passed a resolution that a peerage could be neither alienated nor surrendered, but this does not detract from the prerogative, though probably the Lords would not allow the alienee to sit. Mr. Cruise, however, gives several instances of such alienations. Ranulph, Earl of Chester, alienated to his sister, and Almeric de Montfort alienated his barony to his brother, Simon de Montfort. Again, Edmund Deyncourt alienated his barony with the King's permission in the reign of Edward II., and this fact is attested by Lord Coke.

It was, however, decided in the *Norfolk Case* that a peerage could not be alienated or surrendered to the Crown. These cases show that there was a supposed prerogative as to consenting to the alienation of or accepting surrenders of titles of honour, but if there was a prerogative power it has for centuries been obsolete. The most recent decision as to surrenders of baronies was the *Norfolk Case* in 1908, where it was held that a barony could not be surrendered. Barony by tenure, however, was not favoured by the Sovereign and the charters, and later the patents, paved the way for its gradual extinction.

Nevertheless, up to the days of the Stuarts, and even up to the celebrated *Berkeley Case*, the idea, though discouraged frequently by decisions of Committees of Privilege, did not perish utterly.

In the *De Lisle Case* (Palmer, p. 181) it was claimed that Henry VI. had granted a charter to one John Talbot, his heirs and assigns for ever, being tenants of the manor of Kingston Lisle. It was recited in this charter that one Warren de Lisle and his ancestors had from time immemorial sat as Barons de Lisle by reason that they held the manor and lordship of Kingston Lisle. This claim, which was one to a barony by prescription rather than by tenure, succeeded.

In the *Abergavenny Case* (A.D. 1604) there were two claimants, viz., Sir Thomas Fane, who claimed a barony by writ in right of his wife, who was the only daughter and heir of the last Lord Abergavenny, and Sir Edward Neville, the nephew and heir male of the last Lord Abergavenny. Neville claimed by tenure, but the legality of barony by tenure was not seriously gone into owing to a compromise whereby Neville, the claimant by tenure, got the peerage of Abergavenny, and Fane the peerage of De Spencer.

In the *Arundel Case* Sir John Fitzalan claimed the title of Earl of Arundel by reason that his ancestors sat in the House of Lords as Lords of the Castle of Arundel whereunto the title was united and annexed, and that the said castle was then in his possession. This claim was made good on the ground of tenure (Palmer, p. 179).

The first decisive case against barony by tenure was the *FitzWalter Case*, where the claimant by tenure lost the day, the committee holding that barony by tenure had been discontinued for many ages, and was not in being, and so not fit to be revived (Palmer, 182). In the *Berkeley Case* a claimant by tenure failed to establish his alleged right, the court holding *inter alia* that—

(1) Barony by tenure transgressed the principle that the King is the fountain of honour, because if a peerage were attached to land, the alienee of the land could claim it.

(2) Barony by tenure is inconsistent with the theory of hereditary nobility.

(3) It is of the essence of a peerage that it be inalienable.

(4) A right to a peerage is evidenced by the records of the House, its traditions, usages, and precedents, whereas if it was alienable the right thereto must be determined by courts of law.

(5) It is needless to enquire what was the position of a baron before 1295. Subsequent to 1295, there is no evidence of anyone coming to sit in Parliament without a writ of summons.

Degradation of peers and loss of peerages used to be effected by an attainder (unless the estate was entailed), but this no longer occurs, since forfeiture and corruption of blood was done away with by the Forfeiture Abolition Act, 1870.

"A peer cannot lose his nobility but by death or attainder, though there was an instance in the reign of Edward IV. of the degradation of George Neville, Duke of Bedford, by Act of Parliament on account of his poverty, which rendered him unable to support his dignity" (Blackstone (21st ed.), vol. 3, ch. 12, p. 401).

But though the King cannot deprive a peer of his title, he can still perhaps—though this is very doubtful—refuse to summon him to Parliament. During the recent war writs of summons were not sent to the Dukes of Cumberland and Albany on the ground that they were German Sovereigns, and this was effected without a statute, though an Act was passed some time afterwards. Were it not for this event, the case of the Earl of Bristol would have been sufficient ground for asserting that the King could not under any circumstances refuse a writ to a man who had once been summoned. Charles I., to protect his favourite, Buckingham, refused a writ of summons to Lord Bristol. Bristol complained to the House of Lords of this violation of privilege, and as that assembly exercised pressure on his behalf, Charles I. issued the writ of summons, but informed Bristol in a private letter not to avail himself of it. This letter was laid upon the table of the House, and the following day Bristol was charged with treason, and he promptly retaliated by procuring the impeachment of Buckingham. To save Buckingham, Charles dissolved Parliament.

Alienation and surrender of Peerages.—According to Prynne, peerages could be surrendered and even alienated, but modern writers are sceptical of Prynne's accuracy in this and other matters. It has now, however, long been settled that these dignities are incapable of surrender (see Redesdale Committee, 1st Report, p. 397). But in mediæval days instances occur of surrenders with the King's consent. Lord Coke says "that he heard Lord Burghley vouch a record in the reign of Edward IV. that Lord Hoe having no issue male, by deed granted his dignity over, but, not having the King's license, the same was in Parliament adjudged to be void" (Cruise, p. 111).

"The power of alienating dignities by tenure appears to have almost ceased before the time of Henry VI. In the case of the Barony of Lisle the gift of the manor, to which that dignity had been annexed, by the Countess of Shrewsbury to her son John Talbot, does not appear to have conferred on him a complete right to that dignity, for Letters Patent were also obtained in order to confer the baronage upon him" (Cruise, p. 111). In the *Ruthyn Case* (1640 A.D.), which decided the principle that a peerage must originate in matter of record (Anson, vol. 1, p. 199), the Lords resolved that no person that hath an honour in him as a peer of this realm may alien or transfer the honour to any other person (Cruise, p. 111). These resolutions have been criticised as contrary to history (*vide* Round's Peerage and Pedigree) and the law may be said now to rest on the *Berkeley Case*, settling that barony by tenure cannot exist.

There are several instances, according to Cruise, of surrenders of baronies to the Crown. He mentions how, in the reign of Henry III., Simon de Montfort, the youngest son of the Earl of Leicester, surrendered that title to the King, who made a regrant thereof. In 1660 Lord Purbeck surrendered all his dignities to the King (Cruise, p. 113).

The point arose in the *Norfolk Case*, decided in 1907. Lord Mowbray claimed the Earldom of Norfolk under the following circumstances. In 1302 Roger le Bygod, Earl of Norfolk, surrendered his earldom to Edward I. In 1312 Edward II. granted this earldom to Thomas de Brotherton and the heirs of his body. Brotherton was frequently summoned to Parliament and took his seat. Lord Mowbray claimed as heir to Brotherton the earldom, which had fallen into abeyance. The committee held that Bygod's surrender was invalid and that, therefore, the grant to Brotherton was also invalid, that sitting in Parliament under the King's writ could not create an earldom, and that the claimant had not made out his claim. (The legality of this decision appears to rest on the report on the Dignity of a Peer (3rd Report, vol. 2, pp. 25, 46)).

Restrictions on the Crown's right to create peers:—

(1) The King cannot create a man a peer of Scotland, as the Act of Union does not provide for this contingency.

(2) By the Act of Union with Ireland, 1800 (39 & 40 Geo. III. c. 67, s. 4) one new Irish peer may be created for every three becoming extinct until the number of such peers falls to one hundred, and in order to keep up the number of peers who do not hold hereditary peerages of the United Kingdom up to one

hundred, the King may create fresh peers up to that number if he chooses to do so.

(3) The King is restricted as to the creation of lords spiritual, as follows :—

Only twenty-six prelates are allowed to sit in the Lords. The two Archbishops and the Bishops of London, Durham, and Winchester are immediately on appointment Lords of Parliament, but other bishops have to wait their turn, according to date of appointment, before they become entitled to a writ of summons. Most of the statutes founding new bishoprics contain provisions that the number of lords spiritual shall not be increased.

Before the disestablishment of the Irish Church in 1869 one archbishop and three Irish bishops had seats in the Lords by virtue of the Act of Union, but the Irish Church Act, 1869 (41 & 42 Vict. c. 68, s. 5), abolished the right of these prelates to be summoned.

(4) It has now been universally held that the King cannot grant a peerage which descends in a manner unknown to the law, but there was a time when a contrary view prevailed. In the *Devon Case* it was held that the grant of honours is not regulated by the same laws as the grant of land, and, therefore, where the Crown granted a peerage to a certain man *et hæredibus suis masculis in perpetuum*, and the grantee died without issue, the title was held to descend to the male heir of a collateral branch of the family. The Lord Chancellor remarked that the Crown was the fountain of honour and that such fountain was inexhaustible. He also quoted as a precedent the case of Lord Scrope in the twenty-first year of the reign of Richard II.

The Lord Chancellor also remarked that in the third year of Charles I. a peerage granted to a man *et hæredibus suis tam de latere quam de corpore*, was held good, though that was a limitation which would clearly include collaterals.

In the *Wiltes Case* ((1862), 4 House of Lords, p. 126), however, it was held that a grant of a peerage to a man and his heirs male was bad because "the Crown cannot give to the grant of a dignity or honour a quality of descent unknown to the law." These two cases contradict one another, but the *Buckhurst Case* ((1876), 2 App. Cas. 1) may be considered as settling finally the law on the subject. In this case Lord Cairns stated that "a peerage partaking of the qualities of real estate must be made in its limitations by the Crown, so far as it is descendible, descendible in a course known to the law" (*vide* Palmer, p. 91).

(5) The King cannot at common law create life peers.—There are two points as to the King's power to consider: (1) Can the King make any man or any woman a peer for life? (2) Can the King by making any man a peer for life confer on that man a right to sit and vote in the House of Lords? As to the first point, Lord Coke says, in his Commentary on Littleton, that the King can make any man or any woman a peer for life. Blackstone says: "The King may create either men or women noble for life." Selden agrees with Lord Coke, and so does Comyn.

In the *Abergavenny Case* the opinion of Lord Coke was endorsed. The question of the King's ability to create life peers was raised in the *Wensleydale Case* ((1856), 5 H. L. C., p. 958), where it was held that, though the Queen might have power by virtue of her prerogative to make any man or woman a peer or peeress for life, yet such grant could not confer on the grantee a right to sit and vote in the House of Lords.

In the course of the proceedings the Barony of Hay was mentioned, where, though the right of the Crown to confer on Lord Hay a title of honour was clearly admitted, yet the patent distinctly excluded him from sitting and voting in the Lords (*ibid.*, p. 963). During the proceedings Lord Campbell stated that the House had a right of its own authority to enquire into a new patent, though it might have no power to examine into the claim of an old peerage except upon reference from the Crown. This *dictum* may be considered sufficient to settle the question that the King by his prerogative can refer old peerage claims to any tribunal he chooses, and of this the FitzWalter peerage forms an instance. But, conventionally speaking, the King is bound to refer these cases to the House of Lords, who, in their turn, depute a Committee of Privileges to enquire into the matter and report to them.

It is noteworthy fact that the *FitzWalter Case* was originally referred to the Lords, where it was actually heard, though no resolution was passed. It was subsequently referred by the King to the Privy Council owing to the prorogation of Parliament (Cruise, p. 117).

Peerages are classified as to date of creation as follows : Peers whose peerages were created before the Union with Scotland in 1707 are peers of England. Peers whose peerages were created between 1707 and 1801 are peers of Great Britain, whilst those whose peerages were created after 1801 (Union with Ireland) are peers of the United Kingdom (Ilbert on Parliament, p. 198).

Classes of peers.—These classes are : (1) Temporal hereditary peers of England holding English peerages. (2) Spiritual English peers. (3) Sixteen Scotch elected peers. (4) Twenty-eight Irish life elected peers. (5) Lords of appeal in ordinary.

Peers of realm not necessarily lords of Parliament.—A person can hold a peerage without being a lord of Parliament, *e.g.*, an unelected Scotch or Irish peer, or a peeress in her own right. Many Scotch and Irish peers also hold what are popularly called English peerages.

Again, an infant or a bankrupt peer cannot sit in Parliament.

Various lords of Parliament.—Of lords of Parliament some hold during tenure of office, others for life, and others again are hereditary peers. A bishop on retirement loses his seat, but a lord of appeal retains his seat during his life.

If a lord of appeal retires, he remains a lord of Parliament (50 & 51 Vict. c. 70, s. 2).

Grades of peers.—There are various grades of peers, viz., dukes, marquises, earls, viscounts and barons.

Dukes.—The word "duke" comes from the latin *dux* (general). As the first Norman kings were dukes of Normandy, they did not relish making a subject a duke. Edward III. gave the first dukedom to his son, the Black Prince, and till the time of James I. all dukes were kings' descendants. In the days of Elizabeth there were no dukes, but her successor made one,

Villiers Duke of Buckingham, and this man was the first duke not of royal blood. A dukedom is the first grade of nobility, but at functions dukes take a lower precedence than certain high dignitaries who hold office (Stephen, vol. 2, p. 578 (14th ed.)).

Marquises.—Like the word "duke," the word "marquis" betokened an office-holder, the special function of a marquis being to guard the Scotch and Welsh marches, or frontiers. The term now is a pure title of honour, and has been so since Richard II.'s time, when one Vere was created Marquis of Dublin (see Stephen's Commentaries, vol. 2, p. 579).

Earl (ealdorman).—The earl was formerly head of a shire. In Norman times the title was changed to "comes" or count, but the ancient title was afterwards reverted to. An earl's wife, however, is still styled a countess (May, 11th ed., pp. 8, 9).

Earls used to be invested, a belt being buckled round the waist, and then a sword was attached to the belt. Hence the expression "belted earl."

Viscount.—The word "viscount" comes from the "vice-comes," or sheriff, who presided at the county court when the bishop and ealdorman ceased to attend.

Barons.—This is the lowest grade. For these, see *ante*, p. 219.

Peeresses.—When a peeress in her own right contracts a marriage with a commoner she retains her title and dignity, but a peeress by marriage on afterwards marrying a commoner loses her rank, which is both gained and lost by marriage (Stephen's Commentaries, vol. 2, p. 585), but by courtesy she usually retains her title (*i*).

A peeress of higher degree by intermarriage with a peer of a lower grade does not lose her title, but she loses precedence; thus, where a dowager-duchess became Lady Portmore by a

(*i*) Where there are two co-heiresses entitled to a peerage, the King chooses which is to have the title.

second marriage she was refused precedence as a duchess at George III.'s coronation (Stephen, vol. 2, p. 640, 11th ed.) (*k*).

Scotch peers.—Sixteen Scottish peers, who are not peers of the United Kingdom, are elected to each Parliament. The royal proclamation which directs the election bids the Scottish peers assemble at Holyrood to choose their representatives. The Lord Clerk Register presides, and when the election is over forwards the list of elected peers to the Clerk of the Crown in Chancery. See the procedure at the election fully described in Anson, vol. 1, p. 219.

As the Act of Union does not provide for the creation of fresh Scotch peers, the Crown cannot make a man a Scotch peer, though it may nullify an attainder, and thus perhaps purify corrupted blood.

When a Scotch peer is created an English peer, such Scotch peer loses his electing power as a Scotch peer (*vide* Resolution of Lords in 1787), but no vacancy is created (May, 11th ed., p. 11).

Irish peers.—As to creation of Irish peers, see *ante*, p. 226.

When one of the twenty-eight Irish peers, who are elected for life, dies, the Lord Chancellor despatches to the Irish Lord Chancellor a mandate directing the preparation and subsequent issue of voting papers. The Irish Clerk of the Crown gets ready these voting papers and transmits them in duplicate to each Irish peer entitled to vote. During the thirty days of the poll the Irish peers take the oath of allegiance and transmit the necessary documents to the Irish Crown Office. The peer with the largest number of votes is elected, and where the votes are equal a lot is cast, the name drawn by the Clerk of Parliaments coming out the winner of the election.

Lords of appeal in ordinary.—These lords are selected under the Appellate Jurisdiction Act, 1876. They act as permanent judges in the House of Lords in its appellate capacity.

(*k*) Until the *Willoughby Case*, a man who married a peeress in her own right had a seat in the House of Lords for life by the curtesy (Collins, p. 11)

They receive £6,000 per annum whilst they act as judges. Like other judges, they are removable on an address from both Houses, but they retain their title for life. The qualification for the post is (1) fifteen years' standing as a barrister in England, Ireland, or Scotland; (2) having held high judicial office for two years.

All lords may be present at judicial appeals, but no appeal shall be heard unless there be a quorum containing three at least of the following persons :—

(1) Lord Chancellor.

(2) Lords of appeal in ordinary.

(3) Peers of Parliament who hold or have held high judicial office (Appellate Jurisdiction Act, 1876, s. 5).

The lords can hear appeals during a prorogation and even after dissolution of Parliament (Yearly Practice Notes to Appellate Jurisdiction Act, 1876).

In cases of difficulty the lords may at common law invoke the assistance of King's Bench Division judges (Yearly Practice, p. 1757).

By convention lay peers do not sit to hear judicial appeals (Stephen, vol. 3, 14th ed., p. 380; Yearly Practice, p. 1757).

CHAPTER XXXI.

PRIVILEGES OF THE LORDS.

Judicial privileges.—The privileges and powers of the Lords are either judicial or extra-judicial. The judicial privileges are—

1. Right to act as court of final appeal from the superior courts of law in the three kingdoms.

2. Right to try, as court of first instance, peers and peeresses (including Irish and Scotch peers and peeresses) for treason or felony, and, conversely, the right of a peer or peeress to be so tried (May, ed. 11, pp. 667 *et seq.*).

These rights have belonged to peers from time immemorial, but the first instance of a peeress being so tried occurred *temp.* Henry VI. Whilst Parliament is sitting the accused is tried before the peers, a functionary called the Lord High Steward, who is almost universally the Lord Chancellor, acting as chairman. When Parliament is not sitting the Lord High Steward acts as judge and certain other lords as jurymen (Stephen, Digest of Criminal Law, Art. 17).

Though all the lords can demand to attend, spiritual peers do not vote for guilt or innocence, as they must retire after protesting before the delivering of the verdict. A peeress who has intermarried with a commoner loses the privilege of being thus tried, and a bishop does not possess the privilege though (whilst in office) he is a lord of Parliament. Bishops may vote in a non-capital case (Stephen, Digest of Criminal Law, Art. 131).

3. The right to try impeachments by the Commons (May, ed. 11, c. 24).

4. The right to try disputed peerage claims. This last is a semi-judicial privilege only, as lay peers may take part in the proceedings and no quorum of legal peers is necessary. The Attorney-General, however, is usually at the trial to give legal assistance when needed, and there is also almost always, if not always, a law lord or two to help.

A claimant to a peerage first addresses his petition to the Crown. The Crown, on the report of the Attorney-General, refers the matter to the House of Lords, who, in turn, refers it to its Committee of Privileges (Palmer's Peerage Law, p. 9).

The Lords have also a statutory right to hear criminal appeals when the Attorney-General certifies that the case is a proper one for an appeal (Criminal Appeal Act, 1907).

Extra-judicial privileges.—These are as follows :—

1. Freedom of speech (May, ed. 11, p. 96).

2. Freedom from arrest (May, ed. 11, p. 103).

This includes civil arrest only. The privilege commences forty days before Parliament sits, and lasts during session and forty days thereafter.

The servant of a peer of Parliament has a similar privilege, but the number of days is twenty and not forty (May, ed. 11, p. 111).

3. The right of each peer to demand audience of his Sovereign in order to tender him advice (May, ed. 11, p. 61).

4. The right of each peer of Parliament to record a written protest in the journals of the Upper House against a measure disapproved of.

5. The right of each peer to decline to attend in court as a witness on a subpœna. This right is not supposed to be taken advantage of (Anson, vol. 1, p. 226; May. ed. 11, p. 111) (*m*).

6. Right of each peer to vote by proxy. This right has been waived since 1868, according to Sir W. Anson.

7. Exemption from service as a juryman (see Jury Act, 1870) (*n*).

8. Peers temporal and spiritual *en route* to or from Parliament when passing through a royal forest may kill one of the royal deer without warrant in view of the ranger if present, or on blowing a horn if he be not present, that the peer may not seem to take the royal venison by stealth (Stephen's Com., vol. 2, p. 376, 14th ed.).

(*m*) Where a peer attends Court as a witness, he is sworn like anybody else (*in judicio non creditur nisi juratis*).

(*n*) A juryman who is a peer can have his position challenged by prisoner *propter honoris respectum*."

9. The right of the Lords to commit for breach of privilege and for contempt. The Lords may commit for a period of fixed duration, but where they do not fix a time, the person committed is released when Parliament is either prorogued or dissolved (May, 11th ed., p. 63).

In the case of Lord Shaftesbury the facts were as follows: Lord Shaftesbury with two other lords were committed by the Upper House for contempts. They applied for release under a writ of *habeas corpus*. The return stated that the prisoners were committed for high contempts, and, no other reason being given, it was contended that the return was insufficient. The King's Bench held that had the case been one of the ordinary kind the return would have been insufficient, but that it could not interfere with a court like that of the Lords.

The prisoners remained in custody, and the following session the Lords voted that the application to the King's Bench was a breach of privilege. Lord Shaftesbury was called on to apologise to their lordships, and, on his doing so, was released.

Judicial notice.—The courts take judicial notice of the privileges of the two Houses of Parliament (Taylor on Evidence, § 5).

Of persons who cannot sit in the Lords.—The following persons cannot sit, viz.:—(1) Peeresses in their own right; (2) infants; (3) felons who have not endured their punishment or been pardoned; (4) outlaws; (5) persons who will not take oath or affirmation of allegiance; (6) misdemeanants during incarceration; (7) bankrupts. No bankrupt can sit or vote in the Lords, or on any committee thereof, neither can he be a Scotch representative peer or an Irish life elected peer, unless the adjudication is annulled or the peer be discharged with a certificate that the bankruptcy was caused by misfortune and not misconduct.

CHAPTER XXXII.

THE LORDS AND COMMONS IN CONFLICT.

There was no serious conflict between the Lords and the Commons till 1407 A.D. In this year the Lords voted a subsidy to the Crown, and Henry IV. requested the Commons to send a deputation to the Lords "to hear and report to their fellows what they should have in command from the King to the end that they might take the shortest course to comply with the intention of the said Lords" (Langmead, p. 249). The Commons resented this conduct to such an extent that a rule was made that no report be sent to the King until the money had been voted in both Houses.

In *Floyd's Case* (1621 A.D.) the Commons tried to exercise criminal jurisdiction outside the scope of their privileges, but surrendered their rights at the request of the Lords. The Lower House had, in the reign of Henry IV., resolved that they had no right to exercise criminal jurisdiction. In 1640 the Commons, led by Pym and Hampden, were desirous that redress of grievances should precede supply, and a committee was appointed to wait on the Lords with a list of grievances. Charles I. wanted the supply in a hurry, and called on the Lords to assist him; the Lords then resolved that supply should precede redress of grievances. The Commons resolved that this was a breach of their privileges as to money votes. In *Skinner's Case* there was a serious controversy as to the claim of the Lords to exercise original jurisdiction in civil cases. The dispute lasted a year and a quarter. For further information see Langmead, 7th ed., p. 585.

In 1671 the Commons successfully resisted the claim of the Lords to reduce a tax. In the case of *Shirley* v. *Fagg* the Lords successfully upheld their claim to hear equity appeals (Langmead, p. 490).

In 1678 the Lower House passed a resolution that all money bills must commence in the Commons and that the Lords had no right to alter or amend them. The Lords yielded in this particular instance, but resolved that the right should be reserved to them in future. In the second year of Queen Anne's reign (1704) the Lords and Commons had a very serious dispute over the case of *Ashby* v. *White and the Aylesbury men*, and the only way out of the difficulty was a prorogation which set free prisoners arrested for contempt.

In 1832 there was a severe controversy over the Reform Bill. The Commons prevailed against the Lords, William IV., much against his inclination, supporting Lord Grey by threatening to use the prerogative right of creating sufficient peers to carry the measure.

In 1860 the Lords exercised their undoubted legal right of rejecting money bills by throwing out a measure for the repeal of the paper duty.

On the motion of Lord Palmerston three resolutions to the following effect were carried in the Commons as to this matter. (1) That the right of granting aids and supplies is in the Commons alone. (2) That, although the Lords could reject money bills, yet the exercise of that power was regarded by the House with peculiar jealousy. (3) That the Commons had the power to impose and remit taxation and to frame bills of supply, and that the right of the Commons as to the matters, manners, measure and time should be maintained inviolate. In the following year, Gladstone being then Chancellor of the Exchequer, the opposition of the Peers was overridden by the insertion of the provision regarding paper duties in a general financial measure for the services of the year. In 1869 the Irish Church Disestablishment Bill was violently opposed by the Lords, but the difficulty was surmounted by Lord Cairns's influence and the clearly expressed wishes of the electorate.

There was considerable friction between the two Houses when the Lords rejected the Representation of the People Bill in 1884.

In this case Queen Victoria stepped into the arena of party politics and acted as mediator between the disputants. Lord Salisbury on the one hand, and Mr. Gladstone on the other, by their temperate conduct and their readiness to make mutual concessions were instrumental in securing the passage of a measure which harmonised with popular opinion.

There was another memorable dispute over the rejection of the Army Purchase Bill in 1872. In this case the Commons carried their point by the cancellation of a royal warrant authorising purchase, and thus gained their object in the following session without a direct conflict with the Lords.

The next dispute was over Mr. Gladstone's first Home Rule Bill, but as the Lords were in this case supported by the electorate at a general election their position was for the time being maintained.

It was doubtless this event which encouraged Lord Lansdowne to state, as he did in 1906, that it was the duty of the Upper House to reject a measure when there was good reason for supposing that it was unpopular with the electorate or where such measure was carried in the Commons hastily or without sufficient consideration.

In 1905-6 the Liberals returned to power with a gigantic majority, only to find that their principal measures continued to be rejected by the Upper House. In 1907 the Commons passed resolutions to the effect that the veto of the Lords should be curtailed. These resolutions, which indicated the nature and extent of the curtailment desired, afterwards became the basis of the Parliament Act, 1911. In 1908-9 Liberal measures—and notably the Licensing Bill—were again thrown out by the Lords. The climax was reached when the Budget for 1909 was rejected *in toto*. At two general elections in 1910, in both of which the veto was the principal issue, the Liberals were returned with reduced, but still substantial, majorities. After an abortive conference at Buckingham Palace between the leaders of the Government and the Opposition, and in the face of passionate protest and recrimination, the Parliament Act was passed in 1911, the Lords reluctantly yielding after being informed that the King had consented to the creation of a sufficient number of peers to carry the measure over their heads.

In effect, the Parliament Act wholly abolished the Lords' veto over money bills, and substituted for their absolute veto over other legislation a suspensive veto of two years. It further reduced the duration of Parliaments from seven to five years.

The words of the Act are to the following effect : After reciting (*inter alia*) that it was intended to substitute for the House of

Lords, as it then existed, a second chamber constituted on a popular instead of an hereditary basis, it was provided :—

(1) That if a money bill having been framed by the Commons and sent to the Lords at least one month before the end of the session is not passed by the Lords without amendment within one month after it has been sent up, the bill, unless the Commons direct to the contrary, shall be presented to the King and become a statute on receipt of the royal assent without consent of the Lords.

(2) A money bill means a public bill which, in the opinion of the Speaker of the House of Commons, contains only provisions dealing with the following topics :—

(a) Imposition, repeal, remission, alteration, or regulation of taxation.

(b) Imposition for any financial purposes of charges on the Consolidated Fund, or on money provided by Parliament, or the variation of such charges.

(c) Supply.

(d) The appropriation, receipt, custody, issue or audit of accounts of public money.

(e) The raising or guarantee of any loan or the repayment thereof.

(f) Subordinate matters incidental to the above topics or any of them.

Bills as to rates and other local burdens, corporation loans, etc., are not to be regarded as money bills.

(3) There shall be endorsed on money bills when sent up to the Lords, and when presented to the King for assent, the Speaker's certificate signed by him that a given bill is a money bill, and before so certifying the Speaker is to consult, if practicable, two members to be appointed from the Chairman's panel at the beginning of the session by the Committee of Selection.

(4) If any public bill other than a money bill, or bill containing any provision to extend the duration of Parliament beyond five years, is passed by the Commons in three successive sessions, whether of the same Parliament or not, and having been sent to the Lords at least one month before the end of the session, is rejected by the Lords in each of these sessions, such bill shall, on the third rejection by the Lords, unless the Commons direct to

the contrary, be presented to the King for the royal assent without further consent of the Lords. But the foregoing provision is not to be effectual unless two years have elapsed from the date of second reading in the first of the sessions and the date of its passing the Commons in the third session.

(5) When a bill is presented to the King for assent, the signed certificate of the Speaker that the requirements of the Act have been complied with shall be endorsed thereon.

(6) A bill shall be deemed rejected by the Lords unless passed by them without amendment or with amendments agreed on by both Houses.

(7) A bill shall be deemed identical with a former bill if, when sent to the Lords, it is identical with the former bill, or contains only such alterations as are certified by the Speaker to be necessary owing to lapse of time since the former bill or to represent amendments made by the Lords in the former bill in the preceding session and agreed to by the Commons.

The Commons may, if they choose, in the second or third session suggest further amendments without inserting them in the bill, and such amendments, if agreed to by the Lords, shall be treated as amendments agreed on in both Houses.

But exercise of this power by the Commons shall not affect the operation of this section in the event of rejection of the bill by the Lords.

The Speaker's certificate shall not be questioned in any law court.

When the bill is sent up for the royal assent without the consent of the Lords the enacting formula is as follows :—

Be it enacted by the King's most excellent Majesty, by and with the advice and consent of the Commons in this present Parliament assembled in accordance with the provisions of the Parliament Act, 1911, and by authority of the same, as follows, etc.

CHAPTER XXXIII.

PRIVILEGES OF COMMONS—CONFLICT BETWEEN COMMONS AND LAW COURTS.

Of the nature of privilege.—The following is a well-known conundrum set by university examiners, viz. :—" Privilege is to Parliament what prerogative is to the Crown." This expression means that just as prerogative denotes the common law powers which the Sovereign can exercise without infringing a statute or coming into conflict with the judicial bench, so privilege denotes that power which either the Lords or the Commons can exercise unfettered by statute law or the judiciary.

It is a well-known rule that within the orbit of it either House of Parliament is supreme and that no appeal lies from its decisions.

Classification of privileges.—These privileges are divided by Sir W. Anson into two classes :—(1) those claimed by the Speaker at the opening of a new Parliament (2) those not so claimed.

The fact of a privilege being claimed by the Speaker carries with it no superior force, for all privileges are of equal validity. The privileges claimed by the Speaker are :—(1) Freedom of speech; (2) freedom from arrest; (3) access of Commons to Crown through the Speaker; (4) that the Crown will place the most favourable interpretation on the deliberations of the Commons (May, 11th ed., p. 59). The privileges not claimed by the Speaker are :—

1. Right of Lower House to regulate its own constitution (Anson, vol. 1, 4th ed., p. 162). This includes the right to settle disputed elections, and to pronounce on the legality of an election and on the legality of qualifications for membership. It includes also the right to suspend and expel members (Anson, vol. 1, 4th ed., p. 178; cf. May, 11th ed., p. 52).

2. Right to take exclusive cognizance of what transpires within its own walls (Anson, vol. 1, 4th ed., p. 174; *Bradlaugh* v. *Gossett*, *post*, 12 Q. B. D., p. 281).

3. Right to punish members and outsiders for contempt as any other court of record can (May, 11th ed., p. 83; Anson, vol. 1, 4th ed., p. 147).

4. Right of impeachment, see p. 223, and May, 11th ed., c. 24.

5. Right to control finance and initiate financial legislation, see Ch. XXXV.).

Freedom of speech.—Freedom of speech was first demanded by the Speaker in 1541 (Anson, vol. 1; cf. May, 11th ed., p. 96).

Freedom of speech, says Mr. Taswell-Langmead, is the essential attribute of every free legislature, and may be regarded as inherent in the constitution of Parliament. Quoting Elsynge, the learned writer continues :—" The Commons under Edward III. debated amongst themselves many things concerning the King's prerogative, and agreed upon petitions for laws to be made directly against his prerogative, as may appear by divers of the said petitions, yet they were never interrupted in their consultations nor received check for the same " (Langmead, Const. Hist., p. 268, ed. 5).

The proceedings against Haxey for treason when he introduced a bill for the curtailment of Richard II.'s household expenses were the cause of Henry IV.'s recognition of the right to parliamentary freedom of speech. Henry IV. said " It was his wish that the Commons treat of all matters amongst themselves in order to bring them to the best conclusion . . and that he would hear no person before such matters were brought before him by the consent of the Commons " (Langmead, Const. Hist., p. 269).

In Henry VI.'s reign one Yonge was imprisoned for moving that the Duke of York be declared heir-apparent. Yonge was afterwards released and his conduct condoned (Langmead, p. 269).

In Henry VIII.'s reign one Strode was imprisoned at the instance of the Stannaries Courts for introducing bills to regulate those courts. After the expiration of three weeks he was released by writ of privilege, and Strode's Act was passed, which provided "that all suits, accusements, executions, . . . punishments, &c., against all persons of that particular or any other Parliament . . . for any Bill, or speaking . . . of any matter concerning the Parliament be of none effect" (Langmead, p. 269).

In Elizabeth's reign members were punished by the Crown for words used in Parliament, and members were warned in Parliament not to be free with their language.

In 1629, Elliot, Hollis and Valentine were imprisoned for injudicious language in Parliament. The court held that Strode's Act was not a public Act, and the Commons resolved that it was. These proceedings were reversed in Charles II.'s reign (Anson, vol. 1, p. 159; May, 11th ed., p. 99; Fielden, p. 108).

In the reign of George III., General Conway lost his command for statements and conduct in Parliament, and similar oppressions are attributed to Walpole (Fielden, p. 109; Anson, vol. 1, p. 150; 3rd ed. of Macaulay's Essay on Lord Chatham).

Finally, what is said within the walls of Parliament cannot form the subject-matter of an action for defamation, but where a member gets inserted in a newspaper the contents of a defamatory speech, he can be proceeded against for libel (*R.* v. *Creevy*, 1 M. & S. 273; distinguished *Wason* v. *Walter* (1868), L. R. 4 Q. B. 75).

Punishment by the House itself for parliamentary misbehaviour.—The House of Commons punishes improper conduct of all kinds in Parliament. "No member may allude to any debate of the same session, or any debate in the other House, neither may he use the King's name in an irreverent manner nor for the purpose of influencing the House, nor may he refer to any other member by name." "He must not speak insultingly of either House, or any member of either House." It is the Speaker's duty to preserve order, and his ruling must be obeyed by members. He, or (in committee) the Chairman of Ways and Means, or the Deputy-Chairman, can stop speeches either on the ground of improper language or tediousness (Const. Year Book; May, chap. 12, 11th ed.).

Closure.—This is a device for extinguishing a debate or speech at once. A member moves that the question be now put, and if the Speaker or Chairman accepts the motion, and it is carried, not less than 100 members voting in its support, further debate on the subject must cease.

The Speaker has a duty cast on him of stopping the motion for closure where he considers that the rights of the minority have been infringed, or the motion operates as an abuse of the rules of the House (Ilbert's Manual of Procedure, pp. 113, 271).

The guillotine.—This is a device for curtailing the length of a debate, a definite period being set apart for stages of a bill, and for speeches thereon.

"The Kangaroo."—During the debate on a bill in a committee of the whole House the chairman may choose the amendments for discussion. The same power is vested in the Speaker or other occupant of the chair at the report stage.

Suspension.—Where a member disobeys the Speaker or the chairman or deputy-chairman in committee, is guilty of obstruction, or behaves objectionally, the Speaker or chairman may be asked to name him. The question of suspension is then put, and if carried he can be expelled for as long as the rest of the session (*o*).

Right to exclude strangers.—This may be regarded either as a deduction from the principle of freedom of speech, or as necessary for the orderly conduct of business, where there is a danger of disorderly interruption.

Formerly any commoner could object to strangers being present, but now he must direct the Speaker's attention to the fact, and the question of turning out such strangers is deter-

(*o*) For further information on this subject and procedure generally, see Ilbert's Manual of Procedure.

mined by vote. The Speaker also has the power of ordering strangers to withdraw (Ilbert, p. 219).

Right to restrain publication of debates.—This is another deduction from the privilege of freedom of speech. Mr. Langmead says that members formerly desired secrecy of debate to protect themselves from the Crown, and that they subsequently desired it to protect themselves from their constituents. Mr. Langmead quotes Pulteney, who in 1738 said that "to print or publish the speeches of gentlemen in this House looks like making them accountable without doors for what they said within" (Langmead, p. 582).

In 1771 matters reached a crisis owing to action taken by Colonel Onslow. Certain printers of debates were summoned to the bar of the Commons, and one of them named Miller, who refused to attend, was arrested in the City. Miller gave the messenger of the House into custody for assault. The case was heard by the Lord Mayor, Alderman John Wilkes and Alderman Oliver, who released Miller and committed the arresting messenger. The Lord Mayor and the two aldermen were committed by the House to the Tower, but such a commotion ensued that publication of debates has not been since interfered with (Langmead, pp. 584, 585).

For some time after this reporters were beset with difficulties. They could not get seats, or take notes, and the presence of strangers was often objected to (Langmead, p. 585). The year 1834 was marked by the provision of reporters' galleries, but publication of division lists was not permitted till 1836 (Langmead, p. 585).

The year 1835 witnessed the publication and sale of parliamentary reports and papers at a cheap rate.

In *Wason* v. *Walter* ((1868), L. R. 4 Q. B. 73) it was held that true and faithful reports of parliamentary debates could not form the groundwork of an action for libel.

Freedom from arrest.—Mr. Langmead says that by a law of the Saxon Ethelbert it was provided that if the King call his people to him, and if anyone do them evil, let him pay a bot (compensation) and 50*s*. to the King.

The privilege commenced forty days before Parliament sat, and lasted during session and forty days thereafter. It formerly extended to the goods of members and their servants.

In Edward I.'s reign the Master of the Temple petitioned the King to distrain on the goods of his tenant, the Bishop of St. David's. The King refused the request on the ground of the above privilege *re* the goods of members of his council (May, 11th ed., p. 104).

In the case of the Prior of Malton, who was arrested *en route* to Parliament, the privilege was again acknowledged (Langmead, p. 259; May, 11th ed., p. 105).

In the reign of Henry VI. an Act declaratory of the common law was passed, which awarded double damages in the event of the assault of persons *en route* to Parliament (Langmead, p. 259).

In the same reign Speaker Thorpe, a Lancastrian and a judge, was arrested for seizure, in a judicial capacity, of certain property of the Duke of York. The Commons demanded Thorpe's release and the point was referred to the judges, who, though favourable to a release, did not act on their opinion, with the result that Thorpe was detained in prison (Langmead, p. 260; May, 11th ed., p. 106).

Mr. Langmead says that prior to 1541 members were released by special statute or writ of privilege, but that in 1541, in the case of Ferrers, the Commons demanded release on their own account, and committed the sheriff for contempt (Langmead, p. 262). They continued after this the practice of demanding release of their members (cf. May, 11th ed., p. 105).

In 1575 Smalley, a member's servant, was arrested for debt, and afterwards freed by order of the House of Commons. As the arrest was a collusive one, in order to get rid of a debt, Smalley was sent to gaol for a month and ordered to pay the creditor £100 (Langmead, p. 275, 5th ed.; May, chap. 5).

In 1603 Shirley was imprisoned for debt in the Fleet. On the Commons demanding release the same was refused by the warden on the ground that he would be liable to an action for escape at the instance of the execution creditor. The King procured Shirley's release, but 1 James I. c. 13, was passed, providing: (1) that a prison governor releasing a member of

Parliament was to be free from liability to an action, and (2) that the creditor after the expiration of the privilege be at liberty to re-arrest (Langmead, p. 263).

The statute also recognized the right of the House to set at liberty members of Parliament when arrested, the privilege of freedom of speech, and the right to punish persons procuring the arrest of members of Parliament during time of privilege (Langmead, p. 263; May, 11th ed., p. 107).

The privileges as to the persons of members and servants and the goods of members were put an end to by the combined effect of 12 & 13 Will. III. c. 3, 2 & 3 Anne, c. 18, 11 Geo. II. c. 24, and 10 Geo. III. c. 50, and only the actual persons of members were exempted from civil arrest (Langmead, p. 263; May, 11th ed., p. 108).

The privilege of freedom from arrest has never extended to cases of treason, felony, and breach of the peace, neither does it now extend to cases of contempt of court. In 1839 Mr. Long Wellesley was imprisoned by the Chancery Court for taking one of its wards without the jurisdiction.

A Mr. Charlton was also arrested for contempt, and in 1873 Mr. Whalley and Mr. Guildford Onslow were arrested in a similar way, *re* the great *Tichborne Case* (Langmead, p. 264).

When a member of Parliament commits a crime he is arrested just like anyone else, and if convicted the judge notifies the Speaker. The papers are then laid before the House at their request, and the question of expulsion is considered.

Mr. Alcock, who became insane during his membership, brought about an Act which provided that persons who have received a lunatic member into an asylum must notify the Speaker at once. A report as to mental condition is then asked for, and a further report at the end of six months. If by that time there is no immediate prospect of recovery the seat may be declared vacant (see the Lunacy (Vacation of Seats) Act, 1886 (49 & 50 Vict. c. 16), and Anson, vol. 1, p. 77).

Right of House to regulate its own constitution.—This privilege, as before stated, embraces the minor privilege as to control of elections.

Since *Goodwin's Case*, in the reign of James I., the Crown

has never directly interfered with parliamentary elections. Indirect interference was in vogue till 1832, at any rate. Corruption was, moreover, pretty general till the Ballot Act, 1872. The Corrupt and Illegal Practices Acts contributed greatly to its abolition. By the Parliamentary Elections Act, 1868 (as subsequently amended), the trial of cases of disputed elections was handed over to the judges, and two judges from the rota of election judges now decide these cases. The statute leaves nominally intact the ancient privilege of the Commons, who, as a matter of fact, carry out the judicial views. It enables defeated candidates and persons entitled to vote to present a petition to the King's Bench Division for the election to be declared void, and lays down rules of procedure. As regards England and Ireland, the petition must be presented within twenty-one days after the proper returning officer has made his return to the writ, and £1,000 must be paid into court or secured to meet respondents' costs should they succeed. The election may be declared void where corrupt and illegal practices have been traced to the candidate or his agents, and also in cases where corruption has been sufficiently prevalent to constitute the election unfair. The judges have power to waive irregularities where there has been no actual miscarriage of justice, and have, moreover, ample discretion as to costs.

In Scotland election petitions are tried before a judge of the Court of Session, and certain modifications of procedure are made by section 58 of the Act of 1868.

The following cases decide important points as to parliamentary elections :—

Ashby v. *White.*—One Ashby, a voter of Aylesbury, was refused a vote by the returning officer. On proceedings being taken judgment was recovered on the principle of *ubi jus ibi remedium.* No damage was sustained, as the candidate for whom Ashby would have voted was elected.

Mr. Langmead tells us that on motion in arrest of judgment it was held (Holt, C.J., dissentiente) that no action lay, but the Lords on appeal decided otherwise. This resulted in the Commons passing a resolution that this constituted an infringement of their privilege (*Ashby* v. *White* (2 Anne), 1 S. L. C., p. 240).

Case of the Aylesbury Men.—After this case, five Aylesbury voters brought actions on similar lines to Ashby's, and for their pains were sent by the Commons to prison for contempt. Writs of *habeas corpus* were unsuccessfully applied for. On appeal to the Lords upon writ of error the men nearly gained their liberty, but Queen Anne, on being petitioned about the privilege by the Commons, got rid of all difficulties by proroguing Parliament, thus setting the captives at liberty. This right of the Commons to decide contested elections was, according to Mr. Langmead, prostituted to party purposes, the abuse culminating during the reigns of George II. and George III. Grenville tried to put matters on a right basis by an Act whereby a sworn committee of thirteen persons selected by the House and petitioner was appointed to decide these cases, but the House, which resented the imputation of bias cast upon it at times, finally agreed to the passing of the Parliamentary Elections Act, 1868.

Barnardiston v. *Soame.*—In this case a returning officer was sued for making a double return for one vacancy. Plaintiff won, but the verdict was upset, and afterwards the making of a double return was, in theory, deemed illegal; a custom arose of the Commons allowing them in difficult cases.

By 7 & 8 Will. III, c. 7, s. 3, returning officers *falsely* making double returns are exposed to the penalties specified therein.

This Act disposes of all contentions as to double returns being illegal, and it is now fully recognized that a returning officer, when the voting is equal, has a casting vote, but that he need not exercise the option, but may return two or more members for one vacancy instead. Though the House has practically transferred to the law courts judicial cognizance of disputed election cases, it may still, if it chooses, question the legality of any given election.

The House can also expel and refuse to admit persons whom they deem unworthy to be members of their assembly, and they do not concern themselves as to whether interested parties have moved in the matter or not.

Rossa was expelled in 1870, O'Donovan and Mitchell in 1875, and Davitt in 1882. In the matter of expulsion, a new Parliament is not affected by the conduct of a former one (Anson, vol. 1, p. 167; May, 11th ed., p. 657). When the Ilonse expels, it cannot prevent the re-election of the man who has been expelled.

Right to decide matters arising within the walls of the House.—The great case as to this is *Bradlaugh* v. *Gossett*, 12 Q. B. D. 271. The Serjeant-at-Arms, acting under orders, prevented the entrance of Bradlaugh to the House. Bradlaugh thereupon sued for a declaration that the order of the House for his exclusion should be pronounced invalid. The court decided against the plaintiff on the ground that the Commons could not be controlled by the law courts as to the decision of matters arising within the precincts of their House. Stephen, J., however, was of opinion that the line must be drawn somewhere, and that the Commons could not try, say, a murder which took place under its roof.

Right to punish members and outsiders for contempt.—In the case of *Gossett* v. *Howard*, where a person was arrested by the Serjeant-at-Arms for refusing to appear as a witness before the House, judgment to the following purport was pronounced by Baron Parke :—" The House, which forms the Grand Inquest of the nation, can compel attendance of witnesses, and in case of disobedience bring them in custody to them for examination; and secondly, if there be a charge of contempt and breach of privilege, and an order for the person charged to attend and answer, and then a wilful disobedience of that order, the House may cause offender to be brought in custody to answer the charge, and the House is the proper judge as to when these powers should be exercised " (*Gossett* v. *Howard*, 10 Q. B., p. 451).

In the *Case of the Sheriff of Middlesex* it was held that a parliamentary warrant of detention was not bad because of its omission to state the grounds of that detention (10 Adolphus & Ellis, p. 273).

Burdett v. *Abbott* ((1811), 4 Taunt. 401) was an action of trespass against an officer of the Commons for breaking into the plaintiff's house and carrying him to the Tower. The court held (1) that the power of either House to commit for contempt is reasonable and necessary and well established by precedents;

(2) that the execution of a process for contempt justified the breaking into the plaintiff's house.

Shaftesbury's Case shows the power of the Lords to commit for contempt, and *Burdett* v. *Abbott* shows that the Commons have a similar power. But there is this exception, that the Commons can only commit till the close of the session, whereas the Lords can commit for a definite period.

In the case of *Burdett* v. *Abbott* Lord Ellenborough said: "If a commitment appeared to be for contempt of the House of Commons generally, I would neither in the case of that court nor of any other of the superior courts enquire further; but if it did not profess to commit for contempt, *but for some matter appearing on the return* which could by no reasonable intendment be considered as a contempt of the court committing, but a ground of commitment palpably arbitrary, unjust, and contrary to every principle of natural justice, I say that in case of such a commitment we must look at it and act upon it as justice may require from whatever court it may profess to have proceeded."

Modes of punishment adopted by the Commons.—The modes of punishment are four, viz., admonition, reprimand, fine and imprisonment.

When an admonition is on the "*tapis*," the offender is asked to attend at the bar of the House, and lectured by the Speaker. In cases of reprimand he is brought by force to the bar and then reprimanded (cf. May, 11th ed., p. 93).

Fines are now obsolete, though an offender may be detained till he has paid House fees (cf. May, 11th ed., p. 93).

When a man is committed by order of the House, he is at times, but not necessarily, given an opportunity of apologizing. He may, however, be committed straight away, whichever course is pursued. He is, of course, set free at the end of the session, and if not set free could, of course, demand a *habeas corpus* (see Anson, vol. 1, 3rd ed.; May, p. 94).

Conflict between Parliament and law courts.—Of these conflicts the cases of *Ashby* v. *White* and the *Aylesbury Men* are memorable instances; but the leading decision on the subject is that of *Stockdale* v. *Hansard* (1839), 9 A. & E. 1. The House of Commons instructed Messrs. Hansard, the parliamentary printers, to publish copies of reports of certain inspectors of prisons. These reports were distributed to members and sold to the public. Stockdale, considering himself libelled by these reports, sued Messrs. Hansard and won, the court holding that it is no defence to a libel action that the defamatory matter was part of a document which was by order of the House laid before it, and thereupon became part of its proceedings, and which was afterwards by like order printed and published by defendant.

"This denial of parliamentary privilege," says Mr. Langmead, "was met by a resolution of the Commons that the power of publishing their proceedings and reports was an essential incident of the constitutional functions of Parliament, and that any person instituting a suit as to, or any court deciding on a matter of privilege contrary to the determination of either House would be guilty of a breach of privilege." Stockdale brought other actions, and won.

The sheriff levied execution, and he (the sheriff), Stockdale and his solicitor were committed for breach of privilege. Finally, the deadlock was removed by the passing of an Act which provided to the purport that all actions like that of *Stockdale* v. *Hansard* should be stayed on production of a certificate or affidavit that the paper complained of has been published by order of either House (Langmead's Constitutional History, pp. 586, 587, and see the Parliamentary Papers Act, 1840 (3 & 4 Vict. c. 9)).

The above case also caused a dispute between the two Houses as to the Upper House exercising its appellate jurisdiction to deprive the Lower House of its privileges, and the controversy was so acute that Parliament had to be prorogued.

CHAPTER XXXIV.

HISTORY OF LEGISLATION—PUBLIC BILL LEGISLATION—PRIVATE BILL LEGISLATION.

History of Legislation.—We can trace three distinct epochs: (1) Royal legislation by the King and his council. (2) Legislation by petition, the period when the estates of the realm, and afterwards the two Houses, petitioned the King for a given law, and the King either satisfied their desires or not as he pleased, and in what way he pleased. (3) The epoch of legislation by bill, when both chambers of the Legislature drafted the measure petitioned for, which was called, as at the present day, a bill, and the King assented to it, as he does now. Legislation by bill dates from the time of Henry VI., though the way had been prepared for it in the preceding reign (*p*).

Royal Legislation.—The laws made by the King went by various names. There were (1) charters or quasi-treaties made between King and people; (2) constitutions, probably so called after the imperial constitutions of the Roman Empire; (3) Assizes (*q*).

(*p*) The word "bill" meant a petition—*e g.*, a Bill of Complaint, the well-known old Chancery pleading

(*q*) The word "assize" denoted, in the first place, a sitting of the King and his Great Council—*e g.*, Assize of Northampton; afterwards it came to mean a law made at the meeting—*e.g* , Assize of Novel Disseisin; and, lastly, it assumed its present meaning, which is that of an institution created by a King's law—*e g* , the Maidstone Assizes. (Cf. Maitland, Const Hist , p 13) The word was also used to denominate the mediæval equivalents for juries—*e.g.*, the Grand Assize, the Petty Assize. We have several instances of assizes in the reign of Henry II —(1) The Grand Assize, consisting of twelve knights chosen by four knights in the presence of the King's justices, which tried questions of ownership of land and rights issuing out of land under a writ of right; (2) The following possessory assizes, which protected possession as opposed to ownership, and which were granted without prejudice to a writ of right. Here the object was to prevent the use of force, whether the individual who employed such force had a good claim to the ownership of the property or not. The possessory assizes were as follows: (a) *Novel Disseisin*—*e g* , if A.

It is difficult to fix a precise date for the commencement of legislation by petition, but we notice in the reign of Edward I. that the statute Quia Emptores was passed *instantia magnatum*, and in the reign of Edward III. the Statute of Treasons was passed at the instance of the Commons, who wanted a declaration by Parliament as to what was treason and what was not. (4) Ordinance laws, *i.e.*, laws made by the King in Council.

Legislation by petition had the following drawbacks : (a) the King might alter the wording of the law required by the petitioners; (b) he might grant an ordinance which, being a law made by the King and his Council, could be annulled, say, the next day by the same body which made it. The ordinance was not like a statute, publicly enrolled and only revocable by statute.

In the reign of Henry V. the Commons petitioned the King that they, being assentors as well as petitioners, request that from that time no law be made and engrossed as a statute which varied from the wording of the petition by additions, eliminations or difference in language. The King assented to this petition, saving his royal prerogative to grant or deny what he chose. The King still legislates by ordinance for conquered and ceded colonies. Ordinances as regarded the United Kingdom were later on styled Orders in Council.

Legislation by Bill is the form of legislation now existing. Its introduction in the reign of Henry VI. had important cousequences. Rules of debate and also of procedure sprang up and a necessity arose for committees to consider bills. Legislation by bill has the following advantages. Numerous experts, in the

recently was in possession of the land in dispute, let him not be forcibly dispossessed but remain in possession without prejudice to a writ of right; (b) *Mort d'Ancestor*, or assize "de morte antecessoris." If A.'s ancestor died possessed of the land, let him not be dispossessed by force, but let the ejector have his writ of right (if any); (c) *Darrein Presentment*. If A. presented a clerk to the living in dispute on the last vacancy, let him present on the present occasion without being forcibly molested, but without prejudice to a writ of right; (d) *Utrum*, to decide the question whether a given piece of land was lay or church land. In all these cases the question of possession was decided not by twelve knights, as in the case of the Grand Assize, but by twelve lawful men summoned by the sheriff.

case of a Government bill, at any rate, will have been consulted before its introduction. The bill is published and sold, the Press can comment on its provisions, and thus the opinion of the governed can be sounded beforehand. There have been rare instances lately of legislation by resolution of both Houses, such resolutions, of course, resting ultimately on statutory powers. In the case of the Church of England Assembly (Powers) Act, 1919, the Church measure, after being examined first by the legislative committee and afterwards by the ecclesiastical committee, becomes law if both Houses pass it by resolutions on the subsequent receipt of the royal assent.

In the Emergency Powers Act, 1920, the King is enabled by proclamation to issue regulations, disobedience to which is temporarily a criminal offence; and provision is furthermore made by the Act for making these acts of disobedience permanent criminal offences if both Houses pass resolutions in favour of this course. It would be premature at the present time to assert that legislation by resolution is creeping in as a substitute for legislation by bill. In the case of ecclesiastical legislation it is decidedly arguable that the Church Assembly's legislation is its own affair, just like the legislation of a county council, and that in the case of the Emergency Powers Act prompt legislation of a very drastic kind was imperatively necessary. Sudden disorders call for prompt and fearless treatment.

Various kinds of bills.—A project of law during its passage through Parliament is called a bill, and its sub-divisions are called clauses. Every bill must have a short title. There are four classes of bills :—

1. Public bills, *i.e.*, measures affecting the community at large or altering the general law.

2. Private bills, *i.e.*, measures dealing with local or personal matters, such as railway bills, and bills giving special powers to municipal corporations, or altering settlements.

3. Hybrid bills, *i.e.*, bills brought in as public bills, but which affect private interests in such a way that if they were private bills preliminary notices to persons affected would have to be given under the Standing Orders, *e.g.*, the Port of London Bill, 1903. As to the special procedure adopted in the case of hybrid

bills, see Ilbert's Manual of Procedure, pp. 144—145; May, 11th ed., p. 468.

4. Provisional order bills, *i.e.*, bills confirming orders and schemes made by public departments under statutory powers which otherwise would have to be dealt with by private bills. The delay and expense of private bill legislation is thus saved. The bill merely confirms the schemes or orders which are scheduled to it, and is introduced as a public bill by the Minister in charge of the department concerned. As to the subsequent special procedure, see Ilbert's Manual of Procedure, p. 235, and May, 11th ed., chap 30.

Public Bills.—Most public bills may originate either in the Commons or the Lords, but there are certain classes of bills, such as money bills and bills dealing with the representation of the people, which can only be brought in in the Commons. The normal course of a bill in the Commons is as follows :—When a member wishes to introduce a bill, he must either move for leave to bring it in or, according to a new practice, present it at the table. Notice must be given before either course is adopted. The bill is ordinarily laid on the table in "dummy," *i.e.*, a sheet of paper on which is the name of the member and the title of the bill. The first reading of the bill is usually a matter of form. The title only is referred to, but sometimes if the bill is likely to be opposed a short explanatory statement is allowed. When the bill has been read a first time it is ordered to be printed, and the print is then circulated to members and put on sale. The next stage is second reading, which is the stage for discussing the main principles of the bill. The member in charge can put it down for any day he likes, and if it is not reached on that day then on any subsequent day. If no one objects to the bill, it can be read a second time when unopposed business is taken, but if it is opposed it can only come on on one of the days fixed for taking opposed bills. The Government, of course, can arrange their own order of business, but the days for private members' bills are limited, so precedence on those days i balloted for. When a second reading is opposed, the opponent does not move the rejection of the bill, but he moves "that it be read a second time on that day six months," and if his motion is carried the bill is disposed of for that session. When a bill (other than a money bill) has been read a second time it goes to one of the six standing committees, unless the House otherwise orders. In that case it may be referred to a committee of the whole House or to a select committee, or occasionally to a joint committee of the two Houses. The committee stage is the stage for amending a bill. The bill is taken clause by clause, and amendments are moved in the order in which they come in the clause. When the clauses are finished new clauses and postponed clauses are then considered. After that the schedules, if any, are taken. The bill is then reported to the House. When a bill has been considered by a select committee, it must afterwards go through committee of the whole House. When the House goes into committee, the Speaker leaves the chair and his place is taken by the Chairman of Ways and Means Committee. If a bill has passed through committee of the whole House without amendment, it may at once be put down for third reading, and then, when read a third time, sent up to the Lords. But in other cases it must be put down for consideration on report. On the report stage the bill may, with certain restrictions, be amended as in committee, only new clauses come first, and the clauses as they left committee are taken afterwards. After the bill has been considered on report, it is put down for third reading. At this stage only verbal amendments can be moved, but the bill as a whole can be opposed. When a bill has been read a third time, the Commons have done with it, and it is sent up to the Lords, and put under the charge of some peer to conduct it through that House. The procedure in the Lords resembles generally the procedure in the Commons, but there are certain points of difference, and there is greater elasticity as to forms. Bills, after going through committee of the whole House, usually go also to a standing committee, and amendments may be moved on third reading and also on the motion that the bill do pass. If a bill coming from the Commons passes through the Lords without amendment, it only awaits the royal assent. But if it is amended, the amendments come back to the Commons for consideration. The Commons may assent to them, or dissent from them, or further amend them, and when they dissent a committee is appointed to draw up reasons. If eventually the two Houses cannot come to an agreement, the bill is lost. But if the two Houses agree, the bill receives the royal assent in the House of Lords. This is usually done by commission, though it might be given by the King in person.

For fuller details see Ilbert's Legislative Methods, chap. 6, and Manual of Procedure.

Money bills and clauses.—The right of initiating taxation or allocating the expenditure of the revenues of the State is the province of the House of Commons. As Sir Erskine May says, "The Crown demands money, the Commons grant it, and the Lords assent to the grant." Money bills, that is to say, bills of which the main object is to raise money by taxation, can only be introduced in the House of Commons, and their introduction must be authorised by resolution in committee of the whole House, moved by a Minister of the Crown. Bills for other purposes, but which contain financial clauses, may be brought in in the ordinary way, but their financial provisions must be authorised by a similar resolution. Bills containing clauses imposing rates or dealing with rates must likewise be initiated in the House of Commons, but no special procedure is then required. The House of Lords cannot amend a money bill or any clause in a bill dealing with taxation, and strictly speaking cannot touch a rating clause, but the House of Commons waives its privileges in respect of pecuniary penalties, fees for services rendered, and rating clauses in private bills. Where a bill is introduced into the House of Lords, and it would be incomplete without some financial provision, the necessary clause is printed in italics. It is no part of the bill itself, and is a mere indication by the Lords to the Commons of what they suggest would be an appropriate financial provision. See Manual of Procedure, tit. "Money Bills."

Bills dealing with the royal prerogative or Duchy of Cornwall.—When the consent of the Crown or the Duke of Cornwall is required to a bill dealing with the proprietary rights of either, such consent is announced to the Commons by a privy councillor (see May's Parliamentary Practice, pp. 170, 171, 451—456).

Standing Committees for public bills.—To economise the time of the House, two standing committees were appointed in 1883 as a substitute for committee of the whole House in the case of public bills. Subsequently two more were added, and at the beginning of 1919 there were four altogether—the A., B., and C. Committees, and the Scotch Committee.

Early in 1919 two important reforms were introduced. First, two fresh standing committees were added, bringing the total to six. Secondly, whereas previously bills were referred after second reading to a committee of the whole House, unless the House otherwise ordered, bills are now referred to standing committees, unless the House orders them to be referred to committee of the whole House. Money bills, however, *e.g.*, any bill whereby a tax is imposed, Consolidated Fund bills, or appropriation bills, continue to be referred without exception to a committee of the whole House; and there seems to be a movement in favour of according the same treatment to any first-class controversial measure.

Nature and Constitution of the Standing Committees.—Each standing committee should be a microcosm of the whole House, so that a majority of votes in the committee, when a party bill is involved, should reflect the views of the predominating party. With the exception of the Scotch Committee, each standing committee consists of not less than forty nor more than sixty members, who are nominated by the Committee of Selection.

A bill may be considered as to part thereof by a standing committee, and as to another part thereof by a committee of the whole House.

When a bill relates to Monmouthshire or Wales, all the members for Monmouthshire and Wales must be on the committee (Manual of Procedure, pp. 74, 298).

The Scotch Committee consists of all the Scotch members plus not less than ten nor more than fifteen other members.

Private bills.—Private bills are usually concerned with schemes of public utility which affect private interests. For example, a new railway may compete unfairly with an existing line, and the addition of a new district to a municipal borough may prejudicially affect the county rates, and a water supply scheme, besides requiring land to be taken compulsorily, may prejudicially affect the neighbourhood from which the water is taken. The procedure on private bills therefore assumes a quasi-judicial character. Parliament requires that full notice should be given, so that the parties affected may come in and oppose, and when the bill is referred to a committee, counsel and witnesses are heard on behalf of the contending parties (cf. May, ed. 11, p. 687).

Outline of procedure.—In the months of October and November the proposals of the bill must be publicly advertised in certain newspapers (see Standing Orders for Private Business, 3 to 10).

On or before November 30th in the year preceding the proposed passing of the Act, plans of the proposed scheme, sections and books of reference, according with directions specified in the Standing Orders, must be left with certain local authorities in the Private Bill Office (S. O. 23—31, and 39—55). On or before December 15th, owners and occupiers of land affected by the scheme must be served individually with notice thereof by post.

A deposit of money by the promoters has generally to be made on or before January 15th as a security of good faith, and is forfeited in certain events (S. O. 57—59).

On or before the 17th December the petition for the bill, a copy of the bill itself, and a formal declaration made by the agent must be deposited in the Private Bill Office.

On the 18th of January the examiners appointed by Parliament begin their sittings for the purpose of ascertaining whether the Standing Orders of Parliament have been complied with, and compliance is certified by indorsing the bill to that effect. These examiners are two in number, one being appointed by the House of Lords and the other by the Speaker. When the examiners report that Standing Orders have not been complied with, this report goes to the Select Committee on Standing Orders, who have power to dispense with non-compliance.

On or before January 28th the Chairman of Ways and Means in the Commons, and the Chairman of Committees in the Lords, fix personally, or through their counsel, in which particular House any given hill is to be considered first (Ilbert's Manual of Procedure, p. 221).

The procedure on private bills when they reach either House of Parliament is exceedingly complicated, because of their semi-litigious and semi-legislative character. Assuming that the Standing Orders have been complied with, or that, pursuant to the report of the examiners, compliance with the Standing Orders may be dispensed with, a private bill is usually introduced by being presented at the table, and when it has been laid on the table it is deemed to have been read a first time, and is ordered to be read a second time at a future date. Intricate questions frequently arise as to the *locus standi* of various parties to appear and be heard before a Private Bill Committee. These questions are determined in the House of Commons by the Court of Referees, and in the House of Lords by the Chairman of Committees. There are special provisions about railway bills, but ordinarily when a private bill has passed second reading it goes to the Committee of Selection, who send it to one of the small committees on private bills. The Private Bill Committee then proceeds to hear counsel and witnesses for and against the objects of the bill, and if they find that a sufficient case for legislation has been made out, declare the preamble proved. The clauses are then gone through before the contending parties, evidence is taken and arguments of counsel heard, and amendments, if necessary, are made. When a bill has been amended in one House, it is hardly ever amended in the other House, unless by consent, but the principle is again gone into, and not infrequently a bill passed by one House is rejected by the other. It must be borne in mind, as Sir Erskine May points out, that though "private bills are subject to notices, forms and intervals unusual in other bills, yet in every separate stage when they come before either House they are treated as if they were public bills. They are read as many times, and similar questions are put except when any proceeding is specially directed by the Standing Orders" (May, 11th ed., p. 689).

It is to be noted that the foregoing sketch relates only to English and Irish bills. A special procedure has been provided for Scotland under the Private Legislation Procedure (Scotland) Act, 1899.

Decline in private bill legislation.—Sir C. Ilbert (*r*) calls attention to a decline in the volume of private bill legislation, which he ascribes (1) to the expense involved; (2) to the absorption by general acts, *e.g.*, the Public Health Act, 1885, of much of the sphere formerly occupied by private Acts; and (3) to the machinery of provisional orders, whereby an order made by a public department after holding a local enquiry may achieve the same results as a private Act with less expense.

(*r*) "Parliament," 1920 ed., pp. 87—88.

CHAPTER XXXV.

TAXATION AND FINANCE.

King's extraordinary revenues.—The Norman King had his ordinary and extraordinary revenues, the ordinary consisting of his feudal dues, money raised from Jews, *bona vacantia*, waifs, strays, whales and sturgeons, and other miscellaneous sources of profit, and he had profits made from his courts of justice by the imposition of fines, &c. When money was required for a war and on an emergency, he asked for extraordinary aids. Henry II. taxed personal property for the Crusades, the tax being known as the Saladin Tithe. The great complaint against John was his unfair taxation, and during his reign taxation was direct, *i.e.*, levied directly on the person who had to pay it, and there was also indirect taxation levied on commodities. The barons in John's time complained of both kinds of taxation and Magna Charta contained provisions as to both sorts. Article 12 of Magna Charta provided that the King should demand no aid other than the three accustomed aids. The City of London again was only to render its accustomed aids. Article 13 of the Charta provided that the City of London should retain its ancient liberties and free customs, and other cities, boroughs, and ports should have the like privilege. By Article 41 foreign merchants were not to be liable to evil tolls, but only to the ancient and proper customs duties, except during war.

By Confirmatio Chartarum (A.D. 1297) the charters of John and Henry III. and the Charter of the Forest were to be confirmed. It provided that aids, tasks, and mainprizes be not taken in future without the consent of all the realm saving the ancient aids. It was further provided that the maltote—a toll of 40s. on each sack of wool—and other like tolls be not levied but by consent of the realm, saving the ancient aids and customs due, and customs of wools, wool skins, and leather already granted by the commonalty aforesaid.

In 1297 A.D. a statute—supposed to be not genuine—was said to have been passed forbidding tallage (*s*), and it was known as *De tallagio non concedendo*.

By the Petition of Right (1628) tallages, aids, forced loans and benevolences (*t*) were forbidden and the Bill of Rights provided that the levying of money to the use of the Crown by pretence of prerogative was to be thenceforth illegal.

In Stuart times import duties were not considered as taxes, but rather in the light of licences or concessions. In 1606 John Bate, a Levantine merchant, refused to pay a duty on currants imposed by James I. The court held that the King's power was both ordinary and absolute : the ordinary or common law power, which exists for the purposes of civil justice, cannot be changed without the leave of Parliament, but the King's absolute power, affecting matters of State, is *salus populi*, and is not directed by rules of common law, but varies according to the royal wisdom (see *ante*, p. 112). Customs are a material matter of State. Judgment in matters of prerogative must not be according to common law but according to Exchequer precedents (*u*).

This decision has been much criticised but has during the recent war been partially supported by the Bench.

In the case of the five knights, also known as *Darnell's Case* (1627 A.D.) the defendants were imprisoned for refusing to pay a forced loan. They applied for a *habeas corpus*, but Hyde, J., and other judges held that detention by special command of the King was legal. This case was largely instrumental in bringing

(*s*) Stubbs doubts the authenticity of this supposed enactment.

(*t*) Forced loans, according to Langmead, were said to have been first imposed in the reign of Edward II , but that they might have been imposed earlier. The first instance of a benevolence was probably in the reign of Edward IV.

(*u*) Reference was here made to customs duties levied by Edward I., Henry VIII., and Mary. All customs are the effect of foreign commerce, and all commerce and foreign affairs are in the hands of the King The seaports are the King's gates, which he may open or shut to whom he pleases. He provides for safety. If he may restrain the person by a writ of *ne exeat regno*, he may *à fortiori* restrain the importation of goods, and if he may restrain these absolutely, he may do so *sub modo*. If the King may impose, he may impose what he pleases (Thomas's Const. Cases, pp. 26 and 27).

about the Petition of Right, which forbade forced loans and benevolences.

In 1637 A.D. John Hampden, a native of Bucks, refused to pay a tax known as "ship money." An action was brought, and on Hampden demurring, the case was argued in the Court of Exchequer Chamber, where Finch delivered judgment to the following effect: "The defence of the kingdom must be at the charge of the whole kingdom. The law which has given the King his interest and sovereignty of defending and governing the kingdom also gives him power to charge his subjects with its defence, and they are bound to obey. The precedents show that though for ordinary defence they go to maritime counties, but yet when the danger is general they go to inland counties also. Acts of Parliament to take away the royal power in the defence of the kingdom are void." This case affords an example of *salus populi suprema lex.*

To sum up. The middle of the 14th century witnessed the first precedent of appropriating moneys voted by Parliament to a special purpose, namely, war, and before its close it was practically impossible for the King to impose indirect taxation.

In 1407 A.D. it was understood that money bills should originate in the Commons and were not to be reported on to the King till both Houses were agreed, and they were to be reported by the Speaker of the Commons. As to the Parliament Act, 1911, see p. 238.

Modern Finance.—Sir Erskine May says: "The Crown acting on the advice of its responsible Ministers being the executive power is charged with the management of all the revenues of the country and with all payments for the public service. The Crown, in the first instance, makes known to the Commons the pecuniary necessities of the Government and the Commons grant such aids and supplies as are required to satisfy these demands, and provide by taxes and appropriation of other sources of public income the ways and means to meet the supplies granted to them. The Crown demands money, the Commons grant it, and the Lords assent to the grant.

See p. 238 for effects of Parliament Act, 1911. The Commons do not vote money unless it be required by the Crown, nor impose or augment taxes unless taxation be necessary for the public service as declared by the Crown through its responsible Ministers.

The revenues of the State are not solely derived from taxation, as there is the King's revenue from Crown lands, which is exchanged for an annual sum known as the Civil List, and there are also other sources of revenue, *e.g.*, Suez Canal profits. Taxes are either permanent or annual, and the greater the amount of annual taxation the greater the control of the Commons over fiscal matters; *e.g.*, the income tax is a tax imposed annually.

The Consolidated Fund.—All revenue of whatever kind goes into the Bank of England, where it is paid to the Government account there, called the Consolidated Fund. Formerly there were two consolidated funds, one for England, Wales and Scotland, and the other for Ireland, and there will probably be two, if not three or more, consolidated funds again in the near future. Before 1787 the taxes were charged without any method on particular sources of revenue, but the younger Pitt established the Consolidated Fund and charged all taxes upon it.

The two kinds of public expenditure.—There are, as we have seen, two kinds of expenditure, permanent and annual. The following kinds of expenditure are permanent items: (1) The King's civil list; (2) the salaries of the judges of the High Court, the Speaker, the Comptroller and Auditor-General, the perpetual curate of Alderney and divers other persons (Anson, vol. 2).

Consolidated Fund services.—The permanent payments out of the Consolidated Fund which go on from year to year are called Consolidated Fund services.

Supply services.—These services are not permanent charges on the Consolidated Fund, but are voted annually and include payment for Army, Navy, Civil Service and the bulk of the expenses incurred by the Government.

The National Debt.—It frequently happens that after payment of all anticipated calls there is a surplus, and this surplus is never retained, but passes automatically by statute to the reduction of the National Debt. Till the days of the Stuarts there was no national debt. During the Civil War many persons left money with the goldsmiths of the City of London, and after the Restoration these goldsmiths began to act as bankers, and they lent money to Charles II. on the security of the revenue. In 1671 payment was postponed for twelve months, but there was further indefinite delay. In 1677 partial relief was given by the Government by the granting of annuities out of the hereditary excise (*x*). These annuities were, though delayed, paid till 1683, but ceased after that year.

About the time of the Revolution suits were brought by petitions to the Barons of the Exchequer for payment of the arrears, and the matter was then argued in the Exchequer Chamber. On this occasion it was held by a majority of the judges that the King could alienate the revenues of the Crown (*Bankers' Case*, Broom's Const. Law, p. 225).

The Crown granted no relief to suppliants until by 12 & 13 Will. III. c. 12, s. 3, the hereditary excise was ordered to be

(*x*) When the King gave up his military feudal dues owing to knight-service being converted into free and common socage, he had certain excise profits settled on him by way of compensation. This is one of the very few instances of the Crown being compensated for loss of its prerogative. The Statute of Tenures indirectly sanctioned a man leaving by his will his entire lands of all kinds save entailed land. Personalty could always practically be left by will, though for some time a man was supposed to divide his property into three parts, one part of which he could dispose of as he chose and was usually given to the clergy, the second part went to the wife, and the third part to the children. If there were no children or wife the testator could dispose of the whole. If there were children and no wife the testator could dispose of half, and he could also dispose of half where there was a wife and no children. This rule was gradually abolished. Before the Statute of Uses it was the custom for a man to grant his property to a friend to hold to the uses of his will. The Statute of Uses (27 Henry VIII c. 10) stopped this practice by making the user of an estate the legal owner and liable to forfeiture and other burdens, but the Statute of Wills (32 Henry VIII. c 1) permitted the tenant by knight-service to will away two-thirds of his land, and the socage tenant the whole of his lands. The Statute of Frauds insisted on three credible witnesses attesting wills of land, but prescribed no attestation for wills of personalty. The Wills Act (7 Will IV. and 1 Vict. c 26) prescribed two witnesses for wills of personalty and realty This statute further provided that no will of realty or personalty could be made by an infant Before the Wills Act, males over fourteen and females over twelve could make wills, and until the Wills Act, 1837, no attestation was necessary

charged with a yearly amount equivalent to interest at £3 per cent. until redeemed by repayment of one-half of the principal sum. Thus arose the £3 per cent. Consolidated Bank Annuities (*y*).

The funded debt.—When a man buys an annuity he does not get back his principal, but if he wishes to realise his interest he sells it in the market. He has only a claim to interest. The Government, however, can redeem a holder of these annuities or funded debt at par.

Unfunded debt.—This consists of loaned moneys repayable at certain fixed dates (Langmead, p. 495).

In 1787 the younger Pitt charged the whole of the National Debt on the Consolidated Fund.

The Sinking Funds.—Any surplus remaining after the annual expenditure goes to redeem the National Debt (Langmead, p. 498). By the Sinking Fund Act, 1878, the Treasury have within fifteen days after the expiration of the financial year (1st April) to prepare a statement of income and expenditure. Any surplus remaining in the Bank of England goes to the National Debt Commissioners and is known as the *Old Sinking Fund*. The Act also imposes on the Consolidated Fund a permanent annual charge for payment of *interest* on the National Debt and directs that *any surplus of this interest* not required for the payment thus directed is to be applied by the National Debt Commissioners in reduction of the National Debt (Ilbert on Parliament, 1st ed., p. 97). This last is the new Sinking Fund.

The estimates.—Every autumn the Government Departments send estimates of the amounts they propose to spend for departmental purposes to the Treasury, and it is the duty of the Chancellor of the Exchequer, as the friend and protector of the

(*y*) These are called the 3 per cents. because 3 per cent. was for a long time paid. They were called consolidated annuities because they were charged on the Consolidated Fund. They are called bank annuities because the dividends are paid by the Bank of England and stock is transferred in its books. They are called annuities because one purchases an annual sum in perpetuity.

taxpayer, to cut down these departmental estimates to the lowest amount compatible with reason, and should any dispute arise between the departments and the Treasury, it behoves the Cabinet to settle the difference.

The Budget.—Every April the Chancellor is supposed to have his Budget ready and when he introduces it in committee, he or some Minister on his behalf (Mr. Chamberlain acted recently for Sir R. Horne, just appointed) makes the Budget speech. This Budget speech reviews the past year's taxation, gives an estimate of what will be required for the present financial year, and a suggestion of what additional taxation will be necessary. If there is to be a reduction of taxation this is also mentioned, together with the taxes proposed to be reduced; *e.g.*, the duty on champagne was mentioned in this year's Budget speech.

Committee of Supply.—This committee of the whole House of Commons considers the estimates and then votes the requisite grants of money (Ilbert on Parliament, 1st ed., p. 100). The Committee of Supply can only decrease but cannot increase the grant voted.

Committee of Ways and Means.—After the Committee of Supply has voted the requisite grants the Committee of Ways and Means authorises the imposition of any given tax and passes resolutions that any sums of money voted shall issue out of the Consolidated Fund (Ilbert on Parliament, p. 100). The Committee of Ways and Means is also a committee of the whole House of Commons.

Comptroller and Auditor-General.—It is the duty of the Comptroller and Auditor-General to see that no money leaves the Consolidated Fund without statutory authority. He is a high official and is not allowed to sit in Parliament, and he holds office during good behaviour. It is a special duty of his to see that the money, after it has left the Consolidated Fund, is properly applied, and he also prepares accounts of income and expenditure for the Public Accounts Committee of the Commons together with a report of anything requiring notice.

The Public Accounts Committee consists of fifteen members of the Commons, appointed at the commencement of every session.

Ways and Means Acts or Consolidated Fund Acts.—It often happens that money is wanted by the Departments before the Annual Appropriation Act, which settles what amounts they are to have, and which is passed at the end of the session. Temporary statutes are therefore passed and these incorporate the decisions of the Committees of Supply and Ways and Means. The Appropriation Act then deals with the balances, if any, undisposed of.

The Finance Act passed at the end of each session authorises and legalises the decisions as to taxation arrived at in Committee of Ways and Means.

Ilbert says that the House of Commons has the two following important duties as to finance :—

(1) The expenditure of such money as has to be provided by annual taxation must be authorised by the Commons (Ilbert on Parliament, p. 198).

(2) The annual taxation has to be authorised.

The former, he continues, culminates in the annual Appropriation Act and the latter in the annual Finance Act (*ibid.*, p. 198).

The proper expenditure of the revenue is secured as follows : "The whole revenue is paid into the bank to the credit of the Government. Grants are then made by Consolidated Funds Acts or the Appropriation Act. Then follows an Order under the Royal Sign Manual countersigned by two Lords of the Treasury directing the Treasury Commissioner to transfer the moneys granted to the credit of the Government Department requiring same. The Treasury Commissioners then send an authority to the Comptroller and Auditor-General, who, after being satisfied that there is statutory authority for the grant and that all statutory requirements have been complied with, issues a formal direction to the bank to pay the money to the Departments wanting the same. The bank pays over the money and the Departments can then spend it."

CHAPTER XXXVI.

PROCEDURE IN THE COMMONS.

Order of business.—The usual order of business in the House of Commons is as follows :—(1) Private business; (2) public petitions orally presented; (3) questions; (4) motions for adjournment under Standing Order 10; (5) matters taken at commencement of public business; (6) orders of day and notices of motions (Manual of Procedure, p. 43).

It is to be noted that " every matter is determined in both Houses upon questions put by the Speaker and resolved in the affirmative or negative, as the case may be," *e.g.*, " That this Bill be read second time " (May, 11th ed., p. 277).

Apart from ordinary legislation, the main work of the House of Commons is financial. The theory of the Constitution with regard to finance is clearly shown in the special enacting formula of the annual Finance Acts. It runs as follows :—" Most gracious Sovereign, We, your Majesty's most dutiful and loyal subjects, the Commons of the United Kingdom of Great Britain and Ireland, in Parliament assembled, towards raising the necessary supplies to defray your Majesty's public expenses, and making an addition to the public revenues, have freely and voluntarily resolved to give and grant unto your Majesty the several duties hereinafter mentioned; and do therefore most humbly beseech your Majesty that it may be enacted, and be it enacted by and with the advice and consent of the Lords Spiritual and Temporal, and Commons, in this present Parliament assembled, and by the authority of the same as follows."

As soon as the debate on the Address is finished, committees of the whole House, called the " Committee of Supply " and the " Committee of Ways and Means " are formed, and the estimates for the ensuing year are brought before the Committee of Supply. The estimates are divided into naval, military and civil. Twenty days are allocated for their discussion, with a possible addition of three days if the business of the session permits. After the conclusion of the allotted time, the estimates are voted on without discussion. When the estimates are under discussion, members cannot move an increase; and if, as is usually the case, members desire increased expenditure on some particular subject-matter, this has to be done under the form of a motion to reduce the salary of the Minister in charge of the estimate.

The duties of the Committee of Ways and Means are to authorise grants out of the Consolidated Fund, and to vote the necessary taxes for the year. The financial year commences on the first of April, and the Chancellor of the Exchequer usually makes his financial statement, commonly called the Budget, somewhere near that date. When the Budget resolutions have been passed, fixing the new taxation for the year, they are afterwards embodied in the Finance Act, and the allocation of the revenues of the country made in Committee of Supply are afterwards embodied in an Act called the Appropriation Act. As this Act is only passed towards the end of the session, and the Treasury require money for the service of the State in the meantime, they are authorised to obtain the necessary funds by means of Acts known as the Consolidated Funds Acts (May, 11th ed., Chap. 22; Ilbert's Manual of Procedure, Chap. 10).

A certain amount of the time of the Commons is spent in passing resolutions, which, in more or less abstract terms, point to future legislation, and the House often finds itself embarrassed by having assented to a principle when the matter afterwards comes up in the concrete form of a bill.

Public petitions.—The following rules must be observed :—(1) They must be written and not printed, lithographed, or typed; (2) they must be addressed to the House of Commons; (3) if not in English, they must be accompanied by a translation, for the correctness of which the introducing member is responsible; (4) there must be neither interlineations nor erasures; (5) the petitions must conclude with prayers; (6) they must be signed by the petitioners if they are neither ill nor incapable of signing; (7) no documents must be annexed to petitions; (8) they must be temperately and also respectfully worded; (9) no references must be made to debates in Parliament or to notices of motion not set down in the paper; (10) the introducing member is responsible for all rules relative to petitions being observed; (11) no petitions for any sums relating to the public service, or for any money which is to be charged on Indian revenue, can be presented without leave of the Crown (Manual of Procedure, p. 53); (12) petitions for leave to compound Crown debts will not be received without a certificate giving certain information to the House (see Standing Orders 66, 68, 70); (13) no member is permitted to present his own petition, but he may present a petition signed by himself in a representative capacity; (14) all petitions presented to the House lie on the table, and are referred to the Public Petitions Committee (cf. May, p. 525, 11th ed.).

In the case of *Lake* v. *King* it was decided that no action for libel lies with respect to the contents of a parliamentary petition (19 & 20 Car. II., 1 Saunders, 120).

Questions.—Unless the Speaker gives special leave, written notice of intention to ask a question must be delivered to the Clerk of the House at the table beforehand.

Where an answer by word of mouth is required an asterisk is affixed to the notice (May, 11th ed., p. 252).

In all cases where there is no asterisk, or the member or some friend of his is not in the House to ask the question, or the question is not reached by 3.45 p.m., the Minister who has to answer it has the answer printed and circulated with the votes. The questioning member may, however, postpone his question. The time for asking the question is signified by the Speaker, who calls out the name of the questioning member (*ibid.*, p. 252).

No question should contain any unnecessary name or statement, and the questioning member is responsible for the correctness of any statement of fact. Opinions must not be asked, and purely legal questions are not allowed; nor may a question refer to any debate that has occurred, or answer that has been given, in the current session. No imputations on private character are permitted, but imputations on official character may be made with certain reservations. No questions can be put as to matters pending in a committee till the report of that committee is issued. No argument or irony is suffered for a moment, and the

Speaker is sole judge of the propriety of a question (for further particulars, see Manual of Procedure, pp. 56—62 inclusive : May, 11th ed., pp. 249—252).

A Minister may decline to answer a question on the ground of public policy, and the Minister for Foreign Affairs has great latitude given him. All questions directed to Ministers must relate to their respective departments (cf. May, p. 228, 11th ed.).

Absence and retirement.—All members are supposed to attend Parliament regularly, and no member may shirk a committee for which his name is down unless a very good reason be assigned.

There must be a quorum at every committee. Formerly members were paid for their attendance, and they forfeited their remuneration if absent. The fact that every member was at his place used to be ascertained by a roll call, but wages and the roll call have long been obsolete. When a member wishes to retire permanently, he applies for some post of nominal profit, like the stewardship of the Chiltern Hundreds, which vacates a seat in Parliament. Leave of temporary absence can be obtained on motion of the member desirous of absenting himself, or some-one else on his behalf.

Royal communications.—These are delivered (1) by speech from the Throne to both Houses. The speech is delivered in the Lords, either by the King or the Lord Chancellor (Manual of Procedure, pp. 6—8); (2) by Lords Commissioners under the Great Seal at any time.

In the Commons, messages are delivered (1) under Sign Manual; (2) through a Minister; (3) through a Privy Councillor.

Royal messages under Sign Manual are sent to announce some event of importance or sudden emergency, necessitating the calling out of reserve forces, or to request provision on account of some person having rendered valuable services to the Crown, or to request a marriage provision for a royal prince or princess (May, 11th ed., p. 446).

The message is brought by a Minister, who informs the Speaker of his mission and then brings it to the Chair. Whilst the Speaker reads the message, members uncover their heads. Notification of a royal bereavement is also of a formal character.

Informal messages are delivered either by a member of the Household, *e.g.*, reply to an address, or a Minister of the Crown. Members do not uncover when it is delivered.

Rules of debate.—No reference must be made to debates in the Upper House, nor to any matter *sub judice* in a law court.

The name of the King must not be mentioned either disrespectfully or in order to influence the House (May, 11th ed., p. 328).

No treasonable or seditious words are allowed, neither may a person speak to obstruct business (May, 11th ed., p. 328).

Members must not be referred to by name, and no offensive expressions against members may be indulged in or personal charges made. No debate of the session must be referred to, neither any question not then under discussion (Manual of Procedure, p. 127; May, 11th ed., Chap. XII.).

A member may refer to notes, but must not read his speech (Manual of Procedure, p. 126).

Committee of selection.—This committee consists of eleven members chosen by the House at the commencement of a session.

The principal functions of this committee are to classify or divide into appropriate groups all private bills, and to appoint the select committee to try each private bill.

They also nominate members of the standing committees, and in certain cases only members of other committees (Manual of Procedure, p. 93; May, 11th ed., p. 745).

Railway and canal bills committee.—As to these bills this committee performs similar functions to the committee of selection. The members of this committee are chosen by the committee of selection.

The committee is composed of eight or nine members, and three members form the necessary quorum for business (Manual of Procedure, pp. 92, 94).

Police and sanitary committee.—This committee is also nominated by the committee of selection.

It gives its attention to private Bills relating to sanitary matters and matters of police (Manual of Procedure, p. 96).

Committee of privileges.—This committee is appointed each session to consider matters relating to the ancient privileges of the House (Manual of Procedure, pp. 7, 8, 92, 95).

The joint committee.—This committee consists of an equal number of members from each House. The sittings are fixed by the Lords. It takes cognizance occasionally of public and private bills and also hybrid bills; but where a bill is either public or hybrid it must subsequently be considered by a committee of the whole House (Manual of Procedure, pp. 90—91).

Committee of public accounts.—This committee is charged with the examination of public accounts submitted by the Comptroller and Auditor-General. It consists of eleven members nominated at the beginning of the session (Manual of Procedure; cf. May, 11th ed., p. 597).

Select committees.—The scope of an inquiry into a matter by a select committee is determined by the order creating it, but the powers of the committee may be increased or curtailed afterwards by the House (Manual of Procedure, pp. 82, 83). Select committees can, if empowered by the House but not otherwise, order the production of documents and witnesses, and insist on witnesses answering on oath questions put to them. When witnesses are disobedient they can be attached for contempt by the House (*Howard* v. *Gossett*, Car. & M., p. 380). The chairman has a casting vote. Not more than fifteen members may be appointed to serve, and the quorum is chosen by the House itself (Manual of Procedure, p. 84). Threatening persons giving evidence before a select committee is a misdemeanour punishable under the Witnesses (Public Enquiries) Protection Act, 1892. Giving false evidence is perjury (Manual of Procedure, p. 209). An oath as to absence of interest has to be taken by each member of a select committee before acting. For further particulars see May, Chap. XV., 11th ed.)

Local legislation committee.—This is a committee appointed each session by the House of Commons. Its business is to consider private bills promoted by local authorities, in cases where such bills confer on a locality powers in relation to local government which conflict with the general law.

Count-out.—When forty members are not present either in debate, or in a committee of the whole House, the Speaker or Chairman, unless satisfied that forty members are present, gives the order for withdrawal of strangers, and for the summons of members from other parts of the building. Two minutes are allowed to get members together. The members are then counted twice, and if less than forty are there at the time of the second count the House adjourns. There is no count-out at dinner time.

Censures.—When a member contumaciously declines to take the ruling of the Speaker, or is guilty of misbehaviour, or flagrantly breaks the rules of the House, the Speaker may be asked to name him. The question is then put that the member be suspended from the service of the House, and if the motion is carried he is suspended till the end of the session or further order (cf. May, 11th ed., Chap. XII.).

CHAPTER XXXVII.

ORIGIN OF MEMBERSHIP OF THE COMMONS AND PERSONS INELIGIBLE FOR MEMBERSHIP IN THE COMMONS.

Origin of membership of the Commons.—After the Conquest till the signing of John's Magna Charta the qualification for attendance at the Great Council was tenure *in capite*. The earliest symptom of representation was in 1213, when the sheriffs summoned to the Great Council four men and the reeve from every township (Langmead, Const. Hist., 7th ed., p. 193).

In 1254 two knights were summoned from each county to vote an aid for the expenses of the French war. In 1261 the rebel barons summoned three knights from each county to a council held by them at St. Albans, *secum tractaturos super communibus negotiis regni* and the King summoned the same knights to Windsor. Simon de Montfort summoned to his Parliament in 1265 two knights from each county, two citizens from each city, and two burgesses from each borough. To Edward I.'s Model Parliament the clergy, consisting of the two archbishops, the bishops and heads of monasteries, were summoned by special writ: Archbishops and bishops were to bring with them deans, archdeacons, canons and inferior clergy. Seven earls and forty-one barons—by no means a fair proportion—and two knights from each county, two citizens from each city, and two burgesses from each borough were also summoned. The three estates thus convened voted taxation separately, according to the theory of the three estates on the Continent. The precise date of the division of Parliament into two Houses is difficult to fix. At first the knights and barons sat together. Later on we find the knights, though sitting apart from the burgesses, joining with them in petitions. From 1347 knights and burgesses formed one House and were known as the Commons (Langmead, p. 212, 7th ed.).

The knights were elected in the County Court, first by freeholders, afterwards by freemen, and in the reign of Henry VI. by freeholders of land of a yearly value of 40s. and upwards.

From an early date the members and voters for counties had to be resident therein (8 Henry VI., c. 7), and by a statute of Henry V. borough members had to be resident within the borough (1 Henry V. c. 1). But these provisions were from an early period evaded. By a statute of 46 Edward III. no lawyer practising in the King's Court, and no sheriff during his term of office, was to be admitted to Parliament. The reason was that, as far as lawyers were concerned, it was desirable to prevent them from presenting petitions on behalf of their clients. This statute also was early evaded. By 8 Henry VI. c. 7 it was provided that county members should be "gentlemen born, as shall be able to be knights," and no yeoman was to sit in Parliament. This meant that no one could sit in Parliament unless he held land of the value of £20 a year and upwards.

By 9 Anne, c. 5, members for counties had to be owners of freehold or copyhold land of the value of £600 per annum or upwards (Langmead, p. 277), and borough members had to own freehold or copyhold land of the value of £300 per annum or upwards.

By 1 & 2 Vict. c. 48 county members possessing personalty yielding £600 per annum or upwards, and borough members £300 per annum or upwards, were admitted to Parliament, and by 21 & 22 Vict. c. 26 the property qualification, which had been frequently evaded, was abolished. Quakers were allowed to sit in Parliament owing to an affirmation being substituted for an oath in 1833. In 1829 the Catholic Emancipation Act threw open Parliament to Roman Catholics, and Jews were admitted to that assembly in 1858, the form of oath being altered to satisfy their religious scruples.

Chief disqualifications.

1. Aliens (who have not been naturalized according to the Naturalization Act, 1870, or otherwise).

2. Bankrupts.—The bankrupt's ineligibility is regulated by section 33 of the Bankruptcy Act, 1883, which states that when

a member is adjudged bankrupt, and the disqualification is not removed within six months from adjudication, the court shall certify the fact to the Speaker, and thereupon the seat shall be vacant. Where a sat thus becomes vacant, the Speaker during a recess, whether by prorogation or adjournment, shall, on receipt of the certificate, cause notice thereof to be published in the London Gazette, and six days thereafter (unless Parliament previously meet) issue his warrant for a fresh election writ. The disqualification is removable if and when (a) the adjudication is annulled; (b) the debtor receives his discharge from the court, with a certificate that bankruptcy arose from misfortune and not misconduct. Bankruptcy adjudications may be annulled (a) when the court thinks no adjudication ought to have been made; (b) when the debtor pays up in full.

3. Bankruptcy officials (see Bankruptcy Act, 1883, s. 116).

4. Barristers appointed to try disputed municipal election petitions (45 & 46 Vict. c. 50, s. 92).

5. Clergy of English Established Church (41 Geo. III. c. 63).

6. Clergy of Scotch Established Church (*ibid.*).

7. Clergy of the Roman Catholic Church (10 Geo. IV. c. 7, s. 9).

8. Commissioner of Metropolitan Police (19 & 20 Vict. c. 2, s. 9).

9. County Court judges (51 & 52 Vict. c. 43, s. 8).

10. English and Scottish peers (39 & 40 Geo. III. c. 67).

11. Felons, unless they have served their time or have received a pardon (33 & 34 Vict. c. 23, s. 2).

12. Governors of colonies (6 Anne, c. 41, s. 4).

13. Governors of Indian dependencies (10 Geo. IV., c. 62, ss. 1, 2).

14. Holders of pensions at the pleasure of the Crown (6 Anne, c. 41, s. 4, and 1 George I., c. 56). This does not include civil service or army pensioners or diplomatic service pensioners. Holders of any contract with the Crown (22 Geo. III. c. 45). Company directors holding Government contracts can sit in Parliament.

15. Infants (7 & 8 Will. III. c. 25, s. 7). Sir William Anson says that Mr. Charles James Fox and Lord John Russell sat in

Parliament during infancy (vol. 1, p. 79, 3rd ed.; cf. May, 11th ed., p. 27).

16. Irish peers. These peers may sit for English constituencies, unless they be life elected peers of Ireland (Fielden, Constitutional History, p. 146; May, 11th ed., pp. 12, 30).

17. Judges of Court of Appeal and High Court of Justice (Judicature Act, 1873, s. 5).

18. Lunatics and idiots.

19. Revising barristers (England), so far as their districts are concerned (6 & 7 Vict. c. 18, s. 28).

20. Recorders, as regards their own boroughs (45 & 46 Vict. c. 50, s. 163).

21. Sheriffs, as to their counties (Rogers 2, 18th ed., p. 6).

22. Stipendiary magistrates in London (Rogers 2, 18th ed., p. 22).

23. Traitors convicted of treason (33 & 34 Vict. c. 23, s. 2).

6 Anne, c. 41, s. 25, enacts that no holder of an office of profit created since 25th October, 1705, nor any person holding a pension from the Crown during pleasure, shall be capable of being elected to or sitting in the Commons; but section 25 qualifies this by saying that if any person, being chosen a member of the Commons, shall accept of any office from the Crown during membership, his election is void, but that he shall be capable of being re-elected "as if his place had not become void as aforesaid." The Act of Settlement excluded all office-holders from Parliament; and had it not been for this later enactment the Ministers of the Crown could not have been in Parliament. Section 27 of the Act of Anne exempts from its provisions officers of the Army and Navy. As regards offices of profit created since 1705, the statutory provisions are numerous, and the acceptance of office, in some cases, not only vacates the seat, but also disqualifies the holder from re-election. A member is not to lose his seat by reason of acceptance of an office of profit under the Crown if that office is an office the holder of which is capable of being elected to or voting in the House and if such acceptance has taken place within nine months of the proclamation summoning a new Parliament (Re-election of Ministers Act, 1919 (9 Geo. V.), c. 2, s. 1).

Where before or after the passing of this Act a privy councillor has been or is appointed to be a Minister of the Crown at a salary without any other office being assigned to him he shall not, by reason thereof, be deemed to have been or to be incapable of being elected to or voting in the Commons (*ibid.*, s. 2).

Persons guilty of corrupt and illegal practices.—Where a person has been convicted of personally committing or being privy to personation or bribery, such person can never sit for the constituency to which the offence relates, and if he is already elected such election is void. He cannot sit for another constituency for seven years after conviction (46 & 47 Vict. c. 51, s. 4).

Where a person has been convicted of bribery, treating, personation or undue influence in reference to any election, he cannot sit in Parliament till seven years after conviction, or for the constituency ever (46 & 47 Vict. c. 51, s. 4).

Where a candidate has been reported of having innocently through his agents committed the offences of personation, bribery, treating, or undue influence, he cannot sit in Parliament for seven years, unless the election judges, on proper evidence being adduced, exonerate him from all blame (46 & 47 Vict. c. 51, ss. 22 and 23).

Where a candidate has been reported as being guilty of an illegal practice, or with having been privy thereto, he cannot sit in Parliament for the particular constituency or any other for seven years; and if he has been elected the election is void. When the above offence has been committed by an agent of the candidate, he cannot sit for the particular constituency during the then sitting Parliament (46 & 47 Vict. c. 51, s. 11) (*z*).

(*z*) Candidates for Parliament who do not act for themselves have agents, and besides the regular agent who is usually employed, the candidate very often employs the services of persons who offer gratuitous help in the election, and for all these persons he is answerable. Lush, J., said in the *Harwich Case* ((1880) P. 227), that "a person may become an agent by actual employment, and by recognition and acceptance of what has been done."

The agent can only bind the person for whom he acts, and he only binds the principal when he is acting within the scope of the authority; ergo, if such agent is to canvass a particular section of voters, and exceeds his authority, then what he does in excess of his authority does not concern the principal (Ward's Practice at Elections, p. 148).

CHAPTER XXXVIII.

THE PARLIAMENTARY FRANCHISE.

The county franchise.—The county electors were originally the freeholders who attended the County Courts, and these freeholders were divided into two classes : (a) tenants in chief; (b) other freeholders. Attendance at the courts was a questionable privilege which fell to the lot of the holder of a particular piece of land. New pieces of land were, owing to *subinfeudation* and other kinds of transfer, split up gradually into numerous sections, but there was no increase in the number of suits due to the County Court (Maitland, p. 88). Those who owned the split-up sections settled between themselves who was to go to the County Courts.

Now the persons who, owing to bargains or otherwise, were bound to attend the County Court voted for the knights of the shire who went to Parliament. The greater and lesser barons were the only persons consulted originally as to taxation or otherwise, but in the reign of Edward I. the county franchise was vested in the freeholders who attended the County Court.

In 1430 the county franchise was regulated by 8 Henry VI. c. 7, which provided that knights of the shire were to be elected by freeholders who owned land of the clear yearly value of 40s. or upwards, residence in the county being indispensable (*a*).

The borough franchise.—The borough franchise has been described as an Augean Stable till the passing of the Reform Act, 1832. It was a good field for corruption and the Crown and its adherents could easily command a majority. Originally, the borough franchise was regulated on a more or less democratic basis

(*a*) Mr. Langmead mentions an Act of Henry IV. to the effect that all freemen might vote for a knight of the shire for Parliament (Langmead, p. 273) The restriction of residence appears to have been gradually evaded, but was not abolished till 1774 (14 George III. c. 58).

(see Langmead, p. 278). Members, and persons who were subject to scot (municipal impositions) and lot (liability to hold municipal offices) had the franchise, but gradually encroachments on the right of election were made and prescriptive rights arose.

The Tudors inaugurated a system of granting charters of incorporation to boroughs, and these instruments specified who were to elect the borough member, or members. Sometimes members were elected by a Crown-chosen mayor and corporation. Obscure villages received corporate rights. The borough of Old Sarum, for instance, consisted of a ploughed field.

To sum up :—in the provincial towns at the time of the Reform Act the franchise was regulated in four different ways. It belonged to :—

1. Burgage tenants; or
2. Freemen of the borough or guild; or
3. Householders liable to scot and lot; or
4. Borough corporations (Fielden, Const. Hist., p. 1).

By a statute of Henry V. residence was essential to a borough vote, but this requirement was gradually evaded and was repealed by a statute of 1774. Tudors and Stuarts granted numerous charters, thus vesting the franchise in a select few upon whom the Crown could rely.

A bill for reforming the franchise was proposed by Wilks in 1776, and a similar measure by the Duke of Richmond shortly afterwards. After this Grey, Sir Francis Burdett, and Lord Russell introduced Reform Bills without results. In 1831 the Reform Bill was thrown out by the Lords. It was re-introduced in 1832 and became law owing to William IV. threatening to create peers.

By the Reform Act, 1832, the following changes were made. The old forty-shilling freeholder lost his vote unless he occupied the qualifying property or had a heritable estate therein or had acquired such estate by marriage, marriage settlement office, devise, or promotion to benefices, or had a life estate of a clear yearly value of £10 or more. Copyholders (legal or equitable) of heritable estates of the yearly value of £10 obtained the franchise, and lessees, sub-lessees, and assignees of land of the yearly value of £10 or more holding for terms of years originally created for sixty years or more, and also lessees, sub-lessees and and assignees of land of the clear yearly value of £50 or more whose terms were created for a period of not less than twenty years, and also leaseholders paying a rent of £50 or upwards, became entitled to the parliamentary vote.

A £10 occupation franchise was (subject to certain restrictions as to previous residence and payment of rates) conferred on certain inhabitants of boroughs.

By the Reform Act, 1867, the £10 qualification as to counties of tenants for life of freeholds, copyholders and leaseholders was reduced to £5, and a £12 occupation franchise (subject to restrictions as to occupation and payment of rates) was introduced. As to boroughs, two new franchises were created, viz., occupation of a dwelling-house of any value, and the lodger qualification in respect of lodgings of the rateable value of £10, if let unfurnished. Eleven boroughs were disfranchised and twenty-three boroughs deprived of a member. Additional boroughs were created, the county seats were increased and certain university seats were called into existence.

By the Representation of the People Act of 1884 the lodger and householder qualifications were extended to counties, and a service qualification, giving the vote to people who occupied houses in the capacity of servants, was created.

The present parliamentary franchise.—Under the Representation of the People Act, 1918, a man to be registered as a voter must (1) be a British subject natural-born or naturalised; (2) be twenty-one years of age; (3) labour under no legal incapacity (section 1).

By legal incapacity is meant "some quality inherent in a person, or for the time irremovable in such person, which, either at common law or by statute, deprives him of the status of a parliamentary elector" (Fraser on the Representation of the People Act, p. 4).

The following are subject to legal incapacities : (1) Aliens not naturalized; (2) infants; (3) holders of certain offices (see Fraser, p. 5, for further particulars); (4) lunatics, save in lucid intervals; (5) idiots (*Burgess's Case*, Bedfordshire (1785), 2

Lud. 567); (6) imbeciles (*Oakhampton* (1791)); (7) English peers; (8) Scotch peers and Irish peers, unless elected or serving for a British constituency; (9) traitors and felons, unless they have endured their punishment or have been pardoned; (10) persons who have been found guilty within the last seven years of corrupt practices at a parliamentary election; (11) persons who have been found guilty of the like conduct at a municipal election; (12) certain persons who have been found guilty of illegal practices at parliamentary, municipal and certain other local elections, for five years after conviction.

A man to obtain a vote must be on the register of voters and the fact of being on the register is, in the absence of evidence to the contrary, conclusive of the right to vote. A man to be registered as a parliamentary elector in a constituency must have either the requisite residence or the requisite business premises qualification (section 1, sub-section 1A). In order to possess the requisite residence qualification he must be residing in premises in the constituency on the last day of the qualifying period, and he must further have resided in premises in or near the constituency (*b*) throughout the qualifying period.

In order to possess the requisite business premises qualification he must on the last day of the qualifying period be occupying business premises in the constituency, and he must further during the whole of the qualifying period have occupied business premises in or near the constituency.

The qualifying period is a period of six months, ending 15th January or 15th July in any given year.

"Business premises" means land or other premises of the yearly value of £10 at least occupied for purposes of a business, profession or trade.

A man can be registered as an elector for an English university constituency if he is of full age, is not subject to legal incapacity and has taken a degree (not honorary), at such university (section 2).

The section also deals with voting for Scotch and Irish universities.

A woman can be registered as an elector if (a) she is over thirty

(*b*) The degree of proximity necessary is set out in section 1 (2) (b).

years of age (section 4); (b) is not subject to legal incapacity; (c) could be registered as a local government elector if she were a man. (Section 3 provides that a man can be registered as a local government elector if he is on the last day of qualifying a person occupying as owner or tenant land or premises in a local government electoral area and has during the whole of the qualifying period occupied land or premises in that area, or, if that area is not an administrative county or county borough, then in any area, county or county borough in which the area is wholly or partly situate.) Provided that for the purposes of this section a man who himself inhabits any dwelling-house by virtue of any office, service, or employment shall, if the dwelling-house is not inhabited by his employer, be deemed to be a tenant or occupier of the dwelling-house.

A woman can be registered as a university parliamentary voter if she is over thirty and has either obtained a degree or has fulfilled the conditions required of women in the university in question as to residence, and has passed all the examinations, which would entitle a man at that university to a degree.

Persons on war service shall be entitled to be registered for any constituency for which they might have been registered but for such war service, but when the right relates to a residence qualification they must make a special claim, together with a declaration in special form, that they have taken steps to prevent registration in another constituency. The declaration is to be presumptive evidence of their right to registration. "Serving on war service" means serving on full pay in the Army, Navy or Air Force, or being abroad or afloat in connection with any war in which his Majesty is engaged.

Service of a military or naval character is to count as war service, also Red Cross service, and being engaged in any employment recognised by the Admiralty, Army Council, or Air Service as work of national importance.

Occupation of business premises means premises of the value of £10 for men and £5 for women, and joint occupiers, if men, must pay £10 each and women £5. The residence qualification is not interrupted if a house is let furnished for not exceeding four months, or where landlord has demanded possession.

A person on the register is entitled to a vote, but no person, whether male or female, may have more than two votes, one of which must be a residence vote; *e.g.*, if a person has a university vote, a business vote, a London livery vote, and a residence vote, he may vote only twice though he is on four registers, and one of the two votes which he exercises must be a residence vote (section 8, sub-section 1).

Receipt of poor relief or other alms is no longer a disqualification for voting.

Conscientious objectors to military service cannot vote until five years after the termination of the late war, but they may be allowed to vote by taking certain steps with special permission and supplying certain evidence to the Central Tribunal.

Registration.—Two registers of electors are prepared each year, viz., the Spring and Autumn registers.

The Spring register comes into force on April 15th and remains in force till October 15th, and the October register comes into force on October 15th and remains in force to April 15th.

If for any reason a new register is not compiled every six months the previous one is to be treated as in force.

Every parliamentary borough or county is to be a registration area and the clerk of the county council is to be registration officer, and the borough town clerk is to be registration officer for the borough, and when there is a vacancy in the offices above mentioned, either the mayor of the borough or the chairman of the county council is to appoint a proper person to act. The registration officer has judicial duties as well as that of preparing and publishing lists of voters. Any person may send notice to such officer objecting to another person's being on the list, and the clerk then notifies the person whose registration is objected to, and a date should be fixed for the clerk to hear both sides.

If either party is dissatisfied with the ruling of the registration officer, he can appeal to the County Court judge, and there is an ultimate right of appeal to the Court of Appeal. Pending an appeal, the person thereby affected may vote. It shall be the duty of the officials of the Appeal Court to notify the registration officer of the result of any appeal.

In lieu of the County Court judge the Lord Chancellor may appoint an assistant judge to hear appeals, and such judge shall have the full powers of a County Court judge for that purpose.

Freedom of the City of London.—Freemen of the City of London who are liverymen of one of the City companies may be placed on the register of liverymen (section 17), but cannot have more than two votes.

University registers.—The governing body of a university are to keep a register of persons entitled to a vote for their constituency, and shall allow inspection of their register (section 19).

Absent voters.—Persons who are entitled to registration as parliamentary electors may, not later than the 18th of February, or for the Autumn register the 18th of August, in any given year, claim to be placed on an absent voters' list, and the registration officer, if satisfied that there is a probability that the claimant, by reason of his occupation, service, or employment, may be debarred from voting during the period the particular register is in force, shall place his name on the absent voters' list, and the officer is bound to place in such list without any claim being made persons in the Army, Navy or Air services (Schedule 1 to Act, rr. 16, 17, 18).

The addresses of absent voters must be kept and proper instructions as to the mode of voting sent to them (*ibid.*, r. 19).

The registration officer may require from any household any necessary information, and the giving of false information constitutes a summary offence.

By section 20 the principle of proportional representation is to be applied at contested elections for university constituencies where there are two or more members to be elected. It may also be applied in certain other constituencies returning three or more members if and when a scheme for the selection of these constituencies is approved by Parliament. But no such scheme has been approved so far. In either case the principle of proportional representation is operated by conferring on each elector one transferable vote (*c*).

(*c*) For definition of the expression "transferable vote," see section 41 (6)

Elections.—At a general election all polls shall be held on the same day.

Every candidate for Parliament is to deposit £150, and if he fails to do so his candidature is forfeited, and if the candidate dies before the election the money deposited is to be returned to his legal personal representative.

If a candidate, who has made the required deposit, is not elected and the number of votes polled by him does not exceed, in the case of a constituency returning one or two members one-eighth of the total number of votes polled, or in the case of a constituency returning more than two members one-eighth of the number of votes polled divided by the number of members to be elected, the deposit shall in each case be forfeited to the Crown; in other cases the amount shall be returned to the member elected so soon as he has taken the statutory oath of allegiance, and to the person not elected as soon as possible.

Where, again, a candidate is nominated in more than one constituency he can recover only one deposit.

The division of the constituency into polling districts rests with the registration officer, as does the appointment of polling places.

Scale of election expenses.—A candidate may send to each elector one free postal communication.

Unauthorised persons are guilty of a misdemeanour if they incur expenses on account of holding public meetings or issuing advertisements or circulars to procure election of a candidate—unless authorised in writing to do so by the election agent.

The fourth schedule to the Act provides for a limited maximum scale of election expenses, which must not be exceeded.

Section 37 and Schedule 9 deal with the redistribution of seats, and the total number of members of the Commons is by these provisions raised from 670 to 707. The Act applies to Scotland and Ireland, with the modifications set out in sections 43 and 44 respectively.

History of right of Commons as to control of elections.—The sheriffs, acting under the Crown, formerly controlled elections.

The writ directed the sheriff to return two knights for each county and two burgesses for each borough, and the sheriff had the selection of the places which he considered ought to have members.

The boroughs shirked representation, as they had to pay 2s. per day to each burgess. The first Statute of Westminster declared that elections ought to be free, and an Act of Richard II. fined sheriffs who omitted to make returns of boroughs which had previously returned members. Mediæval sheriffs made false returns of men not properly elected.

An Act of Henry IV. gave two justices of assize power to enquire into disputed returns, and an Act of Henry VI. awarded additional fines for false returns, and enjoined the sheriff to send precepts to mayors and bailiffs of boroughs directing them to elect borough members (Langmead, pp. 267, 268).

The King and Council formerly settled election disputes, and as early as the reign of Richard II. the Commons remonstrated against this course of action. During the Lancastrian period the Commons continued to remonstrate, but there is no recorded instance of their further complaining till the reign of Elizabeth, when they protested against the county of Norfolk election. James I. interested himself much in the kind of men who were to be elected, as is evidenced by his proclamation at his first Parliament, and in this reign the famous *Goodwin's Case* occurred. In 1604 one Goodwin was returned for Bucks, but Goodwin, being an outlaw, the Clerk of the Crown vacated the return. A second writ was issued and one Fortescue was elected, but the Commons disputed Goodwin's outlawry, and contended that outlawry did not disqualify him. The Crown and the Commons consented to submit the dispute to the judges, but no reference took place. Finally, James I. admitted the right of the Commons to settle election controversies. The Commons also claimed to settle the rights of electors, and this gave rise to the celebrated episodes of *Ashby* v. *White* and the *Aylesbury Men* (see p. 248).

After *Goodwin's Case* select committees of the Commons decided election disputes, and as this system was not altogether popular, mixed committees of members and outsiders were appointed by the House, and this remained the practice till the passing of the Parliamentary Elections Act, 1868, whereby the trial of disputed elections was transferred to the judges. The judges report to the House, which then decides what course to pursue.

APPENDIX A.

UNITED STATES CONSTITUTION.

As this Constitution forms part of the student's curriculum, and as it is the parent of all federal constitutions, except, perhaps, the Swiss, a brief account of it is given here. The Constitution was issued in September, 1787, but it has been amended from time to time.

Its great feature is a distinct line of demarcation between Legislature, Judicature, and Executive, though overlapping occurs here and there.

The Legislature is vested in Congress, consisting of two Houses, viz., the Senate and House of Representatives. Judicature is vested in the judicial bench, and the Executive in the President, who has to be guided in certain instances by the Senate.

The President holds office for four years, and is elected in the following manner : Each State of the Union elects a "college" of electors equal to the number of senators and representatives to which such State is entitled, and the man who gets the largest numbers of the votes of these electors is chosen President. (For further particulars see Dodd's Modern Constitutions, vol. 2, p. 301.) The person chosen must be at least thirty-five years of age and fourteen years resident in the U.S.A. If the President dies during his term of office the Vice-President takes his place for the remainder of the term. The President is commander-in-chief of the army, navy, and militia. He can pardon crimes, impeachments excepted.

The President also can be impeached like other American statesmen, but impeachment can only involve loss of office. By and with the advice of the Senate the President can conclude treaties with foreign Powers, provided that two-thirds of the Senate concur, and the same assent is necessary for declaring war and making peace. As the Senate holds office for a longer period than the House of Representatives, the President occasionally has a hostile Upper House to deal with.

The Senate also has to be consulted about the nomination of public ministers, ambassadors, consuls, and the Supreme Court judges. The President can occasionally and temporarily fill up vacancies in the Senate. He may, on an occasion of great emergency, convene the Legislature and adjourn both Houses when they disagree.

He has, however, no voice in legislation, though he makes a speech at the beginning of the sitting, which may or may not receive attention.

He differs from the English Premier, or Cabinet, in that he does not introduce a legislative programme which he is bound to carry out.

He recommends legislation in his inaugural speech, but has to enlist friends in the Legislature if he wishes to carry a measure.

The Speaker in the House of Representatives, in whose hands are placed all the order of business and general procedure as well as the appointment of all committees, is a party man, and not a judge in any sense. (Ilbert on Parliament, chap. 10, 1st ed.) Congress must assemble once yearly at least. The Upper House, or Senate, consists of two members of each State, chosen by popular vote for six years, one-third retiring every two years. All senators must be over thirty years of age, citizens of the United States of at least nine years' standing, and residents in the States for which they are chosen. The Vice-President is *ex officio* President of the Senate. Each State, whether small or large, elects two senators. The members of the House of Representatives are distributed among the States in proportion to population, so that the more populous States outweigh the others. The House of Representatives was intended to represent the nation on the basis of population, whilst the Senate was to represent the States. The judicial bench can interpret the Constitution, and refuse to give effect to laws which contravene it. Again, the electoral college, who choose the President, vote to a man with their party and vote for the party candidate : to do otherwise being considered dishonourable (Dicey). Furthermore, the Senate lately ventilated the view "that the

President could not exactly be a party man where the rights of the Senate were concerned."

Differences between the English and American Constitutions.

1. In America the President is in practice more of a ruler than the English King, but the legal powers of the former are far more restricted.

2. The President can veto legislation, but by the adoption of somewhat complicated constitutional machinery such veto may be overcome; whilst the English King has, conventionally speaking, a very shadowy power of veto which has been dormant since the reign of Anne.

3. The English Constitution is flexible, the American rigid.

4. The judges, as in all written Constitutions, can disregard an Act of the Legislature which is *ultra vires*.

5. The American Constitution is written, whilst the English Constitution is unwritten.

6. In the American Constitution Montesquieu's doctrine of the separation of powers is followed as closely as possible, whilst in England this is not the case.

7. Parliament in England is the legal sovereign, whilst in America, as in most federal States, sovereign powers are split up amongst a number of co-ordinate bodies.

8. In England all laws, constitutional or otherwise, can be altered with equal ease, whilst in America complicated machinery is necessary.

9. In England the impeachment of Ministers is obsolete, whilst in America it is part of the written Constitution.

10. The English Crown is inherited under a statutory entail, whilst the American President is elected for a term.

11. In England the treaty-making power is legally vested in the Crown (*i.e.*, the Cabinet by convention), whilst in America it is vested in the President and the Senate.

12. Declaration of war and the making of peace rests with the Crown in England, whilst in America it is vested in the President and Senate.

13. The American President is not dependent on the vote of Congress, whilst in England the Cabinet is.

England is the only country possessing hereditary legislators. Even Germany and Austria do not possess these, though Germany possessed many hereditary Sovereigns.

CANADA.

Canada enjoys responsible government, but the Upper House, unlike that of America, is Crown-nominated, members holding for life; and the chief executive officer is a Governor-General appointed by the Crown.

Like the United States, Canada possesses a written Constitution, but, unlike the United States, her senators hold for life; whilst United States Senators hold office for six years, one-third retiring at the end of two years.

Unlike the United States and Australia and South Africa, the Canadian Constitution does not provide for a constituent assembly, an Imperial statute being necessary for change of fundamental or constitutional laws.

The Canadian Constitution was created by, and rests mainly on, the British North America Act, 1867, as amended by the British North America Acts, 1871 and 1886.

By the first Act the provinces of Ontario, Quebec, Nova Scotia and New Brunswick were united under the name of the Dominion Government of Canada. Two other Acts provided for the addition of six senators for British Columbia, six for Alberta, and six for Saskatchewan.

The Lower House, known as the House of Commons, is elected on a basis of population, as in the U.S.A.

Every senator must be over thirty, a born or naturalized subject of the King, a resident in the province for which he is chosen; he must also possess a property qualification. In the choice of senators the Governor-General must act on the advice of his responsible ministers, who represent more or less the predominating party in power in the House of Commons at the time he is nominated. The House of Commons is elected by the people for four years. The numbers of the House have been altered from time to time on the basis of population.

By the British North America Act, 1875, the Canadian Parliament has adopted the privileges of the Imperial House of Commons.

The Canadian House of Commons now consists of over two hundred members.

The Executive Government is carried on by the Governor and his acting Privy Councillors, which consists of the eighteen departmental heads and certain other Privy Councillors without portfolios. There are also honorary Privy Councillors, who are not consulted as in England.

Money bills must originate in the Commons, and no money bill, as in England, can be valid save on the recommendation of the Governor-General.

Section 55 : When a bill is presented to the Governor for his assent he must declare whether he assents or dissents or reserves it for the King's pleasure. A reserved bill has no effect unless within two years from presentation to the Governor for assent it has received assent of the King in Council.

The Provinces.—These are presided over by Lieutenant-Governors appointed by the Governor-General. The provinces possess responsible Legislatures, and these Legislatures, being also constituent assemblies, can change their Constitutions. They may not, however, interfere with the functions of the Lieutenant-Governor. Two of the provinces have bi-cameral Legislatures, the rest uni-cameral.

Powers of Provincial and Dominion Legislatures.—The provinces are, by section 92 of the Act, empowered to legislate exclusively on sixteen specific topics of a local nature enumerated in that section. Section 91 enumerates other specific topics in respect of which the Dominion is to have exclusive legislative jurisdiction. These two enumerations to some extent overlap, and when this occurs Dominion Acts, falling strictly within one of the heads enumerated in section 91, prevail over corresponding Provincial Acts, notwithstanding that the subject-matter may to a greater or lesser extent fall also within one of the enumerated heads of section 92. As to topics falling within neither enumeration, the Dominion has exclusive powers of legislation under its general authority to make laws for the peace, order and good government of Canada : but a Dominion Act resting on this power will be overridden by a Provincial Act if the Provincial Act rests on one of the enumerated heads of section 92.

The fact that the undefined residue of legislative power is vested in the central authority and not in the units is an idiosyncrasy of the Canadian Constitution, distinguishing it from America, Australia, and other federal States. It has, indeed, been said that this peculiarity excludes Canada from the class of federations proper.

Judicature.—By a Canadian Act of 1875 (38 Vict. c. 11), there were established a court of common law and equity, with appellate jurisdiction, called the Supreme Court of Canada and also the Exchequer Court of Canada. The judges of these courts are appointed by the Sovereign by Letters Patent under the Great Seal of Canada, hold office during good behaviour, and are removable by an address to the Governor-General from both Houses (sections 4, 5). "All the provinces can appeal to the Privy Council without going through the Supreme Court of Canada" (Wheeler's Confederation Law of Canada, p. 396).

SOUTH AFRICAN CONSTITUTION.

South Africa Act, 1909.—The Constitution evolved by this Act is formed on the Canadian pattern, as laid down in the British North America Act, 1867, and not on that of the United States of America. The conditions in South Africa at the time of the Act were, however, quite unlike anything in Australia in 1900, and were certainly not such as to lend themselves to a Constitution similar to that of the United States. The Supreme Court, in its interpretation of the South Africa Act, will therefore be guided largely by Canadian decisions. There is this great and fundamental difference, however, between South Africa and Canada, considered as federations : that there are not in South Africa two co-ordinate systems of government, not a federation with the sovereignty divided between the federation and the component States, but a genuine union. Questions of unconstitutionality in bills before the Parliament can, therefore, scarcely arise. In a manner of speaking, it may be said that South Africa is no federation (*a*).

Four provinces compose the Union, namely, Cape Colony, Natal, the Orange Free State and the Transvaal. The Governor-General is appointed by and represents the King. He is assisted by an Executive Council of Ministers.

The Legislature consists of the King, a Senate of forty members, one-eighth of whom are nominated by the Crown and the remaining thirty-two selected by the Legislatures of the four former colonies—eight for each colony. All hold office for ten years.

The Lower Chamber is called the House of Assembly, and consists of 121 members, elected for five years. No coloured subject of his Majesty is eligible as a member of the Legislature, but only persons of European extraction being also British subjects. Electors for Cape Colony need not be of European descent, but this law can be changed by statute passed by two-thirds of the Senate and House of Assembly.

Members of both Houses must take the oath or make affirmation of allegiance; must not be office-holders under the Union, but may be Ministers of State, members of the army or navy, or Crown pensioners.

Members can resign on giving notice of intention so to do. The South African Parliament can make laws for the peace, order, and good government of the Union, and it must assemble at least once annually. The Upper House cannot originate or amend any money bill. No other matter can be tacked to an appropriation bill, and, as is the case in England, financial measures can only be proposed by a Minister of the Crown at the instance of the Governor-General.

If the Upper House rejects a bill in two successive sessions a fresh legislative chamber has to be created which consists of the Upper and Lower Houses assembled together in joint session, and then the decision of the majority prevails; but where the bill in question is a money bill, then a majority of both chambers sitting together can settle the matter at once.

(*a*) See 9 Edw. VII. c. 9, the Act for constituting the Union of South Africa

The Governor-General may

(1) Assent to bills.
(2) Veto bills.
(3) Remit bills with his suggestions thereon for further consideration.
(4) Reserve bills for consideration by the Home Government.

If the Crown in this instance does not assent within one year the bill drops. Even where the Governor assents the Crown may veto a bill within twelve months. The provinces are controlled by administrators appointed by the Governor-General, who is assisted by a council of twenty-five members elected triennially.

The Council can legislate as to a very limited number of local matters, and this legislation can be repealed by the Union Parliament. Thus the South African Constitution is unitary, not federal : the Union Parliament's authority overriding that of the Provincial Council on all matters, and the Provincial Councils having exclusive legislative powers in regard to none.

There are in the Supreme Courts courts of first instance and appeal. Appeal to the Privy Council is by leave of the Supreme Court in most cases.

Judicature.—The South Africa Act, 1909 (9 Edw. VII. c. 9), constitutes a Supreme Court of South Africa, with original and appellate jurisdiction. The judges of appeal and other judges of the Supreme Court are appointed by the Governor-General in Council (section 100), and are only removable on an address from both Houses of Parliament in the same session praying for such removal on the ground of misbehaviour or incapacity (section 101). "There is to be no appeal from the Supreme Court of South Africa, or from any division thereof to the King in Council, but nothing is to impair any right which the King in Council may be pleased to exercise as to granting special leave to appeal from the Appellate Division of the Supreme Court to the King in Council."

"The South African Parliament may make laws limiting the matters in respect of which special leave to appeal may be asked, but bills containing such limitation shall be reserved by the Governor-General for the signification of his Majesty's pleasure, provided that nothing shall affect any right of appeal to his Majesty in Council from any judgment given by the Appellate Division of the Supreme Court under or in virtue of the Colonial Courts of Admiralty Act, 1890."

CONSTITUTION OF AUSTRALIA.

It is worthy of note that the Constitution of Australia, as framed by the Commonwealth of Australia Constitution Act, 1900, partakes of the characteristics of both a flexible and a rigid Constitution. It is rigid in so far as the exigencies of the notion of a federation require, but flexible in so far as the traditional British dislike of unyielding forms has found expression in well-understood conventions. The key to the proper understanding of the somewhat anomalous Australian Constitution is to be found in the fact that, for the first time in history, the endeavour has been made to harmonize the conception of a federal constitution with one that is essentially opposed to it—the monarchical or unitarian. Thus stated in terms, the endeavour would seem to be necessarily foredoomed to failure; but when it is realised that the relations of the Mother Country and the largest of her self-governing colonies are really unlike anything in the history of the world, and that the framers of the Constitution have ignored the forms and taken merely those of the conventions of our Constitution which truly represent the spirit and the actual facts, it may not unfairly be thought that the Act will effect its purpose. The chief features of the Constitution of the Australian Commonwealth are these: the government is avowedly federal in form, the federal or national Legislature having power to legislate on certain topics only, while the separate States have apparently unlimited power to legislate on the residuum of subjects (*b*); the composition of the Houses is such as to ensure, to a certain extent, the immunity of the Senate from the vicissitudes of popular feeling; for whereas the House of Representatives represents the mere numerical

(*b*) It should be noted here that whereas the Federal Government of the United States of America can legislate on only some eighteen topics, that of Australia can legislate on forty-two, ranging from such general matters as "external affairs" to such detail as "invalid and old age pensions."

majority, the Senate represents the individual States in an equal proportion, *i.e.*, each State is entitled to an equal number of senators (63 & 64 Vict. c. 12, s. 9 (7)). The senators, however, are elected for a longer term, viz., six years, whereas the House of Representatives can never exist for more than three years (c).

The federal executive is a Council to advise the Governor-General chosen and summoned by him, sworn as Executive Councillors, and holding office during his pleasure (section 9 (6)). The Ministers of State also hold office during the pleasure of the Governor-General; they must be members of the Federal Executive Council, and after the first general election no Minister may hold office for a longer period than three months, unless he is or becomes a senator or a member of the House of Representatives (*d*).

We may safely regard this executive as a parliamentary cabinet responsible to the Federal Parliament and to temporary majorities, as in England. It can dissolve Parliament (in effect) and so appeal to the electors from the authors of its own being. In the United States the administration of affairs rests with an elected President, *i.e.*, a non-parliamentary executive; in Switzerland, with an executive elected by the Federal Parliament, which cannot, however, be dismissed by its electors. This compromise brings out strongly the cabinet traditions with which the framers of the Commonwealth of Australia Constitution Act are so familiar. The Constitution of the Commonwealth is, in reality, as flexible as that of England, notwithstanding its federal form; for though strictly the Federal Parliament cannot alter it fundamentally, yet so wide is the range of topics or "articles" about which it can legislate that, apart from the seemingly efficient means of amendment, there is but little of fundamental importance upon which it cannot legislate. The actual machinery of amendment is a process indicative of a compromise between

(*c*) It may be here remarked, Professor Dicey observes, that though the above-noted sections of the Constitution Act would seem intended to secure a conservative element in the Senate, that body has so far shown itself "absolutely hostile to the maintenance of State rights, and far more so than the House of Representatives"

(*d*) This is in accordance with the spirit of our own Constitution, although an exception was once made in the case of Mr. Gladstone.

the principle that a measure passed by both Houses represents the will of the people and the principle of the referendum. Any measure altering the Constitution must be passed by an absolute majority of both Houses and then submitted to the electors for their ratification. Presumably the Law Courts are the guardians of the Constitution as the Courts are in the U.S.A.

In one way, of course, the Constitution of Australia must necessarily be different from that of any other federation, in that it must in express terms maintain the relation of the Commonwealth with the United Kingdom. Whether the Act expands and deepens the feeling of Australian nationality at the expense of the tie with the Mother Country is a matter which time alone can show.

The Act itself requires that no bill, whether an ordinary one or one that alters the Constitution, can become law unless it receives the assent of the Crown. Moreover, an Imperial Act can, in express terms, bind the Commonwealth (Colonial Laws Validity Act, 1865).

In short, the sovereignty of the Imperial Parliament is maintained in its integrity.

The Legislature consists of the King, represented by the Governor-General, an Upper House called the Senate (six for each of the States) the members whereof are elected for six years, and the House of Representatives, consisting of twice the Senate's number, elected on a basis of population for three years.

The Commonwealth Parliament can legislate as regards forty-two topics, whilst the State Legislatures have a supposed free hand as to other topics, and the Federal Government cannot nullify State legislation.

Every member of either House may resign on giving notice of his intention. He must be a natural-born subject of the King or else a naturalized subject for five years, and he must be of full age.

Judicature.—The judicial power of the Australian Commonwealth is vested in a federal court called the High Court of Australia and in such other federal courts as the Parliament creates. The High Court consists of a chief justice and other judges, not less than two in number. These judges are appointed by the Governor-General in Council, and are to be removed only by the Governor-General in Council on an address from both Houses of the Parliament in the same session praying for such removal on the ground of proved misbehaviour or incapacity (Australian Commonwealth Act, 1900, ss. 71, 72).

The High Court has, subject to regulations made from time to time by the Australian Parliament, a right to hear appeals from the courts of the States, from the judges of the Supreme Court exercising original jurisdiction, and as to points of law from the Inter-state Commission, and the judgment of the High Court shall in all such cases be conclusive (section 73). But no exception or regulation prescribed by the Parliament shall prevent the High Court from hearing any appeal from the Supreme Court of a State in any matter in which at the establishment of the Commonwealth an appeal lies from such Supreme Court to the King in Council (section 73).

No appeal shall be permitted to the King in Council from a decision of the High Court upon any question as to the limits *inter se* of the constitutional powers of the Commonwealth and those of any State or States, or as to the limits *inter se* " of the constitutional powers of any two or more States, unless the High Court shall certify that the question is one which ought to be determined by the King in Council " (section 74). The High Court may so certify at their discretion, and thereupon an appeal shall lie to the King in Council without further leave (section 74). Except as provided in this section, this Constitution shall not impair any right which the King may have by virtue of his prerogative to grant special leave of appeal from the High Court to the King in Council. The Commonwealth Parliament may make laws limiting the matters in which leave to appeal may be asked, but proposed laws containing any such limitations shall be reserved by the Governor-General for the King's pleasure (section 74).

The probability is that, with the exception of the cases mentioned in section 74, there is a concurrent right of appeal from the provincial courts to the Privy Council. The Judiciary Act [of the Commonwealth], 1903, s. 39, has restricted in certain cases the right of appeal to the King in Council (Tarring's Law relating to Colonies, 4th ed., p. 158).

In the case of *Webb* v. *Outrim* ((1907) A. C., p. 81) it was held by the Judicial Committee that the Australian Parliament could not under its Constitution take away the right of appeal to the King in Council from a judgment of the Supreme Court of Victoria as to the validity of the income tax of a Commonwealth officer in respect of his salary, or apparently from any judgment of the States Supreme Courts (Tarring, p. 158).

The question as to the concurrent right of appeal is, on the whole, a somewhat doubtful point.

APPENDIX B.

THE TREATY-MAKING POWER OF THE CROWN.

Blackstone says : " It is the Sovereign's prerogative to make treaties, leagues and alliances with foreign States. It is essential to the goodness of a league that it should be made by the sovereign power, and this power is vested in the King. Whatever contracts he engages in, no other power in the kingdom can annul." Maitland contends that a treaty made by the Crown has no legal effect (Maitland's Const. Hist., p. 424), and instances the Extradition Acts to show that the King is precluded from surrendering persons accused of crime contrary to our law without the aid of a statute. No treaty, except under very exceptional circumstances, should collide with the rights of the subject.

In the case of the *Parlement Belge* ((1879) 4 P. D., p. 429) Sir R. Phillimore quotes Blackstone's *dictum*, and then says, " Blackstone must have known very well that there were a class of treaties the provisions of which were inoperative without the confirmation of the Legislature," and then says that a treaty affecting private rights requires the sanction of the Legislature (cf. Maitland's Const. Hist., pp. 424-425).

By the making of a treaty the Crown may bind the Legislature by a moral obligation to carry it into effect. " Treaties of peace when made by the competent power are binding on the whole nation. If a treaty requires money to carry it into effect, and the money cannot be raised but by an Act of the Legislature, the treaty is morally obligatory on the Legislature to pass the law, and to refuse it would be a breach of public faith " (Kent's Comm., p. 166, 1873 ed.).

In *Walker* v. *Baird* ((1892) A. C., p. 49), Lord Herschell said : " The learned Attorney-General . . . . conceded that he could not maintain the proposition that the Crown could sanction an invasion by its officers of the rights of private individuals whenever it was necessary to compel obedience to a treaty, and . . . that if this be so the power must extend to the provisions of a treaty having for its object the preservation of peace, that an agreement arrived at to avert war was akin to a treaty of peace and subject to the same constitutional law, and then finally said (p. 497) that their lordships would express no opinion on this question."

The sovereign members of the Covenant of the League of Nations are probably not so free as formerly to make treaties with other States, as there is, in the opinion of certain political thinkers, a super-Parliament controlling the formerly existing powers of sovereign States, both foreign and domestic. Any day further doctrines may be laid down as to treaties, and the authors, who have delayed dealing with this subject to the last moment, regret that there are no fresh developments to record.

French statesmen, rightly or wrongly, think that they can make whatever treaties are necessary for the well-being of France without reference to the Treaty of Versailles.

APPENDIX C.

CESSION OF TERRITORY.

Professor Maitland is of opinion that the King may cede territory, at all events, territory acquired during war, but he is uncertain as to the extent of the power. He also considers that the King cannot without a statute cede land subject to the British Parliament (Maitland's Const. Hist., p. 424). He says that parliamentary sanction was obtained to the treaty of peace after the War of Independence. Florida was ceded to Spain without a statute, but by a treaty of peace.

In the following cases the Crown alienated British territory by a treaty which was neither a treaty of peace nor a treaty to avert war :—(1) Case of the surrender in 1817 to the Sikhim Puttee Rajah of territory formerly belonging to Nepaul. (2) In 1833 a surrender to Voorunder Singh of a portion of Assam, the Rajah undertaking to abstain from torturing his subjects. The Rajah was also under the treaty to pay a large annual tribute (Forsyth, Cases and Opinions on Const. Law, p. 185). Mr. Forsyth also says that since the Mutiny there have been several of these cessions to Indian rulers, but remarks that Indian necessities cannot be judged by European precedents (*ibid.*, p. 186).

APPENDIX D.

THE EMERGENCY POWERS ACT, 1920 (10 & 11 Geo. V. c. 55.)

This statute provides that, if at any time it appears to his Majesty that action has been taken, or is threatened, to interfere on an extensive scale with the supply of food, fuel, light, or other necessaries of life or with the means of locomotion, whereby the public or a large section thereof would be seriously affected, his Majesty may, by proclamation, declare a state of emergency. No such proclamation shall be in force for more than a month, without prejudice to the issue of a fresh proclamation during that period. Where proclamation of emergency has been made Parliament is to be informed thereof forthwith, and if the Houses be then adjourned or prorogued, they shall be summoned to meet within five days.

Where proclamation of emergency has been made, and so long as it shall be in force, his Majesty may in Council by order make regulations for securing the essentials of life to the community, and those regulations may impose on a Secretary of State or other Government Department, or any other person in his Majesty's service or acting on his Majesty's behalf, such powers and duties as his Majesty may deem necessary for preserving the peace, securing to the public the necessaries of life, the means of locomotion, and the general safety. Nothing in the Act is to authorise the making of regulations imposing any form of compulsory military service, the alteration of the rules of criminal procedure, or punishment for the peaceable persuasion of persons to join in a strike.

All regulations made by his Majesty shall be laid before Parliament as soon as practicable, and shall not continue in force after the expiration of seven days from the time they were laid before Parliament, unless a resolution is passed by both Houses providing for the continuance thereof. The regulations may provide for the trial by courts of summary jurisdiction of persons offending against the same, and the maximum penalty for breach of the regulations shall be imprisonment with or without hard labour for three months, or a fine of £100, or both such imprisonment and fine together with the forfeiture of any goods or money in respect of which the offence has been committed.

The regulations so made may be added to, altered, or revoked by resolution of both Houses, but the expiry or revocation of such regulations is not to affect any action taken thereunder.

This Act, as well as the Church of England Assembly (Powers) Act, sanctions important legislation by resolution of both Houses. As regards the Church Act, the legislation only affects a section of the community, but as regards the Emergency Powers Act, criminal offences can be created in the first instance by a royal proclamation, and afterwards made permanent by resolutions in both Houses.

The Act is, perhaps, justified by necessity, but the precedent of altering the criminal law in any other way than legislation by bill, with its usual publicity, is hardly to be commended.

APPENDIX E.

ANCIENT WRITS.

Certiorari.—This is a prerogative writ issued at the discretion of the court (1) to remove proceedings from an inferior court into the King's Bench Division of the High Court of Justice; (2) to bring up a peer for trial in the House of Lords for treason or felony (Blackstone, 4, pp. 262-271). As far as the Crown is concerned, it is a *de cursu* writ, but the King's Bench can exercise its discretion when it is applied for by individuals. A writ of *certiorari* is the recognised mode of procuring through the medium of the King's Bench an inspection of the proceedings of inferior criminal courts in order that they may be reviewed and rectified (Stone's Justice's Manual).

De ejectione firmæ.—This was a process evolved from the writ of trespass *vi et armis.* It gave the tenant of a leasehold ample remedies against practically everybody, but at first such tenant could only obtain damages for ouster from his holding, and he was unable to recover possession of the land demised to him, but about the time of Edward IV. the lessee adopting this writ could recover the land (Maitland's Equity, p. 351; Holdsworth, 3, p. 183).

Braeton mentions a writ whereby in his opinion the leaseholder could get redress from his landlord, and this writ was, according to Maitland and also Digby, the writ of *quia ejecit infra Terminum*, but FitzHerbert (who was probably mistaken) thinks otherwise. FitzHerbert was a judge *temp.* Henry VIII. and the author of *De brevium natura* and the *Grand Abridgment.*

As the real action was risky and unpopular, as well as costly, the writ *de ejectione firmæ* was utilised by the aid of fictions to get rid of a cumbersome process. The claimant to a freehold granted a lease to a friend, and later to a fictitious person called John Doe, who was ousted in imagination by another person called Richard Roe, the casual ejector. In process of time the defendant in adverse possession was compelled by the court to admit (1) the lease to Doe; (2) entry by Doe on the land; (3) ouster of Doe, and the action then went on between the real litigants. In 1852 Doe and Roe died by the hand of a common Law Procedure Act.

Dower.—There were three writs of dower: (1) Dower *unde nihil habet*, which lay where no dower (life interest in one-third of the land subject to certain restrictions) was assigned to the widow of a feudal tenant. (2) Writ of right of dower, which was a more general remedy, extending to the part of the dower the widow desired to claim. (3) Writ of admeasurement of dower, which lay against the widow, where the heir had allotted to her too much dower.

Elegit.—This writ is a *de cursu* writ, and was the first mode of execution against a debtor's land.

By the 2nd Statute of Westminster (13 Edw. I. c. 18) it is provided that a judgment creditor may elect that the sheriff deliver to him all the debtor's rents and profits (chattels, oxen and beasts of the plough excepted) until the debt be levied. The writ was called a writ of *elegit* because it stated that the creditor had elected to take the remedy provided by the above statute instead of having a writ of *fieri facias* against the chattels only of the debtor. The remaining half of the profits of the lands the debtor kept to satisfy his feudal dues. Under 1 & 2 Vict. c. 110 the creditor can take the whole of the profits of the debtor's lands under a writ of *elegit*.

Entry (abolished by 3 & 4 Will. IV. c. 27). This was a writ which disproved the title of the defendant in adverse possession by showing the unlawful means whereby he entered into or contінned in possession. The writ directed the sheriff to command the tenant to render up land in dispute (*præcipe quod reddat*) and into which, as he said, the tenant had not entry but by disseisin, intrusion, or the like (Blackstone, 3, c. 10).

The defendant could contest the writ, which was available where land was conveyed illegally by infants, idiots, or limited owners, who tried to pass the fee-simple. It also lay against tenants by sufferance who remained in possession after their tenancies had expired.

Error.—Prior to the Judicature Acts the writ of error was a method of setting right a common law judgment where the fault appeared by the record itself. It is now superseded by appealing (Stephen's Comm. 3, c. 11).

There were errors in fact and errors in law—an instance of the first kind being that defendant, being an infant, appeared by solicitor instead of guardian (*ibid*).

It may be useful here to mention that another mode of appeal was by bill of exceptions. Where a judge in his directions mistook the law by ignorance, inadvertence, or design, counsel on either side could require him to seal a document called a bill of exceptions, wherein was stated the point in which he was supposed to err. The bill of exceptions was afterwards examined in the Court of Exchequer Chamber (Steph. 3, c. 11).

Fieri facias.—This writ still exists, and it commands the sheriff to seize a litigant's goods and chattels. A judgment creditor is entitled to this writ on production of a judgment, or an office copy thereof.

Formedon.—In the reign of Edward I. the statute *de donis conditionalibus* was passed to secure the rights of the lord and the issue of the body of the donee of an estate tail, where there had been an improper alienation of the property. The writ to recover the land was called a writ of *formedon* because the lord or the issue, as the case might be, claimed *per formam doni*.

Previous to the passing of the statute *de donis* (13 Edw. I. c. 1) a donee of an estate tail could turn that interest into an estate in fee-simple directly he had issue born alive capable of inheriting.

Justicies.—A writ directing the sheriff to try a case in the capacity of judge.

Mandamus.—This writ still exists, and it is a prerogative writ commanding any person or corporation or inferior court to do some particular thing specified in the document appertaining to their office or duty (Steph. 3, c. 12).

Monstrans de droit.—This was a process whereby a suppliant of the Crown put in a claim of right upon facts already acknowledged, *e.g.*, by a record, and prayed the judgment of the court as to whether the King or the subject upon the facts was entitled to the right.

Ne exeat regno.—A prerogative writ obtainable in Chancery and at common law to prevent a person leaving the kingdom. Continuance in the kingdom was secured by imprisonment. This writ has probably ceased to exist.

Pone.—This writ derived its name from its commencing words, "*pone coram me et justiciariis meis.*" It directed the sheriff to bring up a given cause to the King's Court.

Præmunire.—This was a prerogative writ issuing from the Council (*concilium privatum*) forewarning the defendant to attend before the Council on pain of forfeiting £100.

Præmunire was originally the offence of applying to the Papal Court, but as the punishment was imprisonment during the royal pleasure and forfeiture of all property, the name was utilised for other offences which were attended with the like punishment. The Council had other means of securing a man's attendance, to wit, a writ of *subpœna*, followed by a commission of rebellion.

Procedendo.—A writ issuing out of the Chancery where inferior court judges delayed judgment. The writ enjoined delivery of judgment, either for one litigant or the other.

Prohibition.—A prerogative writ issuing out of King's Common Pleas, Exchequer, or Chancery. It was, and is, directed to the judges and parties to a suit in an inferior court directing them to cease from the prosecution thereof upon a suggestion that either the cause originally, or some collateral matter arising therein, does not belong to that jurisdiction, but to the cognisance of some other court (Blackstone, 3, c. 7).

Quia dominus remisit curiam.—The lord of the manor could in old days prevent his tenant from suing in the King's Court and before this writ could issue, the leave of the lord had to be obtained. After a time such leave was not necessary.

Quo warranto.—This writ is, says Blackstone, in the nature of a writ of right for the King against him who claims or usurps any office, franchise or liberty, to enquire by what authority he supports his claim, in order to determine the right. It lies also in case of non-user or long neglect of a franchise, or misuser or abuse of it, being a writ commanding the defendant to show by what warrant he exercises such a franchise, having never had any grant of it or having forfeited it by neglect or abuse.

The judgment on a writ of *quo warranto* is final and conclusive, even against the Crown. The *quo warranto* writ has now been superseded by an information. It was held in *Speyer's Case* recently that anyone can file this information on behalf of the Crown.

Recordari facias loquelam.—This was a writ issuing out of the King's Bench commanding the removal of proceedings from a court not of record into the King's Bench in order that the same might be reviewed. As there was no record kept of the proceedings, the judge of the court was directed by the writ to make one.

Scire facias.—This was a writ issuing out of the Chancery and the King's Bench. In Chancery it was used to repeal patents (Blackstone, 3, p. 260); also to get execution against the bail in a civil action (*ibid.*, p. 416), and to revive a judgment which could not be acted on.

Tolt.—This was a precept whereby the *vice-comes* procured the removal of a case from the Manor Court into the County Court. It derived its name from the words *quia tollit et eximit causam a curia baronis.*

APPENDIX F.

THE CRIMINAL AND CIVIL JURY.

The criminal jury is supposed by some to have originated from Ethelred's jury of presentment, but about this institution little that is reliable is known. Stubbs traces the jury to the Carolingian capitularies. In the reign of Henry II. a similar kind of jury is provided by the Constitutions of Clarendon. In 1166 the Assize of Clarendon ordained that twelve lawful men from each hundred and four lawful men from each township should be sworn to accuse reputed robbers, murderers, thieves, and receivers, and harbourers of murderers or thieves, and that the persons so presented be sent to the ordeal of water. By the Articles of Visitation (*temp.* Richard I.) the constitution of the grand jury established by Henry II. was further regulated and assimilated to the system then already in use for choosing the recognitors of the grand assize. The grand jury of those days were not judges of fact. They were neighbours who knew something of the transaction, either personally or from others they trusted. They had, however, to conceal nothing about which they had heard, and the rolls of the coroner and sheriff served as a check on them in this respect. At times the judges told the grand jury to institute enquiries in order to find out whether a given accusation was genuine. Till about 1215 reputed bad characters were sent to the ordeal, but even before that date we hear of another jury, the forerunners of the present petty jury, being impounded to give the accused a further opportunity for acquittal. All these persons were witnesses after a fashion. In the reign of Edward III. we hear of witnesses giving evidence who had no part in the verdict, but such evidence was given out of court.

In the reign of Henry IV. witnesses, who were clearly not jurymen, gave evidence at the bar of the court, and in Fortescue's time juries were judges of fact, as at the present day.

In 1676 Penn and Mead were indicted under the Conventicle Act, and the jury at the trial, of whom Bushell was one, acquitted the prisoners. Bushell and his colleagues on the jury were fined and imprisoned for disregarding the ruling of the judge. On the application for a *habeas corpus* Vaughan, C.J., decided to the effect that a jury cannot lawfully be punished by fine, imprisonment, or otherwise for finding against the evidence or direction of the judge (*Bushell*'s *Case*, Broom's Const. Law, p. 145). As to Fox's Libel Act, see *supra*.

By the Aliens Act, 1914—1918, any person interested may object in any proceeding, civil or criminal, to a foreigner being on the jury.

Foreigners are liable to serve on any jury after ten years' residence in England, if otherwise qualified. Women, if otherwise qualified, are also liable to serve.

The jury were originally summoned from the hundred, and as long as this practice prevailed they generally knew something about the case, but after a time they were selected from the body of the county. It is a strange fact that a man was not obliged, when charged with a criminal offence, to throw himself on his country for deliverance, and when the crime of which he was accused involved forfeiture he did not forfeit his property unless he pleaded. To make him plead he was crushed by heavy weights till he either pleaded or died (*peine forte et dure*). Strangeways was executed in this fashion in 1658, but the practice was not abolished till the latter half of the eighteenth century. When a man was appealed of felony he could challenge appellant to battle. Trial by battle was abolished in 1820 after *Thornton*'s Case.

The Civil Jury.—In mediæval days there was no weighing or sifting of evidence. There was no trial, but a mode of proof was put forward. The demandant had to satisfy the court that his cause of complaint was genuine before defendant had to do anything (cf. Carter's Eng. Legal Institutions, p. 222).

Cases were proved by compurgation, by an attested written document, or else by battle, or perhaps ordeal. Disputes respecting freeholds were settled by battle. The plaintiff or demandant was unable to fight, but defendant court.

After the introduction of Henry II.'s grand assize, trial by battle, so far as civil cases, at any rate, were concerned, began to decline, for though, according to Glanville, defendant could choose between the assize and battle, the judges probably frightened him into choosing the assize for the settlement of the dispute.

At first the original writ commencing the action summoned a jury, or assize as it was then called, but after the introduction of pleadings the jury were summoned after joinder of issue by writ of *venire facias*, and this jury so summoned was known as the *jurata*. Hence the expression, *Assiza vertitur in juratam.*

The notion of adducing evidence unknown to the jury arose from the judge directing them to investigate facts before delivering a verdict. We see traces of this kind of direction in the functions of the present jury, who hear witnesses *in camera* before finding a true bill or otherwise. In Henry IV.'s reign witnesses gave evidence before the judge and jury, and the custom of taking the jury from the body of the county instead of the hundred contributed to converting the jury into judges of fact. As to challenges of jury and the rest of the law relating to them, the student is referred to the commentaries of Dr. Odgers on the common law.

The remaining history of the law on the subject of civil juries resembles for the most part that of criminal juries.

APPENDIX G.

INDIA.

India Office.—India is not a colony, but it may be said to belong to the same genus. In 1857 the Government of India was transferred by the East India Company to the Crown, and the powers of that company were transferred to a Secretary of State. The secretary is assisted by a consultative council, the majority of whom must have served ten years in India, and all dispatches and orders of the Secretary of State must be laid before this body. Should the secretary and his home council disagree, he can override them, but must record his reasons.

Indian Constitution.—The supreme executive authority is vested in the Governor-General in Council. He is generally known as the Viceroy, and he is appointed by the Crown for five years. The Indian Legislature consists of the Viceroy and two chambers, viz., the Council of State and the Legislative Assembly. There are sixty members of the Council of State, who hold office for five years. Twenty of the members only may be officials and the rest are elected. The Legislative Assembly consists of 144 members, of whom twenty-six are officials, the others being elected. The Viceroy can dissolve the Legislature at his discretion. Subject to certain restrictions, the Indian Legislature can enact laws binding on all persons in India without distinction of race, and the Viceroy may on an emergency not only veto legislation but also pass certain laws over the heads of his Legislature (*e.g.*, he may increase the Budget), but in such a case his Majesty in Council may veto the legislation of the Viceroy. Differences between the two legislative chambers are to be settled by a joint sitting of both Houses.

India is now divided up into fifteen administrations. Each of these provinces possesses a Governor, a small European executive and also a Legislative Council, the bulk of whom are elected by popular vote. The topics for legislation are two-fold, namely, central subjects, *e.g.*, income tax, and minor or less important topics called provincial subjects, as to which latter the Legislature has a comparatively free hand. These latter subjects are dealt with by Indian Ministers on whose advice the Governor is supposed to act. In a word, all these native legislatures and executives constitute a constitutional school.

There are separate High Courts for Madras, Bombay, Bengal, Bihar and Orissa, United Provinces and Punjab, which exercise jurisdiction both civil and criminal, and from whose decisions an appeal lies to the Judicial Committee of the Privy Council.

India comprises all the Indian Peninsula directly under British protection (52 & 53 Vict. c. 63, s. 18). The Indian Constitution rests on the Government of India Act, 1915, as amended by the Government of India Acts, 1916 and 1919.

INDEX.

Printed at Reading, England, by the Eastern Press, Ltd.

LIST D. *May, 1922.*

BOOKS FOR LAW STUDENTS.

SUBJECT INDEX.

SWEET & MAXWELL, LIMITED, 3 Chancery Lane, London, W.C. 2.

Suggested Course of Reading for the Bar Examinations.

ROMAN LAW.

HUNTER'S Introduction or KELKE'S Primer. SANDARS' Justinian

CONSTITUTIONAL LAW.

CHALMERS & ASQUITH. THOMAS'S Leading Cases. HAMMOND'S Legal History.

CRIMINAL LAW AND PROCEDURE.

ODGERS' Common Law, or HARRIS'S Criminal Law, and WILSHERE'S Leading Cases Useful also is WILSHERE'S Criminal Law.

REAL PROPERTY.

WILLIAMS (with WILSHERE'S Analysis), or EDWARDS. For revision, KELKE'S Epitome.

CONVEYANCING.

DEANE & SPURLING'S Introduction, and CLARK'S Students' Precedents. Or ELPHINSTONE'S Introduction.

COMMON LAW.

ODGERS' Common Law (with WILSHERE'S Analysis), or INDERMAUR'S Common Law; or CARTER on Contracts, and FRASER on Torts. COCKLE'S Leading Cases.

EVIDENCE AND PROCEDURE.

ODGERS' Common Law, PHIPSON'S Manual of Evidence COCKLE'S Cases on Evidence, WILSHERE'S Procedure.

EQUITY.

SNELL or WILSHERE. For revision, BLYTH'S Analysis.

COMPANY LAW.

SMITH'S Summary.

SPECIAL SUBJECTS.

Bills of Exchange, JACOBS or WILLIS. *Easements*, CARSON. *Mortgages*, STRAHAN. *Partnership*, STRAHAN. *Sale of Goods*, WILLIS. *Wills*, MATHEWS or STRAHAN. *Master and Servant*, SMITH *Carriers*, WILLIAMS.

Suggested Course of Reading for the Solicitors' Final Examination.

For detailed Courses see Steele's Self-Preparation for the Final Examination.

COMMON LAW.

INDERMAUR'S Principles of the Common Law
ANSON or POLLOCK on Contracts.
RINGWOOD or SALMOND on Torts
SMITH'S Leading Cases, with INDERMAUR'S Epitome, or COCKLE & HIBBERT'S Leading Cases

EQUITY.

WILSHERE'S or SNELL'S Principles of Equity
BLYTH'S Analysis of SNELL.
WHITE & TUDOR'S Leading Cases, with INDERMAUR'S Epitome
STRAHAN on Partnership
UNDERHILL on Trusts

REAL AND PERSONAL PROPERTY AND CONVEYANCING.

WILLIAMS or EDWARDS on Real Property.
WILLIAMS or GOODEVE on Personal Property.
WILSHERE'S Analysis of WILLIAMS
ELPHINSTONE'S or DEANE'S Introduction to Conveyancing.
INDERMAUR'S Epitome of Conveyancing Cases

PRACTICE OF THE COURTS.

INDERMAUR'S Manual of Practice

BANKRUPTCY.

RINGWOOD'S Principles of Bankruptcy.

CRIMINAL LAW.

HARRIS'S Principles of Criminal Law.
WILSHERE'S Leading Cases

PROBATE, DIVORCE, AND ADMIRALTY.

GIBSON'S Probate, Divorce, and Admiralty.

ECCLESIASTICAL LAW.

SMITH'S Summary.

COMPANIES.

SMITH'S Summary.

NOTICE.—*In consequence of fluctuation in cost of printing and materials, prices are subject to alteration without notice.*

ADMIRALTY.

SMITH'S Law and Practice in Admiralty. For the use of Students. By EUSTACE SMITH, of the Inner Temple. Fourth Edition. 232 pages. Price 10s. net.

"The book is well arranged, and forms a good introduction to the subject."—*Solicitors' Journal.*

"It is, however, in our opinion, a well and carefully written little work, and should be in the hands of every student who is taking up Admiralty Law at the Final."—*Law Students' Journal.*

"Mr. Smith has a happy knack of compressing a large amount of useful matter in a small compass. The present work will doubtless be received with satisfaction equal to that with which his previous 'Summary' has been met."—*Oxford and Cambridge Undergraduates' Journal.*

AGENCY.

BOWSTEAD'S Digest of the Law of Agency. By W. BOWSTEAD, Barrister-at-Law. Sixth Edition. 485 pages. Price £1 7s. 6d. net.

"The Digest will be a useful addition to any law library, and will be especially serviceable to practitioners who have to advise mercantile clients or to conduct their litigation, as well as to students, such as candidates for the Bar Final Examination and for the Consular Service, who have occasion to make the law of agency a subject of special study."—*Law Quarterly Review.*

ARBITRATION.

SLATER'S Law of Arbitration and Awards. With Appendix containing the Statutes relating to Arbitration, and a collection of Forms and Index. Fifth Edition. By JOSHUA SLATER, Barrister-at-Law. 215 pages. Price 5s. net.

BANKING.

RINGWOOD'S Outlines of the Law of Banking. 1906. 191 pages. Price 5s. net.

" . The book is in a most convenient and portable form, and we can heartily commend the latest production of this well-known writer to the attention of the business community."—*Financial Times.*

BANKRUPTCY.

MANSON'S Short View of Bankruptcy Law. By EDWARD MANSON, Barrister-at-Law. Third Edition. 351 pages. Price 8s. 6d. net.

A book of 350 pages, giving the salient points of the law. The author follows the order of proceedings in their historical sequence, illustrating each step by forms and by some of the more important cases

"It makes a thorough manual for a student, and a very handy book of reference to a practitioner"—*Law Magazine.*

RINGWOOD'S Principles of Bankruptcy. Embodying the Bankruptcy Acts; Leading Cases on Bankruptcy and Bills of Sale; Deeds of Arrangement Act; Bankruptcy Rules; Deeds of Arrangement Rules, 1915; Bills of Sale Acts, and the Rules, etc. Thirteenth Edition. 431 pages. Price £1 5s. net.

"We welcome a new edition of this excellent student's book We have written favourably of it in reviewing previous editions, and every good word we have written we would now reiterate and perhaps even more so . . In conclusion, we congratulate Mr. Ringwood on this edition, and have no hesitation in saying that it is a capital student's book"—*Law Students' Journal*

"The author deals with the whole history of a bankruptcy from the initial act of bankruptcy down to the discharge of the bankrupt, and a cursory perusal of his work gives the impression that the book will prove useful to practitioners as well as to students The appendix also contains much matter that will be useful to practitioners, including the Schedules, the Bankruptcy Rules, the Rules of the Supreme Court as to Bills of Sale, and various Acts of Parliament bearing upon the subject The Index is copious"—*Accountants' Magazine*

BILLS OF EXCHANGE.

JACOBS on Bills of Exchange, Cheques, Promissory Notes, and Negotiable Instruments Generally, including a digest of cases and a large number of representative forms, and a note on I O U's and Bills of Lading. By BERTRAM JACOBS, Barrister-at-Law. 284 pages. Price 7s. 6d. net.

OPINIONS OF TUTORS.

"It appears to me to be a most excellent piece of work."

"After perusing portions of it I have come to the conclusion that it is a learned and exhaustive treatise on the subject, and I shall certainly bring it to the notice of my pupils."

WILLIS'S Negotiable Securities. Contained in a Course of Six Lectures delivered by WILLIAM WILLIS, Esq., K.C., at the request of the Council of Legal Education. Third Edition, by JOSEPH HURST, Barrister-at-Law. 226 pages. Price 7s. 6d. net.

"No one can fail to benefit by a careful perusal of this volume." —*Irish Law Times.*

"We heartily commend them, not only to the student, but to everybody—lawyer and commercial man alike."—*The Accountant.*

"Mr. Willis is an authority second to none on the subject, and in these lectures he summarized for the benefit not only of his confrères but of the lay public the knowledge he has gained through close study and lengthy experience."

CARRIERS.

WILLIAMS' Epitome of Railway Law. Part I. The Carriage of Goods. Part II. The Carriage of Passengers. By E. E. G. WILLIAMS, Barrister-at-Law. Second Edition. 231 pages. Price 10s. net.

A useful book for the Bar and Railway Examinations.

"Admirably arranged, and clearly written with an economy of language which goes to the heart of a busy man."—*Sittings Review.*

COMMON LAW.

(See also Broom's Legal Maxims *post*)

ODGERS on the Common Law of England. By W. Blake Odgers, K.C., LL.D., Director of Legal Education at the Inns of Court, and Walter Blake Odgers, Barrister-at-Law. Second Edition. 2 vols. 1,474 pages. Price £3 10s. net.

Odgers on the Common Law deals with Contracts, Torts, Criminal Law and Procedure, Civil Procedure, the Courts, and the Law of Persons

The Student who masters it can pass the following Bar Examinations :—

(1) **Criminal Law and Procedure.**

(2) **Common Law.**

(3) **General Paper—Part A.**

And (with Cockle's Cases and Statutes on Evidence)

(4) **Law of Evidence and Civil Procedure.**

(5) **General Paper—Part III.**

SOME OPINIONS OF PROFESSORS AND TUTORS.

1. **The Bar.**—"I have most carefully examined the work, and shall most certainly recommend it to all students reading with me for the Bar Examinations."

"It appears to me to be an invaluable book to a student who desires to do well in his examinations. The sections dealing with Criminal Law and Procedure are, in my opinion, especially valuable. They deal with these difficult subjects in a manner exactly fitted to the examinations; and in this the work differs from any other book I know."

"I have been reading through Dr. Odgers' Common Law, and find it a most excellent work for the Bar Final, also for the Bar Criminal Law"

---

2. **The Universities.**—"I consider it to be a useful and comprehensive work on a very wide subject, more especially from

the point of view of a law student. I shall be glad to recommend it to the favourable attention of law students of the University."

---

3. Solicitors.—THE BOOK FOR THE SOLICITORS' FINAL.—"Once the Intermediate is over, the articled clerk has some latitude allowed as to his course of study. And, without the slightest hesitation, we say that the first book he should tackle after negotiating the Intermediate is 'Odgers on the Common Law.' The volumes may seem a somewhat 'hefty task,' but these two volumes give one less trouble to read than any single volume of any legal text-book of our acquaintance. They cover, moreover, all that is most interesting in the wide field of legal studies in a manner more interesting than it has ever been treated before"

INDERMAUR'S Principles of the Common Law. The Law of Contracts and Torts, with a Short Outline of the Law of Evidence. Thirteenth Edition. Re-written and enlarged by A. M. WILSHERE, Barrister-at-Law. 629 pages. Price £1 7s. 6d. net.

For many years Indermaur's Common Law has been a valued friend of the law student, but after a very careful examination of the book Mr. Wilshere found that, if it was to retain the position its merits had won, it could not be re-edited without substantial changes The rearrangements he has made will assist a student who, after or with Indermaur, reads other books on particular subjects.

INDERMAUR'S Leading Common Law Cases; with some short notes thereon. Chiefly intended as a Guide to "SMITH'S LEADING CASES." Tenth Edition. by E. A. JELF. Master of the Supreme Court. With six illustrations by E. T. REED. 111 pages. Price 8s. 6d. net.

The editor has introduced several new features with a view to assisting the student in remembering the principles of law dealt with, but the unique feature of the edition is the addition of six illustrations by Mr. E. T. Reed. After seeing these illustrations of the bull in the ironmonger's shop, the chimney-sweep and the jeweller, the six carpenters in the tavern, etc, you will find it easy to remember the cases and what points they decided. Every wise student reads this book.

Common Law—*continued.*

COCKLE & HIBBERT'S Leading Cases in Common Law. With Notes, Explanatory and Connective, presenting a Systematic View of the whole Subject. By E. COCKLE and W. NEMBHARD HIBBERT, LL.D., Barristers-at-Law. 962 pages Price £2 2s. net.

This book is on the same lines as Cockle's Cases on Evidence.

Following is a short summary of its contents:—

Nature of the Common Law.	**Void, etc., Contracts.**	**Negotiable Instruments.**
Common Law Rights and Duties.	**Quasi-Contracts.**	**Partnership.**
Contract, including Contracts of Record.	**Agency.**	**Sale of Goods.**
Specialty Contracts.	**Bailments.**	**Torts.**
Simple Contracts.	**Carriers.**	**Damages.**
	Landlord and Tenant.	**Law of Persons.**
	Master and Servant.	**Conflict of Laws.**

"Dr. Hibbert is to be congratulated on the masterly manner in which he has re-edited Cockle's Leading Cases on Common Law. The arrangement and printing are particularly clear, the choice of cases is marked by great discretion, and a short analysis of the law of various departments dealt with in the book is set forth with a view to refreshing the reader's knowledge on the subject before he turns to read the cases which are set out."—*Law Coach.*

"The present work has the merits of thoroughness, accuracy, systematic arrangement and a modern point of view."—*Solicitors' Journal.*

SMITH'S Leading Cases. A Selection of Leading Cases in various Branches of the Law, with Notes. Twelfth Edition. By T. WILLES CHITTY, a Master of the Supreme Court, J. H. WILLIAMS, and W. H. GRIFFITH, Barristers-at-Law. 2 vols. Price £4 net.

This work presents a number of cases illustrating and explaining the leading principles of the common law, accompanied by exhaustive notes showing how those principles have been applied in subsequent cases

JELF'S Fifteen Decisive Battles of the Law. By E. A. JELF, Master of the Supreme Court. Second Edition. 124 pages. Price 6s. 6d. net.

Mr. Jelf narrates with light and skilful touch the incidents and results of fifteen of the most important decisions ever given by the judges, and he shows the effect which each decision has had upon the general body of English Law.

COMPANIES.

KELKE'S Epitome of Company Law. Second Edition. 255 pages. Price 6s.

"No clearer or more concise statement of the law as regards companies could be found than is contained in this work, and any student who thoroughly masters it need have no fear of not passing his examination."—*Juridical Review.*

SMITH'S Summary of the Law of Companies. By T. EUSTACE SMITH, Barrister-at-Law Twelfth Edition, by the Author, and C. H. HICKS 376 pages. Price 7s. 6d. net.

"The author of this handbook tells us that when an articled student reading for the final examination, he felt the want of such a work as that before us, wherein could be found the main principles of a law relating to joint-stock companies. . . . Law students may well read it; for Mr. Smith has very wisely been at the pains of giving his authority for all his statements of the law or of practice, as applied to joint-stock company business usually transacted in solicitors' chambers. In fact, Mr. Smith has by his little book offered a fresh inducement to students to make themselves—at all events, to some extent—acquainted with company law as a separate branch of study."—*Law Times*

"These pages give, in the words of the Preface, 'as briefly and concisely as possible a general view both of the principles and practice of the law affecting companies' The work is excellently printed, and authorities are cited; but in no case is the language of the statutes copied. The plan is good, and shows both grasp and neatness, and, both amongst students and laymen, Mr. Smith's book ought to meet a ready sale."—*Law Journal.*

CONFLICT OF LAWS.

WESTLAKE'S Treatise on Private International Law, with Principal Reference to its Practice in England. Sixth Edition. By NORMAN BENTWICH, Barrister-at-Law. Price £1 7s. 6d. net.

FOOTE'S Private International Jurisprudence. Based on the Decisions in the English Courts. Fourth Edition. By COLEMAN PHILLIPSON, LL.D., Barrister-at-Law. 574 pages. Price £1 5s. net.

'Foote' is the prescribed book for the Solicitors' Honours Examination.

CONSTITUTIONAL LAW AND HISTORY.

CHALMERS' & ASQUITH'S Outlines of Constitutional and Administrative Law, with Notes on Legal History. By D. CHALMERS and CYRIL ASQUITH, Barristers-at-Law. Second Edition. 320 pages. Price 12s. 6d. net.

"A very sound treatise, distinctly above the average This book supplies a long-felt want The whole field is covered in an interesting manner, unusual in a work which does not claim to be anything more than an outline" *New Cambridge*

"The learned authors have very clearly tabulated and defined the technicalities of our constitutional law. The book is well arranged and well indexed"—*Saturday Review.*

THOMAS'S Leading Cases in Constitutional Law. Briefly stated, with Introduction and Notes. By ERNEST C. THOMAS, Bacon Scholar of the Hon. Society of Gray's Inn, late Scholar of Trinity College, Oxford. Fifth Edition. By FRANK CARR, LL.D.

[*In the press.*

TASWELL-LANGMEAD'S English Constitutional History. From the Teutonic Invasion to the Present Time. Designed as a Text-book for Students and others. By T. P. TASWELL-LANGMEAD, B.C.L., of Lincoln's Inn, Barrister-at-Law, formerly Vinerian Scholar in the University and late Professor of Constitutional Law and History, University College, London. Eighth Edition. By COLEMAN PHILLIPSON, LL.D. 854 pages. Price 21s. net.

"'Taswell-Langmead' has long been popular with candidates for examination in Constitutional History, and the present edition should render it even more so It is now, in our opinion, the ideal students' book upon the subject"—*Law Notes.*

"The work will continue to hold the field as the best classbook on the subject."—*Contemporary Review.*

"The work before us it would be hardly possible to praise too highly. In style, arrangement, clearness, and size it would be difficult to find anything better on the real history of England, the history of its constitutional growth as a complete story, than this volume."—*Boston (U S.) Literary World.*

WILSHERE'S Analysis of Taswell-Langmead's Constitutional History. By A. M. WILSHERE, LL.B., Barrister-at-Law. 115 pages. Price 6s. 6d. net.

HAMMOND'S Short English Constitutional History for Law Students. By EDGAR HAMMOND, B.A. 163 pages. Price 7s. 6d. net.

An excellent book for the purpose of refreshing one's knowledge preparatory to taking an examination.

"An excellent cram-book and a little more. The tabulation of the matter is excellent."—*Law Times.*

CONTRACTS.

ODGERS on the Common Law. See page 7.

WILSHERE'S Analysis of Contracts and Torts, By A. M. WILSHERE and DOUGLAS ROBB, Barristers-at-Law. Second Edition. 172 pages. Price 7s. 6d. net.

It is designed as an assistance to the memory of the Student who has read Odgers or Indermaur on the Common Law

CARTER on Contracts. Elements of the Law of Contracts. By A. T. CARTER, of the Inner Temple, Barrister-at-Law, Reader to the Council of Legal Education. Fourth Edition. 272 pages. Price 8s. 6d

"We have here an excellent book for those who are beginning to read law."—*Law Magazine.*

CONVEYANCING.

ELPHINSTONE'S Introduction to Conveyancing. By Sir HOWARD WARBURTON ELPHINSTONE, Bart. Seventh Edition, by F. TRENTHAM MAW, Barrister-at-Law, Editor of Key and Elphinstone's Precedents in Conveyancing. 694 pages. Price 25s. net.

"Incomparably the best introduction to the art of conveyancing that has appeared in this generation. It contains much that is useful to the experienced practitioner."—*Law Times.*

Conveyancing—*continued.*

"In our opinion no better work on the subject with which it deals was ever written for students and young practitioners"—*Law Notes.*

" . from a somewhat critical examination of it we have come to the conclusion that it would be difficult to place in a student's hand a better work of its kind."—*Law Students' Journal*

DEANE & SPURLING'S Introduction to **Conveyancing,** with an Appendix of Students' Precedents. Third Edition, by CUTHBERT SPURLING, Barrister-at-Law. Price £1 1s. net.

This book is complementary to and extends the information in "Williams." It is clearly and attractively written and the text extends to 273 pages. The reader is taken through the component parts of Purchase Deeds, Leases, Mortgage Deeds, Settlements and Wills, and the way in which these instruments are prepared is explained. Previous to this is a short history of Conveyancing, and a chapter on Contracts for Sale of Land dealing with the statutory requisites, the form, particulars and conditions of sale, the abstract of title, requisitions, etc, and finally there is a chapter on conveyance by registration. The second part of the book, covering about 100 pages, contains CLARK'S STUDENTS' PRECEDENTS IN CONVEYANCING, illustrating the various documents referred to in the first part It is the only book containing a representative collection of precedents for students.

"It is readable and clear and will be of interest even to those students who are not specialising in questions of real property."—*Cambridge Law Journal*

"The style is singularly lucid and the writer has deliberately formed the opinion that this book should form part of the course of every student who desires a real practical acquaintance with modern conveyancing . . Properly used, the writer's opinion is that Deane and Spurling should be one of the first books studied after the Intermediate has been negotiated"—*Sittings Review*

INDERMAUR'S Leading Conveyancing and Equity Cases. With some short notes thereon, for the use of Students. By JOHN INDERMAUR, Solicitor. Tenth Edition by C. THWAITES. 206 pages. Price 6s. net.

"The Epitome well deserves the continued patronage of the class—Students—for whom it is especially intended. Mr. Indermaur will soon be known as the 'Student's Friend'"—*Canada Law Journal.*

CRIMINAL LAW AND PROCEDURE.

ODGERS on the Common Law. See page 7.

HARRIS'S Principles of the Criminal Law. Intended as a Lucid Exposition of the subject for the use of Students and the Profession. Thirteenth Edition. By A. M. WILSHERE, Barrister-at-Law. 520 pages. Price 16s. net.

"This Standard Text-book of the Criminal Law is as good a book on the subject as the ordinary student will find on the library shelves . . The book is very clearly and simply written. No previous legal knowledge is taken for granted, and everything is explained in such a manner that no student ought to have much difficulty in obtaining a grasp of the subject. . . ." —*Solicitors' Journal.*

". . . . As a Student's Text-book we have always felt that this work would be hard to beat, and at the present time we have no reason for altering our opinion. . . . ."—*Law Times.*

WILSHERE'S Elements of Criminal and Magisterial Law and Procedure. By A. M. WILSHERE, Barrister-at-Law. Third Edition. [*In the press.*

This book sets out concisely the essential principles of the criminal law and explains in detail the most important crimes, giving precedents of indictments; it also gives an outline of criminal procedure and evidence.

"An excellent little book for examination purposes. Any student who fairly masters the book ought to pass any ordinary examination in criminal law with ease."—*Solicitors' Journal.*

WILSHERE'S Leading Cases illustrating the Criminal Law, for Students. 168 pages. Price 6s. 6d. net.

A companion book to the above.

"This book is a collection of cases pure and simple, without a commentary. In each case a short rubric is given, and then follow the material parts of the judge's opinions. The selection of cases has been judiciously made, and it embraces the whole field of criminal law. The student who has mastered this and its companion volume will be able to face his examiners in criminal law without trepidation."—*Scots Law Times.*

EASEMENTS.

BLYTH'S Epitome of the Law of Easements. By T. T. BLYTH, Barrister-at-Law. 158 pages. Price 6s. net.

"The book should prove a useful addition to the student's library, and as such we can confidently recommend it."—*Law Quarterly Review.*

CARSON on Prescription and Custom. Six Lectures delivered for the Council of Legal Education. By T. H. CARSON, K.C. 136 pages. Price 6s. net.

ECCLESIASTICAL LAW.

SMITH'S Law and Practice in the Ecclesiastical Courts. For the use of Students. By EUSTACE SMITH, Barrister-at-Law. Seventh Edition. 219 pages. Price 12s. 6d. net.

"His object has been, as he tells us in his preface, to give the student and general reader a fair outline of the scope and extent of ecclesiastical law, of the principles on which it is founded, of the Courts by which it is enforced, and the procedure by which these Courts are regulated. We think the book well fulfils its object. Its value is much enhanced by a profuse citation of authorities for the propositions contained in it"—*Bar Examination Journal*

EQUITY.

SNELL'S Principles of Equity. Intended for the use of Students and Practitioners. Eighteenth Edition. By H. G. RIVINGTON, M.A. Oxon., and A. C. FOUNTAINE. 578 pages. Price £1 10s. net.

"In a most modest preface the editors disclaim any intention to interfere with Snell as generations of students have known it. Actually what they have succeeded in doing is to make the book at least three times as valuable as it ever was before Illustrations from cases have been deftly introduced, and the whole rendered simple and intelligible until it is hardly recognisable"—*The Students' Companion*

"It has been stated that this book is intended primarily for law students, but it is much too useful a book to be so limited It is in our opinion the best and most lucid summary of the principles of the law of equity in a small compass, and should be in every lawyer's library."—*Australian Law Times.*

"'Snell's Equity' which has now reached its seventeenth edition, has long occupied so strong a position as a standard work for students that it was not easy to perceive how it could be improved. The new editors have succeeded in achieving this task."—*Law Journal.*

BLYTH'S Analysis of Snell's Principles of Equity, with Notes thereon. By E. E. BLYTH, LL.D., Solicitor. Eleventh Edition. 270 pages. Price 7s. 6d. net.

"This is an admirable analysis of a good treatise; read with Snell, this little book will be found very profitable to the student."—*Law Journal.*

STORY'S Commentaries on Equity Jurisprudence. Third English Edition. By A. E. RANDALL. 641 pages. Price 37s. 6d. net.

WILSHERE'S Principles of Equity. By A. M. WILSHERE. 499 pages. Price £1 5s. net.

In this book the author has endeavoured to *explain* and enable the student to *understand* Equity. He has incorporated a large number of explanations from the authorities and has tried to make the subject intelligible while at the same time he has as much useful and relevant detail as the larger students' works. It is not a mere "cram" book. A useful feature is an analysis of the subject which follows the text.

"Mr. Wilshere has succeeded in giving us a very clear exposition of these principles. The book is far better balanced than the majority of text books, and the law is stated in its modern garb and is not, as in so many elementary works, almost lost to sight beneath a mass of historical explanatory matter."—*Sittings Review.*

KELKE'S Epitome of Leading Cases in Equity. Founded on White and Tudor's Leading Cases in Equity. Third Edition. 241 pages. Price 6s.

"It is not an abridgment of the larger work, but is intended to furnish the beginner with an outline of equity law so far as it is settled or illustrated by a selection of cases. Each branch is dealt with in a separate chapter, and we have *(inter alia)* trusts, mortgages, specific performance and equitable assignments, and equitable implications treated with reference to the cases on the subject."—*Law Times.*

INDERMAUR'S Epitome of Leading Equity Cases.

See page 13.

WHITE & TUDOR'S Leading Cases in Equity. A Selection of Leading Cases in Equity; with Notes. Eighth Edition. By W. J. WHITTAKER, of the Middle Temple and Lincoln's Inn, Barrister-at-Law. 2 vols. Price £4 net.

"'White and Tudor' towers high above all other works on Equity. It is the fountain of Equity, from which all authors draw and drink. It is the book we all turn to when we want to know what the Judges of the old Court of Chancery, or its modern representative, the Chancery Division, have said and decided on this or that principle of law It is the book in which counsel in his chambers puts such faith, and from which in Court counsel reads with so much confidence. It is the book from the law of which Judges hesitate to depart."—*Law Notes.*

EVIDENCE.

COCKLE'S Leading Cases and Statutes on the Law of Evidence, with Notes, explanatory and connective, presenting a systematic view of the whole subject. By ERNEST COCKLE, Barrister-at-Law. Third Edition. 500 pages. Price 16s. 6d. net.

This book and Phipson's Manual are together ***sufficient*** for all ordinary examination purposes, and will save students the necessity of reading larger works on this subject

By an ingenious use of black type the author brings out the essential words of the judgments and Statutes, and enables the student to see at a glance the effect of each section

"Of all the collections of leading cases compiled for the use of students with which we are acquainted, this book of Mr. Cockle's is, in our opinion, far and away the best The student who picks up the principles of the English law of evidence from these readable and logical pages has an enormous advantage over a generation of predecessors who toiled through the compressed sentences of Stephen's little digest in a painful effort to grasp its meaning. Mr Cockle teaches his subject in the only way in which a branch of law so highly abstract can ever be grasped; he arranges the principal rules of evidence in logical order, but he puts forward each in the shape of a leading case which illustrates it just enough of the headnote, the facts, and the judgments are selected and set out to explain the point fully without boring the reader; ***and the notes*** appended to the cases ***contain all the additional information that anyone can require in ordinary practice.***"—*Solicitors' Journal.*

PHIPSON'S Law of Evidence. By S. L. Phipson, Barrister-at-Law. Sixth Edition. 699 pages. Price £2 2s. net.

"The best book now current on the law of evidence in England."—*Harvard Law Review.*

PHIPSON'S Manual of the Law of Evidence. Second Edition. 208 pages. Price 12s. 6d. net.

This is an abridgment for students of Mr. Phipson's larger treatise. With Cockle's Cases it will be sufficient for examination purposes.

"The way of the student, unlike that of the transgressor, is no longer hard. The volume under review is designed by the author for the use of students. To say that it is the best text-book for students upon the subject is really to understate its usefulness; as far as we know there is in existence no other treatise upon evidence which gives a scientific and accurate presentment of the subject in a form and compass suitable to students."—*Australian Law Times.*

"We know no book on the subject which gives in so short a space so much valuable information. We readily commend the work both to students and to practitioners, especially those who, not being in possession of the author's larger work, wish to have an up-to-date and explanatory companion to 'Cockle.'"—*South African Law Journal.*

BEST'S Principles of Evidence. With Elementary Rules for conducting the Examination and Cross-Examination of Witnesses. Eleventh Edition. By S. L. Phipson, Barrister-at-Law. 620 pages. Price £1 5s. net.

"The most valuable work on the law of evidence which exists in any country."—*Law Times.*

"There is no more scholarly work among all the treatises on Evidence than that of Best. There is a philosophical breadth of treatment throughout which at once separates the work from those mere collections of authorities which take no account of the 'reason why,' and which arrange two apparently contradictory propositions side by side without comment or explanation."—*Law Magazine.*

WROTTESLEY on the Examination of Witnesses in Court. Including Examination in Chief, Cross-Examination, and Re-Examination. With chapters on Preliminary Steps and some Elementary Rules of Evidence. By F. J. WROTTESLEY, of the Inner Temple, Barrister-at-Law. 173 pages. Price 6s. net.

This is a practical book for the law student It is interesting, and is packed full of valuable hints and information. The author lays down clearly and succinctly the rules which should guide the advocate in the examination of witnesses and in the argument of questions of fact and law, and has illustrated the precepts which he has given by showing how they have been put into actual practice by the greatest advocates of modern times.

EXAMINATION GUIDES AND QUESTIONS.

SHEARWOOD'S Selection of Questions set at the Bar Examinations from 1913 to 1921. Price 6s. net.

STEELE'S Articled Clerk's Guide to and Self-Preparation for the Final and Honours Examinations. Containing a Complete Course of Study, with Books to Read, Test Questions, Regulations, &c., and intended for the use of those Articled Clerks who read by themselves. Incorporating Indermaur's Articled Clerk's Guide. By E. A. STEELE and G. R. J DUCKWORTH, Solicitors, Principals of the Halifax Law Classes. Price 4s. 6d. net.

This book tells you what are the best books to read, how and when to read them, gives test questions to be answered at the various stages of reading and a set of questions and answers Even if you are being coached, you will find many useful hints and much sound advice in it.

A **New Guide to the Bar.** Containing the Regulations and Examination Papers, and a critical Essay on the Present Condition of the Bar of England. By LL.B., Barrister-at-Law. Fourth Edition. 204 pages. Price 5s.

A **Guide to the Legal Profession and London LL.B.** Containing the latest Regulations, with a detailed description of all current Students' Law Books, and suggested courses of reading. 99 pages. Price 2s. 6d. net.

EXECUTORS.

WALKER'S Compendium of the Law relating to Executors and Administrators. Fifth Edition. By S. E. WILLIAMS, of Lincoln's Inn, Barrister-at-Law. 400 pages. £1 5s. net.

"We highly approve of Mr Walker's arrangement. . . . We can commend it as bearing on its face evidence of skilful and careful labour."—*Law Times.*

INSURANCE LAW.

HARTLEY'S Analysis of the Law of Insurance. By D. H. J. HARTLEY, Barrister-at-Law. 119 pages. Price 4s. 6d. net.

PORTER'S Laws of Insurance: Fire, Life, Accident, and Guarantee. Embodying Cases in the English, Scotch, Irish, American, Australian, New Zealand, and Canadian Courts. Sixth Edition. 490 pages. Price £1 12s. 6d. net.

INTERNATIONAL LAW.

BENTWICH'S Students' Leading Cases and Statutes on International Law, arranged and edited with notes. By NORMAN BENTWICH, Barrister-at-Law. With an Introductory Note by Professor L. OPPENHEIM. 247 pages. Price 12s. 6d. net.

"This Case Book is admirable from every point of view, and may be specially recommended to be used by young students in conjunction with their lectures and their reading of text-books."—*Professor Oppenheim.*

COBBETT'S Leading Cases and Opinions on International Law, and various points of English Law connected therewith, Collected and Digested from English and Foreign Reports, Official Documents, and other sources. With Notes containing the views of the Text-writers on the Topics referred to, Supplementary Cases, Treaties, and Statutes. By PITT CORBETT, M.A., D.C.L. Oxon.

Vol. I. "Peace." Fourth Edition. By H. H. L. BELLOT, D.C.L. 365 pages. Price 16s. net.

Vol. II. "War and Neutrality." Third Edition. By the Author. 579 pages. 15s. net.

"The book is well arranged, the materials well selected, and the comments to the point. Much will be found in small space in this book."—*Law Journal.*

"The notes are concisely written and trustworthy. . . . . The reader will learn from them a great deal on the subject, and the book as a whole seems a convenient introduction to fuller and more systematic works."—*Oxford Magazine.*

JURISPRUDENCE.

EASTWOOD'S Brief Introduction to Austin's Theory of Positive Law and Sovereignty. By R. A. EASTWOOD. 72 pages. Price 3s. 6d. net.

Nine out of ten students who take up the study of Jurisprudence are set to read Austin, without any warning that Austin's views are not universally held, and that his work ought not now to be regarded alone, but rather in connection with the volume of criticism and counter-criticism to which it has given rise.

Mr. Eastwood's book gives a brief summary of the more essential portions of Austin, together with a summary of the various views and discussions which it has provoked.

SALMOND'S Jurisprudence; or, Theory of the Law. By JOHN W. SALMOND, Barrister-at-Law. Sixth Edition. 496 pages. Price £1 net.

"Almost universally read among students of jurisprudence."—*Law Coach.*

LEGAL HISTORY.

HAMMOND'S Short History of English Law, for Law Students. By EDGAR HAMMOND, B.A. 177 pages. Price 10s. 6d. net.

EVANS'S Theories and Criticisms of Sir Henry Maine. Contained in his six works, "Ancient Law," "Early Law and Customs," "Early History of Institutions," "Village Communities," "International Law," and "Popular Government," which works have to be studied for the various examinations. By MORGAN O. EVANS, Barrister-at-Law. 101 pages. Price 5s. net.

A digest of Maine's theories for the student. Much of Maine's writing is absolutely useless for examination purposes This little book saves the student much waste of time and mental energy.

LEGAL MAXIMS.

BROOM'S Selection of Legal Maxims, Classified and Illustrated. Eighth Edition. By J. G. PEASE and HERBERT CHITTY. 767 pages. Price £1 12s. 6d. net.

The main idea of this work is to present, under the head of "Maxims," certain leading principles of English law, and to illustrate some of the ways in which those principles have been applied or limited, by reference to reported cases. The maxims are classified under the following divisions:—

Rules founded on Public Policy.
Rules of Legislative Policy.
Maxims relating to the Crown.
The Judicial Office.
The Mode of Administering Justice.
Rules of Logic.
Fundamental Legal Principles.
Acquisition, Enjoyment, and Transfer of Property.
Rules Relating to Marriage and Descent.
The Interpretation of Deeds and Written Instruments.
The Law of Contracts.
The Law of Evidence.

"It has been to us a pleasure to read the book, and we cannot help thinking that if works of this kind were more frequently studied by the Profession there would be fewer false points taken in argument in our Courts."—*Justice of the Peace.*

Latin for Lawyers. Contains (1) A course in Latin, in 32 lessons, based on legal maxims; (2) 1000 Latin Maxims, with translations, explanatory notes, cross-references, and subject-index; (3) A Latin Vocabulary. 300 pages. Price 7s. 6d. net.

This book is intended to enable the practitioner or student to acquire a working knowledge of Latin in the shortest possible time, and at the same time to become acquainted with the legal maxims which embody the fundamental rules of the common law.

COTTERELL'S Latin Maxims and Phrases. Literally translated, with explanatory notes. Intended for the use of students for all legal examinations. By J. N. COTTERELL, Solicitor. Third Edition. 82 pages. Price 5s. net.

LOCAL GOVERNMENT.

WRIGHT & HOBHOUSE'S Outline of Local Government and Local Taxation in England and Wales (excluding London). Fifth Edition. With Introduction and Tables of Local Taxation. By Rt. Hon. HENRY HOBHOUSE. 214 pages. Price 12s. 6d. net.

"The work gives within a very moderate compass a singularly clear and comprehensive account of our present system of local self-government, both in urban and rural districts We are, indeed, not aware of any other work in which a similar view is given with equal completeness, accuracy, and lucidity"—*County Council Times.*

"Lucid, concise, and accurate to a degree which has never been surpassed."—*Justice of the Peace*

JACOBS' Epitome of the Law relating to Public Health. By BERTRAM JACOBS, Barrister-at-Law. 191 pages. Price 7s. 6d. net.

Specially written for students

"This little work has the great merit of being an accurate guide to the whole body of law in broad outline, with the added advantage of bringing the general law up to date The one feature will appeal to the general student or newly-fledged councillor, and the other to the expert who is always the better for the perusal of an elementary review."—*Municipal Officer.*

MASTER AND SERVANT.

SMITH'S Law of Master and Servant. Seventh Edition. By C. M. KNOWLES, Barrister-at-Law. 350 pages. Price 25s. net.

MERCANTILE LAW.

SLATERS' Principles of Mercantile Law. By JOSHUA SLATER, Barrister-at-Law Third Edition. 308 pages. Price 6s. 6d. net.

SMITH'S Mercantile Law. A Compendium of Mercantile Law, by the late JOHN WILLIAM SMITH. Twelfth Edition. By J. H. WATTS, Barrister-at-Law. [*In the press.*

CONTENTS—

Partners.	**Negotiable Instruments.**	**Lien.**
Companies.	**Carriers.**	**Bankruptcy.**
Principal and Agent.	**Affreightment.**	**Bills of Exchange.**
Shipping.	**Insurance.**	**Master and Servant.**
Patents.	**Contracts.**	**Sale of Goods.**
Goodwill.	**Guarantees.**	**Debtor and Creditor.**
Trade Marks.	**Stoppage in Transitu.**	

"We have no hesitation in recommending the work before us to the profession and the public as a reliable guide to the subjects included in it, and as constituting one of the most scientific treatises extant on mercantile law."—*Solicitors' Journal.*

MORTGAGES.

STRAHAN'S Principles of the General Law of Mortgages. By J. ANDREW STRAHAN, Barrister-at-Law, Reader of Equity, Inns of Court. Second Edition. 247 pages. Price 7s. 6d. net.

"He has contrived to make the whole law not merely consistent, but simple and reasonable. . Mr. Strahan's book is ample for the purposes of students' examinations, and may be thoroughly recommended."—*Law Journal.*

"It is a subject in which there is great need for a book which in moderate compass should set forth in clear and simple language the great leading principles. This Mr. Strahan's book does in a way that could hardly be bettered."—*Law Notes.*

PARTNERSHIP.

STRAHAN & OLDHAM'S Law of Partnership. By J. A. STRAHAN, Reader of Equity, Inns of Court, and N. H. OLDHAM, Barristers-at-Law. Second Edition. 264 pages. Price 10s. net.

"It might almost be described as a collection of judicial statements as to the law of partnership arranged with skill, so as to show their exact bearing on the language used in the Partnership Act of 1890, and we venture to prophesy that the book will attain a considerable amount of fame."—*Student's Companion.*

PERSONAL PROPERTY.

WILLIAMS' Principles of the Law of Personal Property, intended for the use of Students in Conveyancing. Seventeenth Edition. By T. CYPRIAN WILLIAMS, of Lincoln's Inn, Barrister-at-Law. 655 pages. Price £1 1s. net.

"Whatever competitors there may be in the field of real property, and they are numerous, none exist as serious rivals to Williams' Personal. For every law student it is invaluable, and to the practitioner it is often useful."—*Law Times.*

KELKE'S Epitome of Personal Property Law. Third Edition. 155 pages. Price 6s.

"On the eve of his examination we consider a candidate for the Solicitors' Final would find this epitome most useful."—*Law Notes.*

"An admirable little book, one, indeed, which will prove of great service to students, and which will meet the needs of the busy practitioner who desires to refresh his memory or get on the track of the law without delay."—*Irish Law Journal.*

GOODEVE'S Modern Law of Personal Property. With an Appendix of Statutes and Forms. Fifth Edition. Revised and partly re-written by J. H. WILLIAMS and W. M. CROWDY, Barristers-at-Law. 461 pages. Price £1 net.

"We have no hesitation in heartily commending the work to students. They can hardly take up a better treatise on the subject of Personal Property."—*Law Student's Journal.*

PROCEDURE.

ODGERS on the Common Law. See page 7.

INDERMAUR'S Manual of the Practice of the Supreme Court of Judicature, in the King's Bench and Chancery Divisions. Tenth Edition. Intended for the use of Students and the Profession. By CHARLES THWAITES, Solicitor. 495 pages. Price £1 net.

"The arrangement of the book is good, and references are given to the leading decisions. Copious references are also given to the rules, so that the work forms a convenient guide to the larger volumes on practice. It is a very successful attempt to deal clearly and concisely with an important and complicated subject."—*Solicitors' Journal.*

WILSHERE'S Outlines of Procedure in an Action in the King's Bench Division. With some facsimile forms. For the Use of Students. By A. M. WILSHERE, Barrister-at-Law. Second Edition. 127 pages. Price 7s. 6d. net.

This forms a companion volume to Wilshere's Criminal Law, and the student will find sufficient information to enable him to pass any examination in the subjects dealt with by the two books.

"The author has made the book clear, interesting, and instructive, and it should be acceptable to students."—*Solicitors' Journal.*

WHITE'S Points on Chancery Practice. A Lecture delivered to the Solicitors' Managing Clerks' Association, by RICHARD WHITE, a Master of the Supreme Court. 76 pages. Price 3s. 6d. net.

REAL PROPERTY.

WILLIAMS' Principles of the Law of Real Property. Intended as a first book for the use of Students in Conveyancing. 23rd Edition. By T. CYPRIAN WILLIAMS, Barrister-at-Law. 717 pages. Price £1 10s. net.

"Its value to the student cannot well be over-estimated."—*Law Students' Journal.*

"The modern law of real property is, as he remarks in his concluding summary, a system of great complexity, but under his careful supervision 'Williams on Real Property' remains one of the most useful text-books for acquiring a knowledge of it"—*Solicitors' Journal*

WILSHERE'S Analysis of Williams on Real Property. Fourth Edition. 133 pages. Price 7s. 6d. net.

This book is designed as an assistance to the memory of the student who has read the parent work It contains a useful appendix of questions.

"Read before, with, or after **Williams,** this should prove of much service to the student. In a short time it is made possible to him to grasp the outline of this difficult branch of the law."—*Law Magazine.*

KELKE'S Epitome **of** Real **Property Law,** for the use of Students. Fifth Edition. By CUTHBERT SPURLING, Barrister-at-Law. 243 pages. Price 8s. 6d. net.

"The arrangement is convenient and scientific, and the text accurate. It contains just what the diligent student or ordinary practitioner should carry in his head, and must be very useful for those about to go in for a law examination"—*Law Times*

GOODEVE'S Modern Law of Real Property. Fifth Edition. By Sir HOWARD WARBURTON ELPHINSTONE, Bart., and F. T. MAW, both of Lincoln's Inn, Barristers-at-Law. 462 pages. Price 21s.

"No better book on the principles of the law relating to real property could well be placed in a student's hands after the first elements relating to the subject have been mastered"—*Law Students' Journal.*

EDWARDS' Compendium of the Law of Property in Land. For the use of Students and the Profession. By W. D. EDWARDS, Barrister-at-Law. Fifth Edition. 482 pages. Price 25s. net.

"Mr. Edwards' treatise on the Law of Real Property is marked by excellency of arrangement and conciseness of statement."—*Solicitors' Journal.*

"So excellent is the arrangement that we know of no better compendium upon the subject of which it treats"—*Law Times.*

RECEIVERS.

KERR on the Law and Practice as to Receivers appointed by the High Court of Justice or Out of Court. Seventh Edition. 410 pages. Price £1 1s. net.

"What strikes one most on reading the book is the excellent combination of clearness of expression and conciseness."—*Law Journal*

ROMAN LAW.

KELKE'S Primer of Roman Law. 152 pages. Price 5s. net.

"In this book the author confines himself mainly to the system of Justinian's Institutes, and as a student's guide to that text-book it should be very useful. The summary is very well done, the arrangement is excellent, and there is a very useful Appendix of Latin words and phrases."—*Law Journal.*

CAMPBELL'S Compendium of Roman Law. Founded on the Institutes of Justinian; together with Examination Questions Set in the University and Bar Examinations (with Solutions), and Definitions of Leading Terms in the Words of the Principal Authorities. Second Edition. By GORDON CAMPBELL, of the Inner Temple, M.A., LL.D. 300 pages. Price 12s. net.

HARRIS'S Institutes of Gaius and Justinian. With copious References arranged in Parallel Columns, also Chronological and Analytical Tables, Lists of Laws, &c., &c. Primarily designed for the use of Students preparing for Examination at Oxford, Cambridge, and the Inns of Court. By F. HARRIS, B.C.L., M.A., Barrister-at-Law. Third Edition. 223 pages. Price 6s. net.

"This book contains a summary in English of the elements of Roman Law as contained in the works of Gaius and Justinian, and is so arranged that the reader can at once see what are the opinions of either of these two writers on each point. From the very exact and accurate references to titles and sections given he can at once refer to the original writers The concise manner in which Mr. Harris has arranged his digest will render it most useful, not only to the students for whom it was originally written, but also to those persons who, though they have not the time to wade through the larger treatises of Poste, Sanders, Ortolan, and others, yet desire to obtain some knowledge of Roman Law" —*Oxford and Cambridge Undergraduates' Journal*

JACKSON'S Justinian's Digest; Book 20, with an English Translation and an Essay on the Law of Mortgage in the Roman Law. By T. C. JACKSON, B.A., LL.B., Barrister-at-Law. 98 pages. 7s. 6d. net.

SALKOWSKI'S Institutes and History of Roman Private Law. With Catena of Texts. By Dr. CAR SALKOWSKI, Professor of Laws, Konigsberg. Translated and Edited by E. E. WHITFIELD, M.A. Oxon. 1076 pages. Price £1 12s. net.

HUNTER'S Systematic and Historical Exposition of Roman Law in the Order of a Code. By W. A. HUNTER, M.A., Barrister-at-Law. Embodying the Institutes of Gaius and the Institutes of Justinian, translated into English by J. ASHTON CROSS, Barrister-at-Law. Fourth Edition. 1075 pages. Price £1 12s. net.

HUNTER'S Introduction to the Study of Roman Law and the Institutes of Justinian. New Edition. By Professor A. F. MURISON, Barrister-at-Law. 222 pages. Price 10s. net.

"Hunter's Introduction has become a student's classic."—*Law Notes.*

GARSIA'S Roman Law in a Nutshell. - With a selection of questions set at Bar Examinations. By M. GARSIA, Barrister-at-Law. 48 pages. Price 4s. net.

With this cram book and the small Hunter or Kelke the examinations can be passed

SALE OF GOODS.

WILLIS'S Law of Contract of Sale. Contained in a Course of Six Lectures delivered by WILLIAM WILLIS, one of His Majesty's Counsel, at the request of the Council of Legal Education. Second Edition, with the text of the Sale of Goods Act. By W. N. HIBBERT, LL.D. 176 pages. Price 10s. net.

"Those who are familiar with the same author's lectures on Negotiable Securities will find here the same clear grasp of principles and the same luminous explanation of the law."—*Irish Law Times.*

"A careful study of these lectures will greatly facilitate the study of the Act."—*Law Notes.*

STATUTES.

MAXWELL on the Interpretation of Statutes. By Sir PETER BENSON MAXWELL, late Chief Justice of the Straits Settlements. Sixth Edition. By WYATT PAINE, Barrister-at-Law. 750 pages. Price £1 15s. net.

"This is an admirable book, excellent in its method and arrangement, and clear and thorough in its treatment of the different questions involved."—*Law Magazine.*

"The whole book is very readable as well as instructive."—*Solicitors' Journal.*

CRAIES on Statute Law founded on Hardcastle on Statutory Law. With Appendices containing Words and Expressions used in Statutes which have been judicially and statutably construed, and the Popular and Short Titles of certain Statutes, and the Interpretation Act, 1899. By W. F. CRAIES, Barrister-at-Law. Second Edition. 825 pages. Price £1 8s. net.

"Both the profession and students will find this work of great assistance as a guide in that difficult branch of our law, namely the construction of Statutes "—*Law Times.*

TORTS.

ODGERS on the Common Law. See page 7.

WILSHERE'S Analysis of Contracts and Torts. By A. M. WILSHERE and DOUGLAS ROBB, Barristers-at-Law. Second Edition. 172 pages. Price 7s. 6d. net.

It is designed as an assistance to the memory of the Student who has read Odgers or Indermaur on the Common Law.

FRASER'S Compendium of the Law of Torts. Specially adapted for the use of Students. By H. FRASER, Barrister-at-Law, one of the Readers to the Inns of Court. Tenth Edition. 258 pages. Price 12s. 6d. net.

"It is a model book for students—clear, succinct, and trustworthy, and showing a practical knowledge of their needs"—*Law Journal*

RINGWOOD'S Outlines of the Law of Torts. Prescribed as a Text-book by the Incorporated Law Society of Ireland. Fifth Edition. [*In the press.*

"We have always had a great liking for this work, and are very pleased to see by the appearance of a new Edition that it is appreciated by students. We consider that for the ordinary student who wants to take up a separate work on Torts, this is the best book he can read, for it is clear and explanatory, and has good illustrative cases, and it is all contained in a very modest compass. . . . This Edition appears to have been thoroughly revised, and is, we think, in many respects improved"—*Law Students' Journal.*

"The work is one we well recommend to law students, and the able way in which it is written reflects much credit upon the author"—*Law Times*

SALMOND'S Law of Torts. A Treatise on the English Law of Liability for Civil Injuries. By SIR JOHN W. SALMOND. Fifth Edition. 568 pages. £1 10s. net.

"It would be difficult to find any book on the subject of Torts in which the principles are more clearly and accurately expressed or the case law more usefully referred to"—*Solicitors' Journal*

TRUSTEES.

The Trustee's Handbook. Containing his Powers, Duties and Liabilities, the Investment of Trust Funds, and the Powers of a Tenant for Life. Reprinted from Snell's Equity, Williams' Real Property, etc. 69 pages. Price 3s. 6d. net.

WILLS.

STRAHAN'S Law of Wills. By J. A. STRAHAN, Barrister-at-Law. 167 pages. Price 7s. 6d. net.

"We do not know of anything more useful in its way to a student, and it is a book not to be despised by the practitioner." —*Law Magazine.*

MATHEWS' Guide to Law of Wills. By A. G. MATHEWS, Barrister-at-Law. 402 pages. Price 7s. 6d. net.

"Mr. Mathews has produced an excellent and handy volume on a subject bristling with difficulties. . . . There is a scope for a short work of this kind on this subject, and doubtless Mr. Mathews' book will find its way into the hands of many Law Students."—*Juridical Review.*

Printed at Reading, England, by The Eastern Press, Ltd

18462609R00213

Printed in Poland
by Amazon Fulfillment
Poland Sp. z o.o., Wrocław